18-

D0761246

Narcissism
and Character Transformation

Marie-Louise von Franz, Honorary Patron

**Studies in Jungian Psychology
by Jungian Analysts**

Daryl Sharp, General Editor

Narcissism
and Character Transformation

The Psychology of
Narcissistic Character Disorders

NATHAN SCHWARTZ-SALANT

Portions of this book first appeared, in different form, in *Quadrant* (Journal of the C.G. Jung Foundation for Analytical Psychology, New York), 1979, 1980; and in *Journal of Modern Psychoanalysis*, 1980.

Canadian Cataloguing in Publication Data

Schwartz-Salant, Nathan, 1938-
   Narcissism and character transformation

(Studies in Jungian psychology; 9)

Bibliography: p.
Includes index.
ISBN 0-919123-08-2

1. Narcissism.   2. Identity (Psychology).
3. Jung, C. G. (Carl Gustav), 1875-1961.
I. Title. II. Series.

BF575.N35S33   155.2'64   C82-094048-8

Copyright © 1982 by Nathan Schwartz-Salant.
All rights reserved.

INNER CITY BOOKS
Box 1271, Station Q, Toronto, Canada M4T 2P4

Honorary Patron: Marie-Louise von Franz.
Publisher and General Editor: Daryl Sharp.
Editorial Board: Fraser Boa, Daryl Sharp, Marion Woodman.

INNER CITY BOOKS was founded in 1980 to promote the understanding and practical application of the work of C.G. Jung.

Cover: *Echo and Narcissus,* by British painter
J. W. Waterhouse (1849–1917).

Photo page 47 courtesy Jessie.

Glossary and Index by Daryl Sharp.

Printed and bound in Canada by
University of Toronto Press Incorporated

CONTENTS

See last pages for descriptions of other INNER CITY BOOKS

Preface

An old fallen leaf has an interesting taste.
The edges of space roll gently.
Everything will come to this pool.

It has often been said, and with justification, that an analyst, more than anyone else, cannot say anything new, because he is always learning from his patients. To a large degree, that applies to the present book.

But there is another teacher as well. And this book also owes its validity, whatever that may be, to a vision. Words and metaphor can only approximate the ineffable, but I have tried to be true to the ability to *see* that comes from it. William Blake wrote: "He who does not imagine in stronger and better lineaments, and in stronger and better light than his perishing and mortal eye can see, does not imagine at all."[1] A vision taught me the truth of this, and attempting to help patients recover their split-off, Persephone-like souls showed me its absolute necessity.

For Lydia

Narcissus, wall painting from the House of Lucretius
Fronto, Pompeii, 14-62 A.D.

Introduction

1 Narcissism and the Problem of Identity

Narcissism, the common conception of which is extreme self-adoration with an aloofness that denies the need for another person, is a subject of long-standing human concern. Ovid's telling of the myth of Narcissus in 8 A.D., in his *Metamorphoses,* began a long literary tradition, carefully traced by Louise Vinge in *The Narcissus Theme in Western Literature up to the Early Nineteenth Century.* There, as we shall see, one may find ample evidence that Narcissus and his female "companion" Echo have been a rich source of speculation on the condition and salvation of the human soul. Clearly, the popular view of narcissism, while correct to some extent, only touches the surface of a vast and complicated phenomenon.

The term *narcissism* made its appearance early on in psychoanalytic theory, and did so in an especially pejorative manner. It initially indicated self-love to a pathological degree and an associated impenetrability, and carried a pessimistic therapeutic prognosis. To be narcissistic was in effect to be bad. It was a judgment that one was not only self-involved but beyond reach. This decree in psychoanalytic thought extended to meditation, introversion and creative fantasy, so it is hardly surprising that Jung rarely uses the term.[2]

But as the "impenetrable barrier" of narcissism began indeed to be penetrated, for example by investigations into early childhood and schizophrenia, the attitude toward the phenomenology covered by the term began to change. This tendency was further increased by clinical experience with so-called narcissistic character disorders. (In character disorders symptoms may exist, such as anxiety, depression and paranoid tendencies, but these are strictly secondary compared to the person's major complaint, which is a lack of identity and self-esteem. In these disorders we are dealing with a disturbance in the development of the ego-Self relationship, rather than with symptoms stemming from instinctual processes breaking through ego defenses, as in the psychoneuroses.)

Narcissistic character disorders were at first believed to be untreatable because the barrier, known as the narcissistic defense, was thought to preclude the establishment of any kind of relationship (transference) with the analyst. When it was discovered that this was far from true, that in fact very strong transferences are established and that these affect the therapist to a high degree (by inducing countertransference reactions), much more about narcissism entered the psychoanalytic literature. The term then became associated with the general issue of *identity,* for it became apparent that the special defensiveness of the narcissistic character disorder was a defense against injury to an already very poor sense of identity. Analytical insight, often aided by the recognition that counter-transference responses can have an objective quality, increased our understanding of the nature of identity structures behind narcissistic character defenses.

The present study, combining both Jungian and psychoanalytic points of view, is an attempt to further broaden the clinical perspective on the issues posed by narcissism and the problem of identity.

In general, the psychotherapeutic attitudes of C.G. Jung have a growing kinship with certain views of other schools of thought. Jung himself valued the Freudian approach, which he regarded as an extroverted, object-oriented psychology, along with that of Adler, which he considered to be introverted or subject-oriented.[3] Indeed, Jung said that sometimes he worked as a Freudian and sometimes as an Adlerian. And developments over the last few decades have brought other psychotherapeutic views and Jung's into closer alignment. For example, the work of Guntrip, representing the English school of object relations, in his recasting of Freud's libido theory,[4] bears strong resemblances to Jung's concept of psychic energy. And like Jung, the modern psychoanalytic school recognizes that the manifest content of a dream is a symbolic expression of the unconscious meaning; that is, there is no need for the idea of a latent dream content.[5] The modified importance of the oedipal complex and the recognition of a need for a psychology of the Self in later Freudian thought are also within the spirit of Jung's approach to the psyche.

But while these and other developments are invaluable in helping to bridge Jungian and other points of view, and hence allow for better clinical communications, Jung's fundamental concept of the archetype, the basic structural unit of the psyche, is often neither well accepted nor understood.

As a result of personal and clinical experience, Jung recognized that certain events in a person's life, events which may fittingly be described as numinous, can be of central, transformative significance. Narcissus' encounter with his own image is just such an event. Its meaning has never been exhausted in literary or psychological commentary, for the mystery it touches upon cannot be exhausted. It is the mystery of identity: Who and what am I?

As shall be discussed more fully in chapter two, the double seen by Narcissus is properly designated as the Self, the image of the total person and not just the conscious, ego personality. The Self is the root, the matrix, of personal identity. It is here especially that we must distinguish between psychoanalytic and Jungian concepts, a distinction that will be followed throughout by capitalizing the term Self as meant by Jung, and keeping the lower-case designation, self, when referring to other views (although the style of authors quoted here, including Jung, may vary).

In the Jungian model, the Self is both the archetype of wholeness and the psyche's central ordering factor. While the phenomenology of the Self is often similar to descriptions of the psychoanalytic self concept, it also can significantly differ. Accordingly, the concept of personal identity also differs. These are the major issues of this study.

2 Identity and the Self

Identity is a mysterious concept and attempts to define it too simply inevitably lead to a cramped condition in which the ego plays too great a role. The theologian Harvey Cox, in the process of deriding what he calls "identity seekers," thus characterizing those with an over-simplified view, offers an illuminating discussion of the subject:

> For the identity seeker, self appears as some sort of inner essence. It is a core which, though it can grow, never does more than actualize a potential which is already there. The essential self may be covered by layers of encrustation or coiled in compact possibility; nonetheless, it is *there*. It can be realized, laid bare, if one's search is persistent enough. It is the psychological diminutive of the timeless uncreated soul of Neoplatonic philosophy. We may be unable to see it now, so the teaching goes, because of the weight of the flesh, the darkness of the material world, or the blindness of childhood repression. But that inner essence is there, we are assured: the real you, waiting to be pursued until its now-hidden light is sufficiently uncovered to allow its glow to illuminate the darkness.
>
> It is important to understand that this modern psychological view of the self as something to be searched for, an essence to be uncovered or developed, not only runs against the grain of biblical spirituality; it also has nothing to do with the self-as-illusion idea taught by most Buddhist schools....
>
> The quest for identity is neither Buddhist nor biblical. It is the impoverished modern heir to a tradition going back to Plato and beyond, which sees the soul as part of the changeless stuff of the universe. It is impoverished, however, because the characteristics which were once attributed to the universe itself are now packed into the individual soul. Thus the self/soul may unfold and flower, but it only actualizes an original potential. Its development can be foreseen and facilitated. Nothing totally unanticipated or surprising ever occurs. This self/soul exhibits all the qualities of a "surprise-free" phenomenon....
>
> For the individual person, the trouble with basing one's life on the quest for an essential self [is that] the self, instead of enlarging and deepening its capacities, becomes more and more like itself.... If the "real self" I am uncovering progressively becomes the determinant of my behavior, rigidity and sclerosis set in early. My actions become predictable and my perception of alternative modes of life narrows. I lose my vulnerability, my capacity to be shattered, or even to catch myself by surprise....
>
> There is, however, another way of looking at the world and the self.... [it is] centered outside of itself. This view of the self comes to us from the Hebrews, and informs those schools of theology and psychology which stress *novum*—unprecedented emergence and novelty. It is the opposite of the "surprise-free" universe, its world is characterized by singular, unanticipated

events and unique persons. It sees sickness in the average and health in the uncommon. It is the world touched by what Christian theology calls "grace."

In the biblical universe of grace and surprise, the human self is not a timeless essence. It is an open, physico-spiritual field that is both the product of and producer of real change. As St. John says, "It doth not yet appear what we shall be." . . . The self is not an inner essence to be discovered [in this view] but an unfinished and unfinishable poem, a unique statement for which no archetypal pattern exists. In this biblical universe, concrete selves meet each other as combatants and companions, not as separate particles of One Cosmic Self. They are centers of being who grapple, love and hate. This irreducible otherness of the other defines the biblical view of the self. It also provides the only view of the self or psyche on which modern psychology can build a new and liberating science of the soul.[6]

Cox is absolutely correct in his critique of the limitation of the psychological view of identity, but he mistakenly includes Jung's approach with all the others. Jung's view of the Self does share the notion of "something to be searched for, an essence to be uncovered or developed." But Jung's Self is also inherently open and fully in accord with "the biblical universe of grace and surprise," an unfinishable pattern that we at best approximate in terms of completion but never in the sense of perfection. The fact that in the individuation process it does present contents to the ego, and in effect also creates the ego, is not incompatible with its characteristic spontaneity. The Self manifests as both a seemingly well-ordered, continuous process, and one which can burst in upon the ego with unknown energies and shake the very core of the conscious personality.

Cox's critique is one-sided, for identity is *also* built up in a step-by-step fashion. That it does *not only* come into existence in this way, and perhaps not even primarily, is a point of view with which I sympathize. The main question, however, is whether the step-by-step approach, for example in Jungian thought, of integrating complexes, works toward blocking the "universe of grace and surprise," or toward becoming more open to it. Much depends on the way in which the integration of complexes, for example, is approached. If this is done in a mechanical manner, without an underlying awareness that it is a small part of the greater universe, there is no doubt that it can have a blocking effect, as it commonly does have in classical psychoanalysis. But it need not, and in analytic work we cannot very well do without the fantasy of integration of parts, for it belongs to the issue of identity as much as does existence in historical time.

3   The Numinosity of the Self

Jung's view of the Self cannot be grasped without reference to its numinous nature:

Religion, as the Latin word denotes, is a careful and scrupulous observation of what Rudolph Otto aptly called the *numinosum,* that is, a dynamic agency or effect not caused by an arbitrary act of will. On the contrary, it seizes and controls the human subject, who is always rather its victim than its creator. The *numinosum*—whatever its cause may be—is an experience of the subject independent of his will. . . .

Every creed is originally based on the one hand upon the experience of the *numinosum* and on the other hand upon *pistis,* that is to say, trust or loyalty, faith and confidence in a certain experience of a numinous nature and in the change of consciousness that ensues. The conversion of Paul is a striking example of this. We might say, then, that the term "religion" designates the attitude peculiar to a consciousness which has been changed by experience of the *numinosum.*[7]

The numinous strikes a person with awe, wonder and joy, but may also evoke fear, terror and total disorientation. Being confronted with the power of the Self arouses just such emotions, which always and everywhere have been associated with religious experience.

There are at least three major forms that fear of the numinous quality of the Self may take. First, there is a fear of being flooded by archetypal energies and of being overtaken by a will greater than that of one's ego. As Jung has said, the experience of the Self is a defeat for the ego. It is also, I might add, a defeat for grandiose contents and defenses; these too are readily overwhelmed and transformed by an experience of the Self.

Secondly, the fear of the Self and its energies stems from an abandonment fear. Over and over again I have met the following attitude: "If I contact all that strength and effectiveness, no one will be able to be with me, I'll be too powerful and everyone will send me away."

Thirdly, and closely related is the fear of taking hold of the energies of the Self because they can be so appealing and beautiful that one is certain he will become the object of envy. He will sacrifice or hide the Self to avoid envy's "evil eye." He is like the primitive that Schoeck tells us about who has a good hunt but upon returning to his tribe cries and moans over how bad it was.[8] In the meanwhile he had hidden his catch outside the camp and at nightfall sneaks out to eat some of it. The person terrified of envy—and as we shall see the narcissistic character has generally been subject to massive envy attack—acts very much like this, only a bit worse: he also hides his prize from himself.

The role of psychic numina should not be underestimated in healing. But they can easily be overlooked, because they often appear in a dim fashion, always different, unusual, but not necessarily overwhelming and unavoidable. In the case of A., which will be presented in chapter one, the numinosity of the archetype broke through to consciousness with a striking transformative effect. This is the exception, not the rule. The more common situation will be seen in the clinical material in chapter three.

The following remarks by Jung underline the importance of one's *attitude* toward the Self and its numinous quality.

The unconscious does indeed put forth a bewildering profusion of semblances for that obscure thing we call the . . . "self." It almost seems as if we were to go on dreaming in the unconscious the age-old dream of alchemy, and to continue to pile new synonyms on top of the old, only to know as much or as little about it in the end as the ancients themselves. I will not enlarge upon what the *lapis* meant to our forefathers, and what the mandala still means to the Lamaist and Tantrist, Aztec and Pueblo Indian, the "golden pill" to the Taoist, and the "golden seed" to the Hindu. We know the texts that give us a vivid idea of all this. But what does it mean when the unconscious stubbornly persists in presenting such abstruse symbolisms to a cultured European? . . . It seems to me, everything that can be grouped together under the general concept "mandala" [self] expresses the essence of a certain kind of *attitude*. The known attitudes of the conscious mind have definable aims and purposes. But a man's attitude towards the self is the only one that has no definable aim and no visible purpose. It is easy enough to say "self," but exactly what have we said? That remains shrouded in "metaphysical" darkness. I may define "self" as the totality of the conscious and unconscious psyche, but this totality transcends our vision; it is a veritable *lapis invisibilitatis*. In so far as the unconscious exists it is not definable; its existence is a mere postulate and nothing whatever can be predicted as to its possible contents. The totality can only be experienced in its parts and then only in so far as these are contents of consciousness. . . . True, [the self] is a concept that grows steadily clearer with experience—as our dreams show—without, however, losing anything of its transcendence. Since we cannot possibly know the boundaries of something unknown to us, it follows that we are not in a position to set any bounds to the self. . . . The empirical manifestations of unconscious contents bear all the marks of something illimitable, something not determined by space and time. This quality is numinous and therefore alarming, above all to a cautious mind that knows the value of precisely limited concepts. . . .

All that can be ascertained at present about the symbolism [of the self] is that it portrays an autonomous psychic fact, characterized by a phenomenology which is always repeating itself and is everywhere the same. It seems to be a sort of atomic nucleus about whose innermost structure and ultimate meaning we know nothing.[9]

The analyst's attitude toward the Self and its symbolic manifestations, especially their numinous quality, to a large extent determines the manner in which the analysand relates to the Self. The analyst's awareness of archetypal factors and processes can lead to them *feeling seen* in the patient's psyche. As Jung has often emphasized, there is consciousness in the unconscious.[10] Complexes all have an "ego quality," a conscious potential. The unconscious "sees" what we do, often far more accurately than do our conscious egos which are weighed down by considerable unconsciousness. Hence dreams can illustrate the analytical interaction in a manner unknown to the ego-consciousness of either therapist or patient.

Psychic contents such as the Self react and come forth toward consciousness if they are seen, if the therapist has the capacity to see them in dream and fantasy material, but especially if he can imaginally see them in the here and now of the analytical session. (More will be said about this kind of seeing in chapter three.) Unconscious contents respond much as does a child, still embedded in the unconscious, who has an acute awareness of whether he is being seen as he is, or being ignored, or worse, the object of a parental fantasy that has little to do with him.

The analyst who does not see archetypal material will not constellate it, and will in fact contribute to its withdrawal from consciousness. Rather than help overcome resistance to the numinous, he will unconsciously collude in the resistance. Psychic numina are generally the last thing the ego wants to face, for their autonomy, spontaneity and energy content are alien to the world of the ego and its attitudes. The analyst who doesn't see them can, perhaps, be an aid to a "borderline" patient who could be overwhelmed by the unconscious and is thus better off not dealing with it. This situation certainly exists, but is less common than was once thought; we no longer need to be so cautious about "latent psychosis," especially when dealing with the narcissistic character, whose psychic cohesiveness potentially allows him to be transformed by the archetypal realm, rather than be flooded by it.

It is possible to inhibit an archetypal process in different ways. One does not have to prescribe thorazine; the process can as easily be destroyed, banished into unconsciousness and its energy drained, by simply ignoring its existence or by reductive interpretations. The clinical material of A. in chapter one will illustrate how a most sudden and radical emergence of archetypal material could have been destroyed by a reductive interpretation, in this case to guilt. Only the most transcendent levels of the numinosum are able to withstand reductionism and non-mirroring. Others need fostering and care, lest their central, healing source of energy be missed.

The approach of analytical psychology is not, as is sometimes erroneously assumed, dependent upon a patient having an "archetypal experience." Anything like a direct contact with archetypal energies is not a common occurrence; it exists, but this kind of confrontation is not what distinguishes a Jungian from a psychoanalytic approach.

The most general difference in the two approaches, stemming from their disparate views of the unconscious and especially their attitudes toward the archetype, is the more subtle one of the ways in which a patient's material is mirrored. I recall Winnicott's concern that

> there is a core to the personality that corresponds to the true self of the split-personality; I suggest that this core can never communicate with the world of perceived objects, and that the individual person knows that it must never be communicated with or be influenced by external reality. . . . Although healthy persons communicate and enjoy communicating, the other fact is equally true, that *each individual is an isolate, permanently non-communicating, permanently unknown, in fact unfound.*
> . . . I would say that the traumatic experiences that lead to the organiza-

tion of primitive defenses belong to the threat to the isolated core, the threat of its being found, altered, communicated with. The defense consists in a further hiding of the secret self, even to the extreme of its projection and endless dissemination. Rape and being eaten by cannibals, these are mere bagatelles as compared with the violation of the self's core, the alteration of the self's central elements by communication seeping through the defences.[11]

Winnicott is especially concerned with the danger of interpretations, a caution of great value. Consequently, he recognizes the importance of *silence* and the need to accept a patient's noncommunicating as possibly positive. But valuing this, as distinct from withdrawal—the distinction he recognizes we must try to make—depends upon the analyst's ability to be silent in a very special way. It requires a respect for the mystery of the patient's soul and a special awareness of when it isn't being revealed.

There is always a domain of the Self that will never communicate with outer objects, just as there are experiences of the Self (especially in its transcendent nature) that the ego never regains in its space-time existence. The reality of the Self does not require that it be embodied, but the tendency toward becoming embodied is ongoing. It is a process that is never-ending, always incomplete and continuously pressing for fulfillment. As Jung has said, the Self wants to "live its experiment in life."[12] That is its unique thrust.

It is especially in order to distinguish between the withdrawn nature of the Self and its necessary silence and noncommunication that archetypal awareness is essential. The analyst's appreciation and capacity for an imaginal *sight* of the Self's energy field, often dominated by joy, is a vital factor in that Self's ability to exist and affect the patient, rather than being split off and sullen.

4 The Immanent and Transcendent Self

With this we must return to Cox's critique of identity and the other crucial question it raises: the difference between so-called immanence and transcendence. Here there is a difference between Jung's view of the Self and the one Cox criticizes. One aspect of Jung's view is that the unfolding, or deintegration, of the contents of the Self toward temporal life and the ego, leads to the Self being experienced as a content of the ego. That is, the ego becomes aware of the fact that its existence partakes of something greater; this awareness requires a capacity for recognizing symbolic reality.

The existence of the Self, in this sense, depends upon ego-consciousness: The Self is felt as "within" even though it is also felt as greater than the ego. This paradoxical quality of the Self is carried by the biblical metaphor, first found in the Book of Daniel (7:13), in which the Messiah is called the Son of Man.

The Freudian-psychoanalytic view of the self is usually of this nature, as a content of the ego, dependent upon ego-consciousness for its existence. While Jung naturally recognizes this aspect—for it is a crucial element in the experience of identity—he also recognizes another Self experience, which in the biblical metaphor is that of the Father, the prototype of man. Like the Self experienced as a content of the ego, the Self as the Father is an archetypal content, but one experienced as "outside" the ego. But, and this is where Jung somewhat departs from the biblical view set out by Cox, the Self is felt as outside the ego in two ways: 1) as a center about which the ego revolves or orients, a core of wisdom and energy far greater than that of the ego; 2) as transcendent in the sense of beyond psyche, not only outside the ego but also beyond being in any way felt as within, whether as a content of the ego or as a center around which the ego exists.

In its most clear and overwhelming form, the transcendent level is experienced in mystical union, the *unio mystica*. As a *result* of this experience of the Self, there is a consequent formation, an incarnation *into* the psyche of a center, as referred to in the first instance of the Self as Father. Moreover, in time this too tends to incarnate and become a content of the ego: the Self as the Son. But throughout all of this, the original transcendent level is never felt as "inside." It is felt as not only outside the ego, but also as outside the psyche.

There are thus *three dimensions of the Self* that must be recognized: 1) as content of the ego; 2) as a focus and center outside the ego; and 3) as an energy field beyond both ego and psyche, experienced as outside both. As 1) and 2) the Self is, in religious language, immanent; it is the Self as Christ, or as the Messiah ben Joseph in the Kabbalah. In 3) the Self is transcendent; it is the Old Testament Yahweh, the Eastern Brahma, the Transcendent Light, etc.

These two categories have a substantial similarity, which is to say that the experience of transcendence leads in turn to the awareness of an immanent Self "within" the psyche that feels like the same energy, only of lesser magnitude. This is the ontological basis for the theological notion of "homoousia," the identity of the immanent and transcendent Self. Jung refers to this doctrine in empirically equating the Self with an image of God, similar to the Indian notion that Atman and Brahman are One.[13] That is what Jung means when he speaks of "the reality of the psyche"—all we can ever know are the psychic images of the archetypes, not the archetypes per se. In so doing he does tend to blur the distinction between the immanent and the transcendent Self. He does not deny it, but he chooses to focus upon their identity rather than their difference.

And yet a distinction must be kept. Because, in fact, we do not experience the transcendent Self as an image. The various metaphors of Eternity and Light are not psychic images in the sense of something dreamed or imagined. Rather they are the ego's frail way of giving images to something that is beyond imagery, always knowing that the image itself is only an approximation, even if it carries a symbolic sense that helps memory and gains its own numinosity and symbolic value in time. It is always an approximation to the unknowable, yet it stems from a moment of grace.

5 Psychoanalytic and Jungian Views of the Self

The self in psychoanalytic thought, as already noted, is generally taken to be a content of the ego. Its major function is always ego-oriented. Thus Edith Jacobson says: "By a realistic concept of the self we mean a concept that mirrors only or mainly the state of characteristics of our ego: of our conscious and preconscious feelings and thoughts, wishes and impulses, attitudes and actions."[14]

Here the "realistic" nature of the self is emphasized, as against an inflated or in other terms grandiose-exhibitionistic quality with completely unrealistic attitudes, unsuitable as a mirror for our ego. But the ego-oriented bias is clear: there is no sense of the Self as an inner, guiding center whose energies can manifest symbolically. That would be "primary process thinking."

Psychoanalytic thinking in general is in the mold of "identity seeking" as criticized by Cox. The underlying premise is that the self is built up through the process of its structures being first merged with the environment and then assimilated back into the ego. Consequently, the self is always to be "found"—and always in interpersonal relations. The self always exists to, in Jacobson's phrase, mirror the ego.

The Jungian notion, which is that *the ego must also mirror the Self,* has little meaning in psychoanalytic thought because introversion is still not distinguished, save by some analysts such as Winnicott, from schizoid withdrawal. Winnicott does not go as far as to recognize the existence of archetypal processes, but he certainly sees that silent communication with subjective states is essential to the health of the self.[15]

When we come to the problem of how a sense of identity comes into existence, we touch upon the boundaries of our understanding of the nature of the psyche. At bottom, what we call identity is a name for a fluid process which depends upon both the introjective model found in psychoanalytic thought, and another, *acausal* dynamic. The latter is the basis for the mystery that surrounds the idea of identity. It is the process by which archetypal reality incarnates in historical time, described by Jung in his studies on synchronicity and acausal orderedness.[16] Identity cannot be fully explained by a causal view, such as a process of projection and introjection, or one based solely upon early childhood development. There is a causal aspect, to be sure, but most psychoanalytic authors give it far too much importance.

How the ego views the Self has a great deal to do with the way the Self

Analysand's drawing of the dynamic interchange of energy between the sun and its reflection. ("How the ego views the Self has a great deal to do with the way the Self mirrors the ego.")

mirrors the ego.[17] When the ego looks into the mirror of the Self, what it sees is always "unrealistic" because it sees its archetypal image which can never be fit into the ego. From a psychoanalytic point of view this would always be a kind of grandiose-exhibitionism. But there is a vast difference between an archetypally toned Self image and the grandiose-exhibitionistic self which dominates the narcissistic character. That self is a merger of ego functions and archetypal dynamics; it would correspond to what in alchemy is called a premature *coniunctio*, a monstrosity. It has a strong defensive quality and does *not* carry the numinosity of the Self in Jungian terms. The narcissistic character also does not carry the numinous energy of the archetype; instead he carries a forced, power-oriented copy. The lack of genuineness of what he has to offer is generally seen by its lack of staying power, its marginal effect in time. In fact, he is defended against the numinosity of the Self for that power is far superior to his and could easily defeat his grandiose self. It is crucial to understand that the narcissistic character is defended against not only outer object relations, but equally against the inner world of archetypal reality. Both are a great threat. He is in fear of the Self for the Self is always a defeat for the ego, and especially for a grandiose, ego-Self merger.

One must, then, distinguish between the psychoanalytic concept of an inflated, grandiose-exhibitionistic self, and the Self as an image of the "greater man" that attempts to be realized, always pushing the ego beyond its known reality. In distinction to the grandiose-exhibitionistic self, the Self drives the ego in a way that can lead to meaning and a feeling of living one's fate, rather than into continual illusions and the inevitable dead end of power for its own sake.

The sense of identity the ego gains from looking into the mirror of the Self is vast, ever beyond its life in space and temporal reality. But in looking to the Self, mirroring it as it is, the Self also transforms. In this process, further discussed in chapter two, the Self becomes a mirror for the ego, reflecting a stable yet changing identity, while the ego becomes a source of consciousness and transformation for the Self. It is in this mixture of time-bound reality and transcendence that identity lives and continuously changes. The process of projection and introjection, dependent upon outer objects, is essential for ego-strength and separation from the Self, whence the Self can develop into the true other. But the experience of this inner other and its role in the continual creation of identity can never be reduced to a theory of object relations.

6 Kohut's Nuclear Self

Heinz Kohut is the most difficult psychoanalytic author to compare with analytical psychology. On the one hand, much of what he says sounds a good deal like Jung's view of the Self and identity. On the other hand, his view is further from Jung's than is that of most of his psychoanalytic colleagues. This is especially so when it comes to the issue of negative emotions, the "dark side" of the Self. His work on the transference-countertransference process is clinically invaluable, however, especially in what I call Stage One of transformation.

We have seen Jung's emphasis upon the unknowability of the Self, its essential, transcendent mystery. So when Kohut uses similar language it would seem that we have found someone on a similar path. Kohut says:

> My investigations contain hundreds of pages dealing with the psychology of the self—yet it never assigns an inflexible meaning to the term self, it never explains how the essence of the self should be defined. But I admit this fact without contrition or shame. The self is . . . not knowable in its essence.[18]

I was struck by this deviation from usual psychoanalytic thought, as was Mario Jacoby who notes the same quote in his lucid description of Kohut's theories and their relationship to Jungian thought.[19] But while I share Jacoby's appreciation of Kohut, I also see a fundamental difference between his approach and that of Jung.

Kohut's self concept certainly differs from that of his Freudian colleagues in that he recognizes its nature as a center outside the ego, as well as a content of the ego. But his references to its "unknowableness" and "cosmic" quality are only metaphors of little significance.[20] They are not backed up by the central significance of the archetypal realm. Without this dimension to psyche and the existence of the *numinosum,* what difference does it make if the Self is cosmic or not?

My appreciation of Kohut is for his clinical differentiation of the transference-countertransference process; his structural view of the psyche and the Self is very different from Jung's. These differences have importance in the way we view the transformation of the narcissistic character.

For Kohut, the narcissistic character would be a person living the Self but in a marginal manner. Due to the fragmentation of Self images under the impact of poor empathy from "self-objects" (see chapter one), the narcissistic personality is always vulnerable to becoming enfeebled, dominated for example by depressions and a chronic lack of interest in work and relationships. But for Kohut, a basic "nuclear self" is still attempting expression.[21]

The nuclear self Kohut refers to differs from Jung's Self concept in several crucial ways:

1) Kohut's nuclear self is, in Jungian terms, a personalistic version of *one* archetypal pattern. This pattern is the puer-senex archetype.[22]

2) Kohut's nuclear self has a strong defensive quality. In this it is actually a defense of the Self,[23] protecting a split-off archetypal pattern that primarily carries the feminine aspect of the Self.

3) For Kohut the self is structured in two opposites: one is concerned with transforming archaic exhibitionism and the other with idealization. In Jungian terms, this polarity is only one of many. It has affinities with the development of the ego-Self axis as discussed by Edinger,[24] but leaves out not only the central role of the archetype in this process, but that of the contrasexual, and especially feminine, aspect of the psyche.

4) The Kohutian self is largely positive; negative emotions such as hate, envy, rage and so forth are "disintegration products" of poor empathy. (In discussing Kohut later in chapter one we shall have occasion to quote Searle's critique,[25] and therein find a view of the negative, dark side of the Self much more in line with Jung's conception.) For Jung the Self was both good and bad, ordering and disordering, a creature of eros and power, a nexus of instinctual and "drive" processes as much as spiritual ones.[26]

A few remarks on this last issue may shed some light upon why Jungians sometimes gravitate toward Kohut. His approach has similarities with Jung's synthetic or purposeful attitude in distinction to a reductive one. This already is quite a change from most psychoanalytic authors. Beyond this, from experience with the individuation process of the puer aeternus (a man who remains too long in adolescent psychology), Jungians are aware of the fact that negative emotions, issues called shadow problems, are the last thing the puer assimilates. His process (and that of the puella, his female counterpart) is the inverse of the classical view of individuation: It goes from the top down, so to speak, from being concerned first with spirit and then with instinctual and shadow issues.

The attitude toward negative emotions held by Kohut is similar to the *privatio boni* attitude toward evil that Jung stood against so tenaciously.[27]

Evil in Jung's view is not the absence of good, any more than darkness is an absence of light. Kohutian theory proposes that negative emotions exist as a result of an absence of sufficient empathy. While this view is sharply contrary to Jung's idea of man and the Self, it is, as in the Jungian attitude toward the puer, a necessary tactic for the sake of transformation. It is not that the Self is this way, but rather that its inherent dark aspect must be sidestepped for tactical reasons. The puer, like the narcissistic character, cannot handle these emotions; they are too threatening to an already fragile sense of identity.

But the narcissistic character disorder is not identical with puer problems; this is only a stage in its transformation. When this stage is worked through, other issues emerge for which the Kohutian view of the Self is inadequate. All it will accomplish is to keep a patient fixated upon transferences, especially the idealized transference. While the *privatio boni* attitude toward negative emotions, implicit in Kohutian theory, is a good approach and one which Jungians readily understand—Freudians are often less cognizant of its value—it is also one-sided and detrimental to depth transformation.

7   Two Stages of Transformation

For the sake of clarity I set out two distinct stages in the transformation of the narcissistic character. This is a useful abstraction although actually they intertwine; especially issues of Stage One are found in Stage Two (the converse is not so common).

After the narcissistic transferences characteristic of Stage One have dissolved—that is, after a sufficient degree of transformation has occurred —a deeper issue emerges. The clinical picture takes on what looks like a schizoid form, an "in-and-out program" as described by Guntrip (see chapter five). This is *not* a defense against an idealized transference, as it might have been in earlier stages. Rather, it signals the appearance of *the phenomenology of the Self.* It is the Self that is the source of archetypal energies, as opposed to the grandiose-exhibitionistic self that first dominates the clinical picture. Its existence can easily be missed, due to a lack of appreciation of the archetypal dimension and the patient's all-too-ready willingness to avoid the issue. For the Self that now appears has its own autonomous will that threatens to take the person into depths he or she would much rather avoid. These depths and mysteries are associated with the archetypal feminine. Even the person who has succeeded in establishing a positive internal puer-senex relationship tends to resist this change.

My consideration of the first stage of transformation follows much that Kohut describes. There are major points of difference which shall later become clear, but his emphasis on the formation and transformation of the narcissistic transferences is crucial to this stage. It is the stage described by the Narcissus myth according to Ovid. The second stage concerns the redemption of the Self, the emphasis being on its feminine aspects. It is the mystery alluded to in the Narcissus myth according to Pausanius, and in the Homeric Hymn to Demeter.

The mythology of Narcissus according to Ovid will be dealt with in chapter two, with pertinent clinical descriptions in chapter one. The version according to Pausanius and the Homeric Hymn to Demeter, which can be seen as a reconstruction of the Narcissus myth, will then concern us in the chapters that follow.

Stage One of transformation, the Ovidian stage that Kohut has, in my view, greatly contributed to our understanding of, largely results in a transformation in the masculine realm of *doing:* From a compulsive, nonreflective masculine order, dominated by negative puer or senex phenomenology, there emerges a positive capacity for work, love and creativity. There is also some change in the feminine, with an enhanced capacity for *being* and also for empathy.

In Stage Two the emphasis is on the transformation of the feminine. Archetypally this can be related to the rape and redemption of Persephone. The transformation of the masculine also continues here and is extremely valuable, but it is not of the same order of importance. (It has its archetypal correspondence in the figure of Triptolemus in the Homeric Hymn and the Eleusinian Mysteries.)

8   Narcissism and the Fear of the Self

It is clear that notions such as "fear of the Self" or "rejection of the Self" have little meaning within a psychoanalytic framework. At best it is seen as the fear of allowing the formation of the narcissistic transferences, lest the earlier wounding be repeated. But this is quite a different thing from fearing the "will of the Self," whose numinosity far exceeds the energy content of the ego. In terms of Jung's approach to the psyche, however, it would be the rejection of the Self, the failure to live one's true pattern, that leads to what we now call the narcissistic character disorder. This is most clearly formulated in Jung's seminars on Nietzsche's *Thus Spake Zarathustra.*

In considering Nietzsche's question—"Tell me, my brother, what do we think bad, and worst of all? Is it not degeneration?—And we always suspect degeneration when the bestowing soul is lacking"—Jung notes that degeneration in Nietzsche's time meant the deviation of one's development from the original pattern to which one belongs; if you deviate from that *genus* you suffer from degeneration.

Nietzsche refers to a deviation from the pattern which is in man, and that, Jung tells us, is the Self, the individual pattern or condition or form which can be fulfilled according to its individual meaning.

> If you fulfill the pattern that is peculiar to yourself you have loved yourself,
> you have accumulated, you have abundance; you bestow virtue then be-

cause you have lustre, you radiate, from your abundance something over-flows. But if you hate yourself, if you have not accepted your pattern, then there are hungry animals, prowling cats and other beasts in your constitution which get at your neighbors like flies in order to satisfy the appetites which you have failed to satisfy. Therefore, Nietzsche says to those people who have not fulfilled their individual pattern that the bestowing soul is lacking. There is no radiation, no real warmth; there is hunger and secret stealing. [Quoting Nietzsche]: "Upward goeth our course from genera to supergenera. But a horror to us is the degenerating sense, which saith: 'All for myself.'"

You see that degenerating sense which says "all for myself" is unfulfilled destiny, that is somebody who did not live himself, who did not give himself what he needed, who did not toil for the fulfillment of that pattern which had been given him when he was born. Because that thing is one's *genus* it ought to be fulfilled, and in as much as it is not, there is that hunger which says "all for myself."[28]

That is the phenomenology of the narcissistic character disorder: the self-hate, hunger, secret stealing and lack of bestowing warmth Jung describes is exactly the workings of the deep-seated envy which rules the narcissistic character's inner life. But Jung also notes something of essential clinical importance which we shall discuss in chapter one: This state of envy is a result of rejecting the Self. A psychology that recognizes the archetypal power of the Self can also consider the existence and devastating effects of envy, without seeing it simply as a too-negative concept that is consequently of little use. Envy dominates the world of the narcissistic character, but the Self offers a greater order and reality that is a way out.

In his commentary on *Thus Spake Zarathustra,* Jung deals with the Self in ways that are very unlike the descriptions found in his Collected Works. Nietzsche's emphasis was upon the Self being *embodied,* and consequently in these seminars we find a good deal about the body that is most illuminating, and quite useful in considering Stage Two of transformation (see chapter three).

Jung, in the above passage, touches upon an aspect of the narcissistic character disorder not found in psychoanalytic thought. There it is always a result of infantile-developmental conflicts (see chapter one). But narcissistic structuring can occur at any developmental phase. Just as the Self may be hidden away in infancy because the environment is too negative for its embodiment, it may also be denied at later stages in life. And this denial of the Self may contribute to the formation of the narcissistic character disorder quite as much as do its infant origins.

9 Narcissism as a Concept in Jungian Psychology

For many years Jungians have been acquainted with the issue of meaning and the existence or absence of the guiding power of the Self which alone gives a person a sense of direction, and ultimately an awareness of personal identity. This would appear to be the main fare of Jungian psychology. Is not the clinical picture of the narcissistic character disorder covered by well-established Jungian concepts such as the failure to live the reality of the Self, and associated patterns of anima or animus possession?

Contrary to the view often held, that Narcissus has little to do with the clinical notion of narcissism, in chapter two I will show that this is not at all the case. The behavior pattern whose image is Narcissus is the same pattern that determines the development of the narcissistic character. So it would be possible to simply analyze the myth, and avoid the nasty issue of labels and diagnosis. I choose not to do this, for the main feature of the clinical picture of the narcissistic character is *not* covered by certain complexes or archetypal patterns. The clinical picture, especially in the initial stages of transformation, is dominated by the specific nature of the transference-countertransference process. Consequently, the failure to relate to the narcissistic character through an understanding of this process, and especially the objective nature of the countertransference, frequently results in a failure to constellate a healing process. Or worse, one risks causing the patient to be enslaved to his idealizations in the service of feeding the analyst's own narcissistic needs.

Defining these existential disorders in terms of their content, whether it be complexes of the shadow, the contrasexual dominants anima/animus, or of the Self, even if one is very careful in specifying the particular nature of, for example, the "anima/animus possession," is thus off the mark. The very same complex-phenomena found in the narcissistic character disorders are also found in the borderline and schizoid states, yet the transference-countertransference processes can differ strongly from one category to the other. Accordingly, the way of approaching the patient is confused rather than clarified by reference to complexes.

If one fails to heed the specific nature of the transference-countertransference issue, that is if one does not understand its objective meaning and relate out of this understanding, analytical work will most likely become based upon the dialectic model that Jung proposed as one image of the analytical relationship.[29] This encounter between two individuals giving expression to the unconscious is often appropriate when the interacting individuals are capable of somewhat equal participation. But in the narcissistic character disorders this is precisely not the case, a situation often blurred by the seeming authority of the patient.

There is a further difficulty that is more subtle. If the analyst is well related to the Self as an inner directing center, if he is open enough to listen to his own unconscious wisdom as to *when* to interpret or *when* to be still, then the therapy will often proceed as if the analyst were operating through a conscious attitude toward the specific transference mode in question. The narcissistic character disorders would appear to be tailor-made for "working out of the Self," so to speak, and for disregarding very much conscious reflection on the nature of the transference-countertransference process. When this works it is fine, but this approach is often blind, for it tends to be guided by the ordering capacity of the Self, and consequently is oriented toward order and may undervalue certain disordering effects such as envy and rage. It easily fails to understand these all-important elements of the narcissistic character disorder, contents which I view as catalysts to the transformation process. Moreover, when the analyst's Self-connection is disturbed by the impingement of difficult emotions such as envy, the dialectical method of working out of the Self often degenerates into its caricature, a need for being omnipotent.

The transferences that dominate the narcissistic character disorder are often not, in my experience, neatly arranged into the pure forms of idealization or the mirror transference as proposed by Kohut (see chapter one). It is only when the transferences appear in rather pure forms that working out of the Self is a somewhat reliable guide. When there is a "mixed" transference, and when it is vital to analyze rage, *indeed pick it out of analytical material* when it could easily be sidestepped, the conscious awareness of the nature of the narcissistic disorder is essential; then working from a sense of the objectivity of one's own unconscious and the directing power of the Self often falters.

Optimally, it is necessary to blend the approach of working out of the Self with conscious reflection on the meaning of the transference-countertransference process. This offers a way of keeping oneself open to the unconscious in the face of strong transference reactions which tend to constellate one's own narcissistic defensiveness. Similarly, being attuned to the unconscious in the manner captured by that phrase, "working out of the Self," helps avoid the rigidity that often occurs by attending solely to the transference-countertransference dynamics.

The narcissistic character structure is found in personalities of widely varying quality. It can be dominant, or an aspect of any psychological pattern. It may be *the* dominant pattern, in which case we speak of a narcissistic character disorder. It may also be an auxiliary pattern, secondary to another, helpful or destructive to its development. It is a strong aspect of the pattern known as the puer aeternus and its counterpart, the senex. It is always a quality in the creative personality, especially evident as that person struggles to bring his or her creativity into the world. It is a dominant quality of the infantile personality with a strong mother complex. The list can be extended, for the narcissistic character disorder does not correspond to any one archetypal pattern.

The narcissistic character structure is a pattern that is a link between the personal and the archetypal realms. Accordingly, it is found in any archetypal pattern entering space/time reality, and within any personality structure. The narcissistic character disorder per se is a paradigm of a general structuring of psyche, and studying it is of value not only in dealing with personalities dominated by this condition, but also for understanding its manifestation in various psychological conditions.

10   Summary

In this introduction I have attempted to differentiate the Jungian view-point on identity and the Self from other approaches. In the chapters that follow, this differentiation will continue with reference to the transformation of the narcissistic character structure.

Just as there exists a wide variation of approaches within the Freudian-psychoanalytic community, the same is true among Jungians. Some analytical psychologists see a closer relationship between the psychoanalytic and Jungian views of the Self than I do. Others find far less value in the psychoanalytic literature. I have especially come to believe that the factor of the *numinosum,* even when slight as a psychic reality, is of vital importance in terms of the analyst's attitude toward the pre-oedipal disorders. What we believe and see, or believe we see, greatly affects our patients. I have come to recognize more and more that patients that seem to have absolutely no sense of the archetypal dimension, those for whom the Jungian or archetypal approach would seem to be without significance, eventually come to recognize, to some degree or other, the numinous energy of the archetype. And when this occurs, it is often the case that they "knew it all the time."

Throughout this book I note the difference between a personalistic and an archetypal point of view toward narcissism. Both are necessary. The psychoanalytic contribution to the treatment of narcissistic character disorders is valuable in its emphasis upon the transference-countertransference, and upon the personal unconscious comprised of introjected objects. But, as we shall see in chapter one, the Freudian concept of narcissism is actually a description of psychic states and processes similar to the material Jung first set out in 1911 in *Psychology of the Unconscious* (later revised as *Symbols of Transformation*), the book that led to his break with Freud. There Jung was concerned with the transformation of psychic energy, but primarily with the energy-upgrading or value-endowing dimension of the psyche. This was often referrred to by him as the spirit archetype, which he found to be extremely ambivalent and paradoxical.

It is obvious that Jung was discovering then (and later in his work on alchemical symbolism), from an archetypal point of view, what psychoanalysts are now studying from a personalistic point of view under the term narcissism. Not only do psychoanalysts find narcissism to be extremely polyvalent and paradoxical, but many have also stressed that narcissism and its transformations can endow psychic contents with value. It appears that what Freud rejected in Jung's work at the time of their break is now entering psychoanalytic thought through the back door, so to speak, in the subject of narcissism.

Psychoanalysts, especially the school of object relations, work out of a conception of psychic structure as introjects of the experience of personal interactions and the possibility of transformation of inner objects formed in that manner. But they do not generally recognize the existence of archetypal psychic realities or the value of introversion and creative imagination in activating them. Yet there are healing processes in which archetypal factors are clearly the dominant elements. These archetypal factors exist in potential in the collective unconscious, the objective psyche, much as systems in nature can be conceived of as having active and potential forms.

The prejudice against the reality of an archetypal psyche, as distinct from an inner world of introjects, runs throughout psychoanalytic literature. Even Winnicott, generally so sensitive to both the reality of the psyche and the need to respect the secrecy of the patient's inner world, falls back onto the notion of introjects when discussing mysticism:

> In thinking of the psychology of mysticism, it is usual to concentrate on the understanding of the mystic's withdrawal into a personal inner world of sophisticated introjects. Perhaps not enough attention has been paid to the mystic's retreat to a position in which he can communicate secretly with subjective objects and phenomena, the loss of contact with the world of shared reality being counterbalanced by a gain in terms of feeling real.[30]

At least he gives value here to introversion and to psychic reality—unusual for a Freudian-oriented analyst. But the inner objects of the world of mystical experience can hardly be reduced to "sophisticated introjects." At best, there may be meditative aids that are incorporated, but only as a path toward experiences that are always new, always a unique discovery of archetypal reality.

Narcissistic characters experience a deficiency in the areas of introversion and imagination as a result of an extremely negative field of personal introjects. Because the conscious ego of the narcissistic character anticipates no inner support and has no confidence in its own inner resources, it avoids introversion and imaginal activity except of the most passive wish-fulfillment kind. However, when activated, the potential archetypal factors behave as inner objects often far more powerful than personally acquired introjects. The possibility then emerges for the redemption of introversion and imagination. Once these are developed, they in turn facilitate the positive activity of the archetypal processes. Then the energy invested in narcissistic activity, defensiveness and self-adoration can instead find its proper goal: the discovery of individuality guided by the central archetype, the Self.

Unless the introverted dimension is dealt with and the creative function of imagination appropriated by the ego, the healing of narcissistic disorders is incomplete and unstable. The inner domain to which introversion addresses itself is that which has traditionally been called the soul. This is why the narcissistic problem, though it appears so superficial, actually runs very deep. For the issues raised by the narcissistic character disorder are those of the suffering and depths of the soul.

I

Stage One of Transformation:
Clinical Issues

1 Psychoanalytic and Archetypal Points of View

A major difficulty in presenting a coherent psychoanalytic view of narcissism is that writers in this area of study often have divergent opinions. Let us begin with the contrasting views of Otto Kernberg and Heinz Kohut, with regard to the patient with a narcissistic character disorder. For Kernberg,

> These patients present an unusual degree of self-reference in their interactions with other people, and a great need to be loved and admired by others, and a curious apparent contradiction between a very inflated concept of themselves and an inordinate need for tribute from others. Their emotional life is shallow. They experience little empathy for the feelings of others, they obtain very little enjoyment from life other than from the tributes they receive from others or from their own grandiose fantasies, and they feel restless and bored when external glitter wears off and no new sources feed their self-regard.[31]

He especially emphasizes the role of envy, rage and hatred:

> These patients experience a remarkably intense envy of other people who seem to have things they do not have or who simply seem to enjoy their lives. . . . They are especially deficient in genuine feelings of sadness and mournful longing; their incapacity for experiencing depressive reactions is a basic feature of their personality. When abandoned or disappointed by other people they may show what on the surface looks like depression, but which on further examination emerges as anger and resentment, loaded with revengeful wishes, rather than real sadness for the loss of a person whom they appreciated.[32]

The narcissistic character, writes Kernberg, sees others as "shadowy objects":

> People may appear to him either to have some potential food inside, which the patient has to extract, or to be already emptied and therefore valueless. In addition, these shadowy external objects sometimes suddenly seem to be invested with high and dangerous powers. . . . His attitude toward others is either deprecatory—he has extracted all he needs and tosses them aside—or fearful—others may attack, exploit, and force him to submit to them. At the bottom of this dichotomy lies a still deeper image of the relation with external objects. . . . It is the image of a hungry, enraged, empty self, full of impotent anger at being frustrated, and fearful of a world which seems as hateful and revengeful as the patient himself.[33]

Not only is the world of outer object relations robbed of vitality by the patient's envy and hatred, but the internal world also suffers:

> Internalized object representations acquire the characteristics of real, but rather lifeless, shadowy people. . . .
> They need to devaluate whatever they receive in order to prevent themselves from experiencing envy. This is the tragedy of these patients: that they need so much from others while being unable to acknowledge what they are receiving because it would stir up envy.[34]

For Kernberg, the only "plus" for these patients is

> their relatively good social functioning, their . . . impulse control, and what may be described as a 'pseudosublimatory' potential, namely the capacity for active, consistent work in some areas which permits them partially to fulfill their ambitions of greatness and of obtaining admiration from others.[35]

Kernberg's estimation leaves one with a very negative picture of the narcissistic character disorder. The extreme paucity of inner objects matches the narcissistic character's poor object relations; this psychic structure is heavily determined by defenses against experiencing envy, rage and intense hatred. Inwardly, Kernberg sees the narcissistic character as manifesting a cohesive structure which is a regressive fusion of early self and object images and which largely serves a defensive function. The resultant incapacity to deal with other people as real, or to properly assess personal capacities, becomes, for Kernberg, a tragic situation that dominates their lives and gets worse with age.[36] (The "fusion of self and object images" is psychoanalytic language for what analytical psychologists would see as an ego which regressively clings to a uroboric stage, resulting in ego inflation through identity with the archetype.)

But Kernberg's description of the ego-self structure, indeed his general view of narcissistic character disorders, is not shared by Heinz Kohut. Rather than envision the narcissistic character's self structure as a regressive fusion and pathologically distorted, Kohut regards it as a stage of blocked development, with the self not basically disturbed, but only hindered in its evolution. In essence, for Kohut, it is archaic and at an exhibitionistic-grandiose level, but it is basically sound, while for Kernberg the self structure is fundamentally disturbed, especially in the dominance of "splitting."[37]

Kohut also finds symptomatology and phenomenological descriptions of far less importance than does Kernberg. For Kohut the major diagnostic factor and healing element is the transference-countertransference process:

> Despite the initial vagueness of the presenting symptomatology, however, the most significant symptomatic features can usually be discerned with increasing clarity as the analysis progresses, especially as the narcissistic transference in one of its forms comes into being. The patient will describe subtly experienced, yet pervasive feelings of emptiness and depression

which, in contrast to the conditions in the psychoses and borderline states, are alleviated as soon as the narcissistic transference has become established — but which become intensified when the relationship to the analyst is disturbed. The patient will attempt to let the analyst know that, at times at least, especially when the narcissistic transference has become disrupted, he has the impression that he is not fully real, or at least that his emotions are dulled; and he may add that he is doing his work without zest.... These and many other similar complaints are indicative of the ego's depletion because it has to wall itself off against the unrealistic claims of an archaic grandiose self or against the intense hunger for a powerful external supplier of self-esteem.[38]

Intense rage and especially envy are not for Kohut essentially fixed features of the narcissistic character, but are rather transient affects due to empathetic failure. The character structure itself, the grandiose-exhibitionistic self merged with the ego, is for Kohut a blocked development that can unfold once the narcissistic transferences he describes become manifest.

Kohut defines two major transference paradigms, which he calls the mobilization of the idealized self and the grandiose-exhibitionistic self. These are discussed in detail later in this chapter, but here we may note that he regards them as natural, developmental forms of the self, which need to be allowed to unfold during psychotherapy. Kernberg, on the other hand, regards idealization and grandiosity as serving defensive purposes, primarily to ward off the experience of envy. Kohut thus stresses the positive, transformative potential in narcissistic character disorders, while Kernberg stresses their negative, destructive and controlling nature.

The following summary of Kohut's views by Paul Ornstein is comprehensive:

The self as a bipolar configuration contains at one end of the pole the transformations of archaic grandiosity and exhibitionism into the central self assertions, goals and ambitions. At the other pole it contains the transformation of archaic idealization into the central idealized values and internalized guiding principles. The ever-present tension arc which Kohut describes between these poles encompasses the innate talents and skills which the self is able to use to express the basic design which is laid down in the nuclear self. This nuclear self is the earliest complex mental organization and is prone to enfeeblement and fragmentations. At such fragmentations, isolated drives emerge with considerable intensity as disintegration products of the self. Thus, Kohut affirms that neither narcissistic rage and destructiveness nor infantile sexuality are, in isolation, primary psychological configurations. The primary psychological configuration is the relation between the self and its self-objects....

The empathetic response of the self-object allows for the building up of psychic structure through the process of transmuting internalizations. This is the bit by bit acquisition of structure with development. Deficiency in the line of development of the grandiose self-object will lead to an absence of the ability to pursue one's goals and ambitions, an absence of the capacity to experience pleasure in one's mental and physical activities, and the absence of reliable regulation of self-esteem. These are, then, the characteristics associated with the narcissistic personality disorders. In the developmental line of the idealizing parental imago, the other pole of the bipolar self, the deficiency in structure will lead to the absence of drive controlling, channeling, and neutralizing functions, the characteristics of the behavior disorders.

This schema accounts for the specific impact of parental psychopathology, especially self-pathology, on the developing nuclear self and points the direction for the acquisition of psychic structure during treatment via transmuting internalizations during working through of specific self-object transferences.[39]

Kohut's insistence on the basically positive nature of the self, unfolding through empathy, has caused considerable reaction from his psychoanalytic colleagues. Searles especially focuses on the problems posed by negative countertransference emotions:

It's a very fine, and difficult, and I think perhaps essentially not entirely possible thing, to distinguish whether one is empathetically sensing the patient's dissociated images of herself, felt as one's own, or to what extent one is experiencing parts of one's genuinely own self that were never adequately analyzed. . . .

Despite the many things I admire about Kohut's concepts, my main criticism of him is that one gets from him a view of the analyst that is, in my sense of it, a bit unpalatably kindly, wise, non-hating. I simply cannot accept this. It is, to me, too narcissistically gratifying to the analyst to so regard himself. . . .

What Kohut does not mention, and what I think we need to address ourselves to, is the highly negative countertransference phenomenon that the analyst has in working with such a [narcissistic] patient. The analyst inevitably regresses in the course of the session and will experience the patient as being identified with the so-called bad mother of the patient's past. The analyst will inevitably react to the patient as being a very disappointing and enraging unempathetic mother. My impression is that the countertransference experiences in work with these patients are so very, very negative that there's a powerful tendency for the analyst to regress in trying to cope with these negative experiences. As a result, the analyst speaks with a narcissistic rage of the patient whose mother is unempathetic. I would simply put alongside that the inevitable development of the analyst's narcissistic rage in response to the patient's limited capacity for empathy. . . . I would simply again . . . mention how disappointing to the analyst these very difficult patients are—how they mobilize one's idealized self-object reactions to them and then they disappoint one, so that one has to deal with one's own disappointment and rage.

. . . . It is worth simply reminding ourselves of the role of the analyst's ability to hate and to use his hate.[40]

The Kohutian analyst might counter that if one properly understands hate and rage and other negative emotions, especially if one sees them as disintegration products caused by wounds to self-esteem, then they become much less of a problem than Searles believes.[41] The issue, however, is not *being able* to slip out of negative countertransference reactions, but the ability to do so when it is appropriate, or alternatively to use the reactions when that is required. The former situation often pertains to forming an alliance and to creating an environment in which the narcissistic or self-transferences can emerge.

Dealing with negative countertransference reactions prematurely can destroy the cohesive formation of a narcissistic transference, or else turn it into a defensive structure. Idealization can of course be used for both purposes, but the premature use of negative countertransference reactions can turn a potentially nondefensive idealization into a defensive one. Moreover, one also then gets a clinical picture that looks like a borderline state, and this may account for Kernberg's insistence that the narcissistic personality can be an instance of the borderline personality organization.[42] But I find much to recommend Searles' observations, for it is my experience that it is sometimes necessary to deal with extremely negative countertransference reactions at the outset *in order that* a transference can form

For example, a patient came to me after he had had several disappointing analytical experiences in which he was able to totally control his analysts, one a man and the other a woman. Both idealized him and looked to him for interpretations. In our first session I became aware that I was feeling very angry, and realized I was experiencing his own unconscious rage. I told him how I felt and asked if he was angry with me. He then admitted that while driving to my office he had wondered whether or not I allowed smoking, and if not, did I allow guests at parties to smoke? As he spoke he became aware that he was angry. He quickly went on, with a controlling mirror transference to prevent me from saying more or from dealing with his question. But already I had become different from his previous analysts, both of whom he had seduced with his charisma and intelligence. By recognizing his unconscious rage from the start I became someone who could not be easily seduced, and a narcissistic transference was immediately established. If I had not dealt with my countertransference feelings at the outset—and they could easily have been sidestepped in the spirit of gaining a friendly rapport—a defensive idealization would have formed and a good deal of time been wasted.

Returning now to the divergent views of psychoanalytic authors, Béla Grunberger is one who attempts to place narcissism within an extended view of the Freudian drive theory and ego-id-superego model. Grunberger notes Freud's comment on narcissism as "absolutely self-sufficient [in] fetal existence" and his reference to the "narcissism of germ cells," to illustrate his own position that narcissism pertains to prenatal life, and to the loss of that pristine state.[43] For Grunberger, "narcissism is a psychic agency . . . present at [and even before] birth . . . as absolute and forceful in its demands as an instinct."[44] He believes that "narcissism should . . . be recognized as an autonomous factor within the framework of the Freudian topography and be promoted to the rank of psychic agency along with the id, the ego and the superego."[45] Not only is it the energy of the prenatal state of wholeness, but it is the source of value for all later psychic agencies. According to Grunberger, narcissism "follows throughout its existence a development parallel to that of the drives . . . functionally different from the drives . . . constituting a separate dimension of the psychic realm and governed by laws other than those that govern instinctual life proper."[46]

For Grunberger, narcissism is therefore a fourth factor of equal importance to those in the Freudian ego-id-superego trinity, having its own "functionally different laws." (A fourfold structure to narcissism per se has also been described by Ernest Jones.)[47]

Grunberger's is an attempt to bring order to what Freudians themselves consider chaos within their differing views on narcissism:

> Whoever addresses the question of narcissism comes up against the paradoxical polysemy of the concept. An important aspect of the multiplicity of meanings was examined by Andreas-Salome. . . . She tried to explain the contradictory tendencies of narcissists, who seek individuality at all costs and yet cannot live outside a continuing state of fusion. . . . *The fact is that narcissism always has a dual orientation.* . . . Thus we are dealing with a narcissism that is centrifugal or centripetal, primary or secondary. . . . healthy or pathological, mature or immature, merged with the drive component or opposed to it, its antagonist.[48]

And echoing many other investigators of narcissism, Grunberger goes on:

> One could write a voluminous and painstaking study on the historical development of this concept in Freud's work. . . . In practical terms, however, such efforts result in pure chaos in which it is very difficult to find one's bearings. Hart has shown us how many contradictions there are in the notion of narcissism, making an unambiguous definition well-nigh impossible. . . . "Narcissism is reported as inherent in the most sublime of sublimations and in the most psychotic of regressions. In some instances it is held responsible for the heightening of male potency, but in other cases blamed for its diminution. It can be found at work in feminine frigidity and in feminine attractiveness. It is supposed to neutralize any destructive tendencies, yet becomes a source of anxiety to the ego. It is a defense against homosexuality, yet homosexuals are particularly 'narcissistic.' Sleep is a narcissistic withdrawal of libido, yet sleeplessness is the flight of enhanced narcissism from further augmentation. It is used to explain the drag of inertia and the drive of ambition." ("Narcissistic Equilibrium," Int. Jour. Psychoanalysis, v. 28, p. 106, 1947).[49]

Thus we have narcissism as a contradictory concept, easily thwarting rational attempts at definition, and in fact always having a dual orientation. While narcissistic disturbances exist at all levels of psychic disorder, for example in psychoneuroses, borderline states and the psychoses, attention has especially been given, during the last decade, to their role in the character disorders.

The issues of narcissism as dealt with by psychoanalytic authors are subjects that were of concern to Jung, but from a different point of view.

While Freudian approaches are personalistic (parental imagos being the main source of introjected structures), for Jung these all-important imagos are basically a form that the a priori energy of the archetype fills. The distinction is crucial in that Jung's view allows for an indigenous healing potential within the psyche itself, whereas the other restricts healing to a restructuring of objects, internalized in childhood, by means of new introjects provided by present-day relations such as the psychotherapeutic ones.

The ambivalence of the archetype is well known from Jung's researches. And it is precisely this ambivalence that, as we have seen, characterizes narcissism. In *Symbols of Transformation,* as well as in other works, Jung traces the transformations of psychic energy; and while numerous archetypes attend this process, the major one is the spirit archetype, carried by the image of the hero. It is autonomous, value-endowing and highly inflationary when the ego identifies with it. The spirit archetype is the main factor behind the "free energy" or "excess libido" Jung speaks of, and is the archetypal correlate of the "neutral-energy" Freud identifies with narcissism.

Freud's vantage point was extraverted, deductive and clinical; Jung's was more introspective and concerned with those unique events which result in great religious revelations and individual transformation. Freud's data is more repetitive and observable; Jung's are the "points off the graph" of any statistical study. Hence scientifically oriented minds gravitated more to Freud. Now the archetypal point of view is not only becoming more fashionable but is increasingly recognized as essential to an understanding of the deeper psychic conflicts.

Narcissism, in psychoanalytic thought, is not only of a psychic nature. While certain authors such as Kohut lean in this direction—and thereby come quite close to Jung's 1928 view of libido[50]—others, such as Kernberg and Grunberger, are especially concerned with the interaction between narcissism and instinctual processes. Grunberger conceives of this as a mutual transformation, in which "instinct is conferred with narcissistic qualities . . . so it becomes a treasure . . . and narcissism comes to grips with reality."[51] And for Kernberg, narcissism and instinctual processes are strongly intertwined. Thus to the duplex nature of narcissism already noted, whereby it is the value-endowing factor as well as the source of ego inflation, we must add its equal participation in the domain of instinct and the body.

With this addition of the "material factor" we come to Jung's alchemical studies. While his work on psychic energy employed a purely psychological model (the psyche as "a *relatively* closed system"),[52] in his alchemical studies Jung began to wrestle with the immense issue of the relationship between spirit and matter. While his emphasis is most assuredly on the psychic aspect, his researches here lay the basis for a proper archetypal view of the images that transcend matter and psyche and which picture their mutual transformation. More than any other image, the alchemical Mercurius, studied exhaustively by Jung, represents the archetypal analogue of the phenomenology known as narcissism.

Jung summarized his researches on Mercurius as follows:

(1) Mercurius consists of all conceivable opposites. He is thus quite obviously a duality, but is named a unity in spite of the fact that his innumerable inner contradictions can dramatically fly apart into an equal number of disparate and apparently independent figures.

(2) He is both material and spiritual.

(3) He is the process by which the lower and material is transformed into the higher and spiritual, and vice versa.

(4) He is the devil, a redeeming psychopomp, an evasive trickster, and God's reflection in physical nature.

(5) He is also the reflection of a mystical experience of the artifex [the alchemist] that coincides with the *opus alchymicum*.

(6) As such, he represents on the one hand the self and on the other the individuation process and, because of the limitless number of his names, also the collective unconscious.[53]

The similarity between the psychoanalytic concept of narcissism and the alchemical image of Mercurius is striking. A dual nature and even the potential for splitting is common to both. They also share in the participation and mutual transformation of spiritual and material processes. Narcissism is a trickster, leading one to all kinds of inflation and self-importance, with nothing in the end to show for it. It is a once-lived immersion in Paradise (Grunberger) and thus has some relationship with what Jung calls the "mystical experience of the artifex."

In psychoanalysis (Grunberger, Kohut), narcissism represents an agency of the self, and it also pertains to the Freudian view of individuation in both positive (Kohut) and negative (Kernberg) ways. Generally, narcissistic character structures are involved with individuation much as Mercurius is. As we shall see, they represent both the urge toward individuation and the drive toward the regressive fusion of ego and Self images. They represent the power to effectively block the emergence of psychic contents that may be too disordering at a particular stage of psychic development, but equally the power to forestall future growth. They can contain archetypal, healing powers and behave like the "unborn god," or they can be a consistent, demonic urge toward power through ego inflation. They can lead to the emergence of a new spirit, through idealizations, or they can use idealization primarily defensively to control envy. Narcissistic character structures can lead to a birth of the feminine or to the repression of this realm of being and body with its own spirit and consciousness. As well, they can lead to a capacity for reflection, or to its continual suppression under the dominance of a grandiose-exhibitionistic power drive.

I have drawn the analogy between narcissism, narcissistic character disorders and the alchemical god Mercurius to suggest that narcissism has an archetypal background. The descriptions of Mercurius stem from meditative reflections and projections onto matter and its transformations, projections which are transpersonal contents of the collective unconscious, and thus not capable of reduction to repressions or personal material. Archetypes and archetypal processes are potential patterns of the psyche. Just as an equation may have many solutions, each complete in itself, with one or another necessary for any given situation, so too the collective unconscious has many possible forms that may constellate under given conditions. These conditions may be personal and historical, but they can just as well be purely indigenous, psychic factors.

While a Jungian view of narcissistic disorders can certainly benefit from the Freudian emphasis on object relations and instinct, and especially the inclusion of the body image in the Self concept, a Freudian view could benefit from an appreciation of the archetypal dimension. For the ego, in dealing with the various blockages in personality development such as occur in narcissistic character disorders, is actually facing a conflict of powers that are impersonal and of far greater energy content than that of the ego. This awesome fact is easily overlooked by the clinical view which insists that the root of narcissistic problems lies in the interpersonal domain—especially that of parental empathetic failures or constitutional problems with aggression.

Some aspects of narcissism are certainly rooted in the interpersonal, perhaps even in the constitution of the individual, but not to the exclusion of the transpersonal. Narcissistic problems may appear due to transformations attempting to occur in the collective unconscious. These problems must therefore also be understood as purposive, the symptoms of a new Self image attempting to incarnate, either in the individual or in the collective or both. They may represent nothing less than the psyche's response to the call that "God is dead," raised by Nietzsche many years ago, and painfully brought home to us in the fragmentation our modern society suffers and creates.

2   Profile of the Narcissistic Character

The following descriptions highlight the dominant features of the narcissistic character disorder. Everyone has in his or her personality some of these features, but in the narcissistic character they are chronically present.

Lacks penetrability

The experience of being with a person with a narcissistic character disorder is one of being kept away, warded off. Often this is accompanied by a body tightness or tension. Extreme self-reference is dominant in the narcissistic character, so that whatever one says is immediately transformed by that person into a story or fantasy or idea about himself (or herself). One feels like a stimulus to a response which excludes participation.

Rejects interpretation

A common analytic experience is that interpretations, if given, are distorted or have little effect. If the analyst attempts to expand the analysand's self-awareness by interpreting a family or life problem in the light of dreams or other psychic material, the interpretation may be 1) totally ignored or rejected; 2) enthusiastically accepted, only to be totally nonexistent in the following session; or 3) taken in and selectively modified to serve the person's a priori inflated or deflated self concept. In all cases, the resultant experience is that the interpretation was useless or even destructive.

Cannot tolerate criticism

Criticism is met with extreme resistance. The person with a narcissistic character disorder has so little sense of identity—a feature of which is the capacity of the ego to be separate from, yet related to, the Self and the outer world—that any criticism at all is felt as a personal threat. This extends to reductive analysis generally, for viewing himself relative to any psychic content other than his own grandiose (or deflated) self concept threatens his identity. Criticism of any kind, before a good rapport is established (which can take a very long time), may result in the patient's abrupt termination of therapy.

Cannot integrate synthetic approach

While reductive analysis is not feasible, at least until the narcissistic transferences are worked through, it is equally, but more subtly, destructive to employ what Jung calls the synthetic approach.[54] The narcissistic character is presymbolic, unable to appreciate the reality of the symbol because of the ever-present merger between ego and Self, or ego and world. The symbol is the "other," the nonego characterizing the objective psyche, and unless it bursts through in the form of a *unio mystica*[55] (a very rare occurrence) symbolic reality will not exist for the narcissistic character. Thus interpretations along symbolic lines, stressing the positive, synthetic nature of unconscious contents, will only result in inflating an already grandiose ego-Self merger.[56]

Unfortunately, this feeding of a person's narcissism is a seductive approach that often keeps narcissistic characters in therapy for a long time, with little transformation. Furthermore, unconscious rage is built up by the synthetic approach, for the person knows he is really not being related to. If anything, the premature reference to symbolic reality makes it more difficult for the patient to express anger, and as such actually blocks transformation.

Low emphathetic capacity

Just as narcissistic characters are difficult to reach empathetically, so too they can be cruel and self-centered in situations that beg for the slightest degree of empathy. Often one gets the feeling that it is not just a question of a low empathetic capacity, but rather that empathy is withheld for cruel, sadistic purposes.

Takes pride in having no needs

The narcissistic character rejects feelings of need for another human being, for experiencing such needs can unleash rage and envy that could flood the weak ego structure. Narcissistic characters often take pride in having no needs, while doing a great deal for others. "I can do it" is often their motto. If their own needs for sympathy or relatedness are kindled, this often is experienced as a blow to their self-esteem, and can lead to depression and loss of energy.

Lacks sense of history or process

Narcissistic characters experience history in a marginal way.[31] Situations are not really *experienced* because every situation is met out of the weak ego's complex of low esteem. Consequently, historical process is only assimilated to the extent that it aggrandizes the ego. Another class of events remembered with great tenacity are those which wounded the ego's self-esteem.

History is also distorted. We have seen how the narcissistic character can distort interpretations; this can extend to extensive lying. For the internal-grandiose pressure so overwhelms the ego that it causes the ego to meet situations not with a realistic response, but with lies that meet the inner demands of omnipotence. Thus it is not what actually happens historically that is of importance to the narcissistic character, as much as how that event meets—or can be twisted into meeting- inner, grandiose pressure.

A lack of real, historical sense may manifest in other ways. For example, narcissistic characters often feel much younger or older, but rarely their actual age. Their sense of age may be diffuse, varying greatly from one situation to the next. Another example is their tendency to tell the same story over and over again, with no awareness that they are repeating it to the same person. This can be especially painful to a more conscious partner who, pointing out the repetition, gets the response, "That is so new to me," or "I didn't know you'd feel that way," when the same issue has been talked about over and over again. The sense of "newness" is very real for the narcissistic character, but the repetition is confusing and annoying for the person listening.

The narcissistic character's lack of a sense of history includes a poor relationship to inner psychic processes. This may be a response to the grandiose pressure, which (as shall be described later in the section on narcissistic structures) can be characterized as a negative magician or negative senex figure. As such, the rejection of history is a result of the lack of this archetypal potential on an inner level, a potential that would stem from the positive senex or father constellation.

Disturbed masculine and feminine functioning

Both masculine and feminine functioning are disturbed in the narcissistic character. The realm of spirit as a connecting link to creativity and religious values, as well as a positive connection to the "spirit of the times"—and especially as the capacity for reflection—are missing. Instead there is a grandiose power drive. Under its control, certainty must reign and chance be suspended. Along with this constellation, which has affinities with the "black magician" of fairytales and folklore, the feminine realm of *being* (including proper relatedness to the Self and the body) is absent; crushed by the power drive and compulsion of the "magician," but basically under the influence of a negative feminine constellation. In the language of fairytales this is called the "false bride"—the negative mother in the form of the witch who usurps the place of the "true bride." Through the "false bride" the value of the Self is usurped by the ego, leading to inflation and the denial of the positive significance of suffering. All is oriented toward appearances, outer rather than inner beauty (see section ten in this chapter).

While feminine and masculine functioning are disturbed in the narcissistic character disorders of both men and women, the burden of transformation usually falls upon the proper connecting link between consciousness and the unconscious. Thus, for men the anima problem is usually central, while for women the problem is mainly with the animus.[58] (We shall see in the next section how envy of the opposite sex, so common in narcissistic characters, stems from the anima/animus problem.)

When the anima emerges in positive form, the potential exists for internal mirroring, for ego and Self to enter into a relationship of mirror symmetry. Similarly, the emergence of a positive animus yields reflection and objectivity. For both men and women, the transformation of the contrasexual components results in the capacity for union and involvement with another person based upon consciousness and experienced needs. Thus the archetype of connection, the *coniunctio,* both to outer and inner worlds, is born and/or resurrected in the transformations of the narcissistic character disorder.

Potential for positive archetypal constellations

Both the outer and inner world of the narcissistic character have few good objects. Archetypally, the negative aspects of the mother and Self are dominant, so that the inner world is experienced as full of hate, rage, envy and crushing demands. This leads to a feeling of emptiness. But it is crucial to recognize that the narcissistic character is in a sense unborn, and that especially unborn are the positive archetypal constellations. Consequently, while the person's experience of his inner world is one of emptiness and danger, it is not uncommon to find, for example in dream material, a positive inner world ready to be born. But for this to occur (as will be clear from later discussions and clinical material) the transference-countertransference process must be constellated in a stable manner.

Until the inner world constellates in a positive way, reflection and imagination are superficial; flashiness substitutes for depth. But with the emergence of positive, archetypal factors comes the possibility for imagination to creatively function; the person no longer has to stay on the surface of life and the unconscious, but may instead experience a growing ability to penetrate into both realms. This signals the transformation of the narcissistic character.

3   The Problem of Envy and Rage

Kernberg and his followers emphasize the central role of envy in the narcissistic character, while Kohut and his school regard envy and rage, along with other affects, as a result of poor empathy. The issue of the strong negative emotions in the narcissistic character is fertile ground for a *privatio boni* argument, where evil is seen as the absence of good, darkness the absence of light, etc. Jung opposes this view; he insists that the dark side of the soul has a substantial reality.[59]

There is no doubt that emotions such as rage, hate and envy exist to a pronounced degree in the narcissistic character. In fact, narcissistic rage has a special, unforgiving quality. It is striking how this rage can live on in the unconscious, seemingly untouched by events that follow the wounding situation. Years after the fact, one can be astonished to experience the rage anew, as if the precipitating event had just taken place.

My experience is that properly addressing a grievance in relationship does not result in the disappearance of the rage that has built up, but rather in its possible transformation into a creative form. Generally, anger and rage are catalysts that are the driving force for the transformation of the narcissistic character disorder. Analytically, the eruption of rage when a sufficient analytical rapport has not been established is totally destructive, but equally, the denial of rage can result in a stalemate in which little transformation occurs.

Envy, the felt conviction that "anything I need will be withheld from me, so I will spoil or otherwise destroy the withholding object," is one of the most difficult emotions to experience and integrate.[60] Envy, the "evil eye" of folklore, is a central feature of the narcissistic character. It can take a grossly destructive form, but equally a subtle, spoiling one of precisely withholding what a person needs, for instance encouragement, warmth, bodily comfort, etc. In this manner, the narcissistic character often treats people in the way he experiences being treated himself.

This often stems from childhood, for the narcissistic character may actually have been the object of parental envy. It is not unusual for parents to envy the talents or abilities of their children, quite unconsciously. In such cases the child hears, "You have something special," but with the underlying message, "I hate you for it." The child's psyche responds by identifying with the feeling of being very special, and splitting off from the feeling of being hated. The sense of specialness is continually inflated as a defense against the feeling of being hated.

Narcissistic patients often speak of how full of praise and encouragement their parents are, yet they also confess a need to keep their distance from them, a strange sense of dis-ease in their presence. Analysis often reveals an underlying feeling of having been hated, the object of intense envy. Recovering this painful and frightening fact in analysis is essential, otherwise negative emotions remain in a repressed, split-off condition, and grandiosity continues in a negative, defensive way, undergoing no change and in fact getting worse with age.

Envy can dominate the life of the narcissistic character. A man may envy his wife's activities, femininity and way of being. Whatever she has he wants. And the narcissistic woman may envy her mate's physical prowess, business acumen or social ease. They can be totally unaware of their envious feelings, for to admit them consciously would be too "petty" and demeaning to their image of themselves as benevolently interested in the other person.

Envy of this kind appears to be rooted in the fact that the contrasexual components of personality, the man's anima and the woman's animus, are especially undeveloped in narcissistic characters.[61] They are largely assimilated by the exhibitionistic-grandiose form of the self, so that their proper functioning, which is to relate the conscious personality to both the outer and inner worlds, is deficient. Instead of reflection and relatedness there is compulsion and a continual self-reference.

Without a properly functioning anima or animus, identity will be either highly collectively determined or unstable. For the contrasexual dominants, as functions of relatedness between consciousness and the unconscious, are the psychic links between the ego and its root of identity in the Self. The narcissistic character keenly feels the pressure of individuation, and equally the lack of a living relationship between ego and Self when they are merged in a grandiose form. The already intense envy that dominates this merger fuels an envy of the opposite sex. Women become objects who in projection carry the desperately needed feminine side of the man, and men are similarly envied by women for their own needed masculine function.

Envy is the dark side of the narcissistic character. I view it with great importance, because I find it to be the "psychic glue," the element of affinity that keeps the components of the self, in its grandiose form, cohesively together. Dealing with envy and its associated components of rage and sadism can allow the deintegration of this self structure. As a result, a properly functioning anima or animus can emerge.

The psychoanalytic approach to envy and rage generally places its source in outer object relations. But it should be noted that these emotions, and especially narcissistic rage, can also appear as part of an introverted process. Individuals facing the pressure of an inner, creative task often experience rage at their own feelings of inferiority. I have seen this expressed in dreams of creative personalities, temporarily blocked in a creative task, by the image of the dreamer in a murderous rage at some figure who by association turns out to be creatively inept, while showing a great pretense at being creative. The rage stems from the lack of self-esteem, the narcissistic injury suffered by their own creative block and their own ineptitude. This shadow aspect often proves very difficult to integrate, for it contrasts so keenly with the narcissistic character's grandiose self image. However, its integration is often crucial for the creative task to continue in a positive manner.

4   Idealization in Transference and Countertransference

The term *idealization* denotes a process in which another person is viewed as all-good and all-powerful, benevolent and wise, and with no qualities that detract from this perfection – no "darkness" such as the all-too-human realities of anger, hate, deceit, shallowness, power drives, manipulations, envy, etc. The process of idealization can serve a primarily defensive purpose, where it defends against personally experiencing such negative feelings, or else it can represent the healthy mobilization of the positive Self in the form of projection: one's own better or potential qualities are "transferred" to another and experienced as characteristics of that person.

This one-sided projection (or transference) is a necessary stage during which the spiritual aspect of the Self unfolds, becoming a psychic structure that performs vital functions. It is natural in childhood, and it is a path taken by psychic energy during the transformation of the ego-Self merger in narcissistic character disorders. The spirit archetype,[62] often partially experienced through the idealized projection, is behind an individual's sense of creativity and purpose, of values and of psychic structure. Especially important is the role of this archetype in creating the inner capacity to assimilate the energy of instinctual life, so that the conscious ego gains new strength, felt, for example, in enhanced will power and the capacity for self-control.

In childhood, the spiritual aspect of the Self is usually first projected onto the mother, so that she embodies the archetype of wisdom (as does for example the image of Sophia), and later onto the father, who then carries the image of archetypal father. Grandparents or other figures also commonly carry these projections. It is essential that the child, who partially lives in a state of merger or oneness with the outside world, be allowed to merge in a bodily and psychic manner with these idealized objects. For only through an initial eros union (as in infant-parent bonding) can the projections later be assimilated as functions of the child's own psyche.

But if the spirit archetype is not positively constellated in the parents, it is difficult or impossible for them to properly accept the child's projection. The mother and father must accept being treated by the child as if they were invulnerable, without their own feelings and needs, knowing that this is not the child's "selfishness" operating, but rather the "godlike" projection of the spirit; otherwise they will find the projections oppressive, leading to demands that the child "grow up." In turn, the child often does grow up, but prematurely, and at the price of acquiring a narcissistic defense that prevents the archetypal projection from attaching to anyone, thus inhibiting a positive psychological development. This is one function of such a defense: It protects from a repeat of early wounding suffered through rejection of the idealized projection.

As a result of this early rejection, idealization later occurs as part of a defensive operation. Individuals may be idealized but they are eventually rejected with contempt when they fall short of the ideal. Similarly, institutions and causes of all kinds, political and religious, may be rabidly identified with and then rejected with equal finality. In such cases, idealization serves the function of defending against the envy and contempt that resulted from the failure of parental figures to properly accept the archetypal spirit projection. It is then not an easy matter for the positive spirit archetype to constellate in analysis, as the idealized transference. The resistance to this is experienced in the transference-countertransference process.

When a patient is withholding an idealized projection out of an expectation that idealization will be treated as it was in childhood, there are typical countertransference reactions. Common are boredom and the tendency for the analyst's attention to wander. The "message" to the analyst is: "I don't expect you to really be interested and accept my need to idealize you." Interpreting this can reveal underlying rage at the once-rejecting parent, an expectation carried over to the analyst (sometimes due to prior analytical failures with the present or a previous analyst in dealing with the idealizing process). But if this rage is expressed, the positive purpose of idealization can begin to unfold.

Another class of countertransference responses stems from the effect of being the object of idealization.[63] At a minor level this can lead to annoyance and exasperation in the analyst who resists being treated as a god.[64] Far more serious is the countertransference characterized by an energizing feeling of well-being and importance. The analyst's need to be seen in this way, his own unworked-through exhibitionism, can be transmitted to the patient as excitement.[65] This has an envious quality, a *demand* to be seen as omnipotent and a concomitant tendency to take over the analysis so as to ensure being continually seen as valuable, good, etc. Often the analyst will begin to share an inappropriate amount of personal material, or he will offer extensive amplifications in order to exhibit his knowledge. His behavior will generally have a compulsive quality.

The effect of all this on the analysand is that he feels his own process has been spoiled. All he knows is that his analyst feels excited and he is no longer the center of attention. Commonly, this builds up in the patient into a rage reaction.

If the analyst is aware of his countertransference response, and recog nizes that the energies he is filled with are really part of the patient's own process, then his empathetic understanding will return these energies, so to speak, to the patient. The result can then be a successful projection and integration of the idealized transference, leading in turn to the constellation of a stable, spiritual Self in the analysand.

But the experience and integration of the Self can also happen in an introverted way, as a result of a personal creative process or a numinous archetypal experience. Is there any difference between the integration process and its effects when a basically introverted approach is taken, and the more extroverted approach of working with the idealized transference?

There is a difference. The introverted relationship to the spirit archetype can lead to a strong sense of religious values, a healthy respect for and awareness of archetypal processes and surely a creative drive. The energy-upgrading function of the psyche can also be well established in this manner. But the introverted experience will generally be lacking in a ready extension to life, relatedness and especially in an in-body awareness of the spirit. The idea of being "in one's body"[66] will have little meaning to a person whose relationship to the spirit has stemmed from primarily introverted experience. But equally, the more extroverted way of working through an idealization has its deficiencies. This path may lead to a spiritual awareness of the value of relationship, especially of *its* energy-upgrading capacities, but it will lack the keen sense of archetypal reality more readily gained in an introverted way.

In fact, the two ways are complementary; both are necessary, while individually one somewhat excludes the awareness of the other. They form a pair of opposites that must be united for a stable and in-life experience of the spirit archetype.

5 Mirroring and the Mirror Transference

To be mirrored is to be understood, to feel that someone empathetically follows our thoughts, feelings, experiences, etc. It is a glaring deficiency in our culture that being right is more highly valued than being related. Yet to mirror another person requires a willingness to enter into his or her world, to suspend critical judgment and reflect what is being offered.

The need for mirroring from another is lifelong, and represents the inevitable incompleteness that accompanies growth. For mirroring is an externalization of an internal, psychic reality. It is based upon the fact that consciousness and the unconscious exist in a relationship of mirror symmetry. This has been well explained by Jung, and applied in his analysis of the Book of Job.[67] Ego consciousness is a mirror into which the Self gazes, and as such the Self's consciousness of itself and its development depends upon the consciousness of the ego. Conversely, the ego is a reflection of the Self, its attitudes and structure—a mirror replica of the Self.

The ego's stability is dependent upon an inner sense of being mirrored by the Self. But when collective forms of religion fail to contain the numinosity and symbolic presence of the Self, the ego is especially hard put to gain a sense of being mirrored from the Self within. And as individuation is a process in which the ego is challenged to develop toward greater wholeness (as imaged by the Self), at every stage there is a need for external mirroring, all the greater when really radical personality changes are necessary. When this development stabilizes, mirroring of this kind becomes less dependent upon another person's empathetic reflection, but is inevitably required again to meet new challenges. Any creative task is severely hindered by the absence of an external, mirroring presence along the way.

The archetypal image of the hero represents the capacity of the psyche to build up a new mirroring relationship between consciousness and the unconscious. But not to require, to some degree, the external mirroring of another person, or perhaps of a human or divine presence felt through books or other forms, is to identify with the hero archetype.

Mirroring is especially crucial in early childhood, the time when a symbiotic relationship must exist between mother and child. Since they then partake of a common energy field, processes in the child penetrate the mother and vice versa. But most important, the anxiety the child experiences as part of its emerging consciousness must also be experienced, and to some degree absorbed, by the mother.

The fact that disorder or anxiety accompanies emerging ego consciousness is imaged in numerous creation myths in which order or consciousness engenders disorder.[68] One need not adopt the theory of a Freudian or Kleinian "death instinct" to explain this; rather it is a natural consequence of the emergence of consciousness, a new ordering potential, into a time-bound system, whether that be a schedule, any temporal form, or eventually the ego system. A mother must be sensitive to, and capable of mediating, the disorder that accompanies her child's emerging consciousness. For she is the first carrier of the archetypal Self image, the central source of order in the personality. Properly containing the child's anxiety helps constellate the positive Self as an internal reality for the child, and

"Mirroring is especially crucial in early childhood."

with this an inner sense of security and actual inner functioning of the archetype of order. Unless this mirroring takes place, a child will not readily have the inner ground for development. All change will be fraught with anxiety and fear, and its sense of identity will be chronically diffuse.

Another form of mirroring is that of empathetically experiencing the contents of the child's personality. This means recognizing and mirroring its uniqueness, omnipotence, vulnerability and especially its exhibitionism, often manifesting through a field of sexual and aggressive energies For the child, ego and Self have not separated, and when it demands, "Look at me," the *me* is special. It is the quality of the child's Self that is being exhibited, the essence that its emerging ego must gradually reflect. If a child's exhibitionism is properly mirrored, that is if it feels really seen and listened to, then a healthy ego-Self relationship can begin to form. The growing ego will gain a sense of power and effectiveness in the world, and ambition will develop in realistic proportions.[69] Moreover, a sense of self-esteem will exist, rooted in stability in outer tasks, and especially in creative and instinctual functioning. Life will be entered with body-awareness and vitality.

But the evolution of exhibitionistic energies does not stop there. Rather, as individuation proceeds and the Self is experienced as the true center of the personality, the ego becomes a vessel that mirrors the glory of the Self, and at heightened times exhibits it, for example in creative moments or in religious awareness. Ultimately it is the Self, not the ego, that is the proper goal of exhibitionistic energies.

Narcissistic characters have generally experienced a chronic lack of mirroring, often stemming, as already mentioned, from parental envy. When parents lack a sense of their own identity they become sensitive to how their child likes *them,* or how it adds or detracts from *their* sense of esteem. Not only will they be unable to mirror the child's emerging personality, but they will want to be mirrored by the child, who feels this keenly. Often the child feels that it has something special the parents want, yet this specialness must be subverted to mirroring the parents, to giving back responses that make the parents feel secure. Otherwise there will be an uncomfortable feeling in the environment, a disquiet due to the parents' discomfort with their child's uniqueness. This undertone is the workings of envy, the spoiling effect stemming from the parents' insecurity and jealousy of their own children who may create an identity they themselves lack. The end result of this process is that rather than feel its Self loved and accepted, the child feels hated.

It is against this feeling of being envied and hated that the narcissistic character erects defenses. The resultant ego-Self structure can be characterized as both a regressive fusion product and as developmentally retarded. Generally, the child's exhibitionistic energies, usually in an instinctual matrix, have emerged but, meeting rejection, turn backwards and regressively fuse. The resultant structure is called, in psychoanalytic terms, the grandiose-exhibitionistic self. Analytical psychologists are more familiar with the image of the uroboros, the tail-eating dragon, representing the original condition out of which personality develops,[70] and in this model the fusion structure could be called defensive-uroboric. It contains the drive and seeds of personality growth, but has a defensive shell, the narcissistic defense, that denies needs rather than, as in the healthy, self-contained uroboric state, has them readily met.

Yet the original, nascent personality does still exist, ready to unfold, therefore the regressive fusion structure must also be seen in the context of a developmental blockage. The fact that the creative drive to personality formation is not basically injured in the narcissistic character attests to the strong archetypal underpinning to these disorders.

The central feature of the narcissistic fusion structure, the grandiose-exhibitionistic (or defensive-uroboric) self, is its capacity to exert control over others. Kohut has aptly called this phenomenon the *mirror transference,*[71] for through it the need for mirroring emerges, but in a controlling manner in which other persons are used, *forced* to be mirrors. This experience can be mild to intense for one who is the object of the narcissistic control, the intensity varying with the strength of the character disorder, or the need for defensiveness. Being controlled can be felt physically as a difficulty in breathing, as a choked-up feeling, and generally as a problem in staying embodied or "grounded." Psychically, the control often inhibits one's speech, as if anything said would be "thin" in content and certainly intrusive. If this inhibition is overpowered, the resultant feeling may be worse, that of emptiness and of having had no effect at all, except perhaps to evoke rage. Overall, the one being controlled has difficulty in maintaining his or her own standpoint, while the controlling person becomes the absolute center of attention.

When the mirror transference develops in psychotherapy, it is an attempt to undo the poor mirroring process of childhood that originally led to the narcissistic character structure. Understanding the purpose of the control, which at times can be very strong, is of the first order of importance in allowing the mirroring process to assume a natural, positive function. When the controlling effect can be recognized and accepted by the analyst, it becomes clear that one of its functions is to allow the analysand to feel effective.

Although narcissistic characters can have a strong effect on others, and are often seen as confident and powerful, they themselves seldom feel any power or effectiveness at all. They are often amazed at being told of the effect they have. When a patient unconsciously controls the analyst, and the latter recognizes and permits this, a situation is established in which the patient is shown that he has power. If the analyst does not intrude, the control will often be lifted near the end of the hour and the analyst will "be allowed" to say something.

The experience of being controlled is not only unpleasant, but tends to evoke countertransference responses in the analyst to become wise and all-knowing. In a sense the analyst is saying, "I need to be seen, too," or, "I have something to say." There is a compulsion to this intrusion, to this caricature of wisdom; it is usually defensive, a demand to be idealized and an attempt to "gain space," to ward off being controlled. Equally, this compulsion can be an induced countertransference reaction stemming from the analysand's expectation of not being mirrored.

The mirror transference can manifest in the patient talking a great deal, but equally in silence. In either case there is an underlying message: "Shut up and listen!" This communication is a demand that the analyst *do nothing*, but instead that he empathetically recognize that there is a great deal beneath the surface, in fact an entire personality attempting to be born.

Incessant *doing* is a chronic condition of the narcissistic character. His basic belief that no center exists within, no source of rest, results in seemingly endless activity, whether of an internal fantasy nature or an external rush to more and more achievements and tasks. A great deal may be accomplished along the way, but aside from compensatory bouts of depression and diffuse, enfeebled existence, the compulsion to *do* runs the person.[72]

If a therapist consciously understands and to a sufficient extent accepts the narcissistic control, thus allowing that it has a purpose, a healthy transference-countertransference process can take place. Through this vessel the exhibitionistic-grandiose self, which has been "heard" through its captive audience, can transform. Compulsive *doing* can change into reflection, and the archaic-grandiose self structure give way to a positive spirit invested in the Self and in realistic self-esteem.

If the "shut up and listen!" stage is successfully negotiated, the counter-transference reaction to being controlled may also transform. The analyst may feel a greater empathy for the analysand and more ease in penetrating his depths. A control still exists, but now it may be felt as a call: "Be with me!" And this can be experienced as a request to "be with my depth, my real value." This change in the quality of the control is striking. From someone who was experienced often as boring and shallow, there emerges a person who knows what the term *soul* means. It is as if the patient always knew about it, always secretly knew of an inner, religious dimension to life and to his own person, but it was hidden from view. It awaited someone else to constellate it, someone who saw him in his real depth; this was the purpose of his previous alienating and frustrating controlling nature.

Just as compulsive *doing* can give way to reflection, the transformation of the exhibitionistic-grandiose self also results in a capacity for *being*. This represents a positive feminine functioning of the psyche,[73] a development discussed in chapters four and five.

6 The Mixed Transference

As Kernberg has noted in his criticism of Kohut's view of narcissism, the idealized and mirror forms of transference are intertwined.[74] While I disagree with Kernberg's negative assessment of the idealizations of the narcissistic character, and find Kohut's view of a potentially positive process much more in accord with my own clinical findings, it is also my experience that a strong mixture of mirror control and idealization often exists. In many instances, that is, the transferences do not readily sort out into either a pure mirror or idealized form. This is no reason, however, to revert to a negative viewpoint toward the narcissistic personality; rather the mixture may be seen as a form of the *prima materia* of analysis, where a pair of opposites is in need of separation. With this in mind, a Jungian approach, based for example upon the technique of amplification,[75] can in many cases be useful in dealing with the so-called mixed transference.

Consider the following clinical picture. The patient's conscious-unconscious merger extends a controlling transference, but one whose implicit demand is that *the analyst be ideal*, that he be all-knowing and wise. The analyst's response to this is different from the common countertransference reaction to a positive idealization, where the analyst identifies with being ideal and feels marvelous in the process, all to the patient's detriment.[76] Rather the analyst feels a *demand* to be ideal, an enforcement from the grandiose self, which can be something of a healthy paranoia, a process in which an idealization is not only extended but also controlled. It is as if the analyst were being tested to see if he or she *could* be ideal, while the control is protecting the patient from foolishly extending an idealization to (yet another) inappropriate person. I have found this form of controlling idealization in very creative, spiritual individuals.

While amplifications and other storehouses of knowledge often at the fingertips of Jungian analysts can be extremely destructive in the face of a narcissistic transference, operating for the therapist and at the cost of the patient, the enforced state of idealization is one in which this very amplificatory process can be extremely helpful. In many such cases, when I am able to understand the patient's dream material by amplifying an ongoing process—somewhat like dealing with the patient's imagery as Jung did in *Symbols of Transformation,* or Neumann in *The Origins and History of Consciousness*—the effect is that the transference uncouples. Gradually, a positive, uncontrolling idealization develops, and, at the same time, the energies of the grandiose-exhibitionistic self are integrated in the form of realistic ambitions and ego-strength. In these cases the patient's controlling quality is not primarily a sadistic attack, although it often does have this admixture.

A Jungian approach rather than a psychoanalytic one may thus be better able to handle the mixed transference involving enforced idealization. But the opposite situation, in which an idealization is there primarily for the purpose of control, is one in which techniques such as amplification will have the opposite effect. Then there is much to learn from Freudian-oriented writers, as well as those Jungians who have assimilated much of the Freudian point of view (notably Fordham's London school). For one form of the mixed transference the classical amplificatory technique may be a cure, while for the other it is sheer poison.

In the latter instance, when idealization is essentially in the service of controlling the analyst, we have no recourse but to interpret the sadistic nature of the patient's idealization. Two important aspects to this procedure are worth noting. 1) The patient, extending an enforced idealization in the service of control for its own sake, will often become dissociated under the impact of amplifications. Naturally, this is generally brought out near the end of the hour, all the more to make the therapist feel incompetent. 2) This dissociated state stems from a coupling of the patient's and analyst's sadism. It is necessary for the analyst to recognize, and disengage from, his stance of "knowing." Then it is possible to interpret the transference in terms of the patient's goal: having the analyst be ideal is in order to eventually make a fool of him.

The following is a portion of my session notes regarding J., a male patient with a strong, controlling idealization. The notes stem from an aspect of our work in which I was finally getting a grasp on the nature of the transference-countertransference process, after having acted out with "knowing" interpretations.

The transference has been controlling with a mixture of idealizing demand. By acting out this demand I become the attacking father, and as such he becomes angry and splits off, becoming dissociated, "wiped out." When I contained this, it was clear that he had to have me "knowing," for that was the only position in which his father felt real. I could show him that I did exist while not knowing, allowing *him* to discover instead. Then oedipal material began to emerge. His fear of massive attack was no longer hidden behind a masochistic submission, and he then began to ask me directly what I thought of certain life situations or dreams he brought. It was clear that a mixed message still prevailed: I was being asked, but also told to shut up. A part of him was asking, and another part saying, "I don't want to hear anything from you!" He was split from this shadow side, but could gradually accept it. He was protecting from the anal rape he expected, and instead attempted to humiliate me. He does his best to rope me into knowing, and when all else fails, he attempts to be seductive. Eventually, he became conscious of his sadism, which was quite an achievement, for it meant that he could begin to feel the nature of his connection to his mother. He discovered that this was dominated not by love feelings alone, but largely by intense sadistic drives. This was a result of identification with his father's energy, which was highly sadistic toward his mother.

The tragedy in this development was that his father also acted out his sadism on J. in a most common and cruel way: Just when J.'s oedipal feelings were emerging the father emotionally withdrew. As a 3-4-year-old boy J. would behave in a normal fashion: He would ignore father, go away himself, and see if father cared, if he would come after him. The outcome was disastrous: His father just withdrew, leaving J. overladen with the father's own sadistic shadow. Against this J. had no choice but to be stuck at a narcissistic level, for his own sadistic energy left him in an incestuous bond with his mother; with no father to provide tension, his ego could never get beyond or into the oedipal level. The result was a stuck, narcissistic development, appearing in the transference as a controlling idealization, a demand that I be the father that would allow him to find himself, but a demand that also humiliates me—treats me as he was treated.

In getting to this point, J. was integrating his sadistic energy, becoming aware of his desires to hurt women, and equally of the many forms his sadism took when turned back upon himself. Principally, these were negative body images, hating his body, finding it distorted, fat, etc. And with the emergence of his sadism into consciousness, it also was possible to witness how losing this energy resulted in depression, and regaining it led to a lift of his energy, a quick leaving of the depressed mood.

In his state of narcissistic defense against his own sadistic drives, J. has the typical male attitude toward women that characterizes narcissistic relatedness. It is an attitude that wants to be turned on by the woman, wants her energy to make him real. He hates it when the woman is depressed or withdrawn. She is there to make him feel vital, actually to pull together his energy, and especially sexual energy, that is dismembered in his unconscious by his split-off aggression. Women quickly get used up, no longer vital to him. For the last thing he wants to do, or even thinks of doing, is penetrating them, awakening the woman. He has so little sense of his own power that he never moves in this direction. This would also involve a transformation of his sadism, a change from this drive being largely for the purpose of control, a power drive that guarantees the woman will not vanish, to a drive which penetrates in a gentle way. Taking hold of the sadistic energy, and learning that it can be an energy of penetration rather than psychic rape, tends to unfold its archetypal root, as represented in Greek myth by Hades, Pluto or Dionysos.

For J. to recognize the workings of this archetypal power is a source of great fear, for it means that his ego has a kind of power that he feels as alienating. To be strong in this way means to be abandoned.

7 Archetypal Factors in Transformation

The following case is a striking illustration of the transformation of the grandiose self of a narcissistic character into a positive, spiritual form. The extreme nature of the process was probably due to the fact that I did not interpret the elements of the negative transference, because at the time I was unaware of the catalytic importance of envy and rage. Had I consistently interpreted the negative affects that appeared, it is possible that the transformation process may have occurred in a more gentle, contained manner. As it stands, the case represents a remarkable emergence of an archetype which served as the primary healing factor. At the most dramatic moment of its emergence, personalistic, reductive interpretations would have destroyed the creative healing potential inherent in the archetype.

The case concerns a young woman in her early twenties whom I shall call A. Her situation was the common existential one of character disorders; that is, overt symptoms were not of central importance. Even though she was often depressed, this was strictly secondary to her complaint that life held little meaning or purpose and that she was not developing her creative abilities. She had made numerous attempts to "find herself" (such as many briefly held jobs, affairs with a number of men who inevitably rejected her, considerable foreign travel, etc.) and had, as she put it, "failed miserably." She came to analysis with the attitude, "I've tried everything else, so why not this?"

Along with her general condition she mentioned a specific complaint. When she rode on a bus, she was nearly overcome by an urge to scratch out people's eyes. This frightened her as she was not sure she could control the urge, which she said was "like a monster, an *it,* or a *thing* that has nothing to do with me."

A mirror transference was soon established. If I was tempted to say something, anything at all, but reflected for a moment, I felt as if what I had been going to say would have sounded a bit forced and been "thin" in content. If I overpowered this feeling, she would just pause while I spoke and then continue as if I had said nothing. It felt as though she were putting up with me. This was how her archaic grandiose control manifested itself. I was intended to just listen, to be a mirror for what she would tell me; generally this was an account of the week's events in a consecutive, detailed manner. But if her control was respected, near the end of the hour it would be released and I was allowed to say something. The slightest comment, perhaps an empathetic rephrasing of what she had said, seemed sufficient. This telling of events was her exhibitionism unfolding, with me as a captive audience.

Her initial dream referred symbolically to the threatening rage she experienced (as the "monster" on the bus) but showed it in a remarkable form indicative of the containing power of the transference-countertransference union. She dreamed: "I have an egg. The egg has the power of an atomic bomb. If it is broken it could destroy the world. I carry it in a very careless way, even though it could easily explode."

The egg is generally an extremely positive symbol, pointing to the potential creation of new conscious attitudes. Concerning the egg Jung writes: "In alchemy the egg stands for the chaos apprehended by [the alchemist], the *prima materia* containing the captive world-soul. Out of the egg ... will rise the eagle or phoenix, the liberated soul."[77] Her chaos, whose negative aspect is the envious rage that tended to flood her on the bus, is shown in the dream to have the form of an egg. In terms of the analytical relationship the egg represents the containing power of the mirror transference. New psychic contents commonly rise out of chaos, which according to Jung is "the *sine qua non* of any regeneration of the spirit and the personality."[78]

This is a typical situation for a narcissistic character. There is strong, creative potential for the rebirth of the personality, yet there is also a rage which can destroy any transformation process. A. felt so hated and was, in turn, so full of hate, that any premature interpretation at all would have resulted in the breaking of the egg, that is, in the destruction of the transformative vessel represented by the analytical process. In her case, as we shall see, the egg held not only the raging, envious energies of the Self in exhibitionistic-grandiose form, but also the potential for the development of the animus.[79]

After two months she brought the following dream:

> I am shown a child in a covered tube. I only see the tube and I am frightened because the child is so deformed. It is so deformed that it is just a thing in a tube. But because of a doctor and myself it gets better and develops ears, arms and a human shape. It is then a little boy, only its arm is crippled. I feel this is much better. The arm is touched at some point and the pain is mine.

Now the container, once the egg, has a new form, one that is transparent like the alchemical *vas hermeticum,* the sealed vessel in which transformation takes place. This contains the undifferentiated "chaos" of her grandiose-exhibitionistic energies, which now show their transformative potential.

The results of this transformation can be seen: A boy child, an emerging animus, is developing, just as alchemical speculation speaks of an eagle or phoenix rising out of chaos. A. felt the child's pain, indicating a

"In alchemy the egg stands for the . . . *prima materia* containing the captive world-soul. Out of the egg . . . will rise the eagle or phoenix, the liberated soul."[77] (Codex Palatinus Latinus 412, 15th cent.)

growing capacity for suffering and especially an awareness of her own unconscious. The fact that she felt the pain also indicates an awareness that she is not invulnerable, as her grandiose personality that carelessly carries atomic bombs would have it. The transparent nature of the vessel meant that her process could more readily be seen, both imaginally and in behavioral changes associated with positive animus development. For example, she left her mother's apartment, where she had been living, and found a place of her own. She also stopped attending a school which had been not her own choice but her mother's. She got a job and began paying for her own therapy. These changes happened spontaneously; they were not the result of any "educational approach."

After five months she brought the following dream: "There is a little boy left with me for a while. I have my arm around him in a protective way. He needs to urinate. I take him to a toilet."

Here, the child in the *vas* is growing up. Needing to urinate, but controlling it, points to his emerging potency, the beginning of a feeling of power and effectiveness.[80] This child, which represents the young animus emerging out of the grandiose self, may also be seen as the product of the analytical process, born from the fertile union of our unconscious psyches.

As her child, her new attitudes, continued to grow up, she reported dreams of a numinous nature. In the sixth month of analysis she dreamed:

> I look out of an attic window. In the distance I see a white object, hazy and not clear. I know it is a flying saucer and I'm very excited. I call someone to look at it but I am the only one who can see it. It passes right by the window with sparks and stars flying out.

Before this dreams had held relatively little interest for her. But the numinosity of this one really stunned her and captured her attention. This is typical of the attitude of the narcissistic character. The slowly developing process, the growth of her inner little boy, was not sufficiently striking to offset the fear that in her unconscious there would be only violence and hatred. This dream had a dramatic feeling of new life. The flying saucer is a symbol of the Self, as Jung has amply demonstrated;[81] here it represents the center of her new identity. It is a visit from her potential wholeness, separating out, as the animus had, from an archaic-grandiose fusion. With this dream, A. began to have a sense that there might be something interesting and positive "inside" her.

At this time an interruption in the analysis—I took a month's vacation—led to A.'s decision to terminate treatment. Most probably this stemmed from an abandonment rage with me, which I failed to interpret. The rage had, nonetheless, been ignited, and it found its release in an envious attack on her mother. This involved a complete loss of control in which A. physically attacked her mother in a fit of rage. Thereupon she collapsed and became inundated by a vivid sensation of being totally filled up by a black snake. That was the form the unconscious took when it invaded her conscious personality as a result of the overflow of activated rage. This incident frightened her so much that she returned to therapy. It was the beginning of the ninth month since our work began.

The ninth month of analysis is often a special time, as if the psychic process follows a physical gestation model. This was true in A.'s case. A new development appeared in a dramatic form. The day she returned to analysis she had been sitting in a cafe listening to music. Suddenly, she felt a hand touch her back though no one was around. It was a vague feeling but she knew it was there. During our analytical hour, as she was telling me about this experience, she began to feel it again, only more vividly. Soon she experienced it as a terrifying hallucination. It grew red nails and began creeping over her back. It terrified her and she said of it, "It's my judge, judging me for what I did to my mother!"

Since a very positive process had been constellated in the previous months, and since new emergences of an archetypal nature are often preceded by intensely disordering experiences, it was inappropriate to reduce the experience to guilt. I encouraged her by amplifying her experience with mythological parallels. She was experiencing the chaos she had dreamed of and which had threatened her initially on her bus trips. This

Figure One

chaos had been gradually transforming until she was engulfed by the
outburst of rage at her mother. The rage acted as a catalytic agent which
sharply speeded up the transformation process. At this point the question
was whether or not it was too fast and too overpowering an experience for
her. Would she be capable of containing it?

The next day the hand was still there but now it began to change. She
felt there was an eagle on her back and that it was eating her. Her fear
intensified. She drew the eagle (Figure One). When I suggested that she
talk to the eagle she told it to go away. The result was that she felt it get
smaller but immediately had the sensation that she was being filled with a
black fluid until she nearly burst. It was clear that the eagle was not
intended to go away. When she asked it to come back, the black receded
as well. Instead of talking to it she drew it again as well as the feeling of
blackness (Figures Two and Three, page 58). During all this time the
controlling transference had ceased and had shifted to a mild form of
idealized transference which allowed me to be a guide for her through her
ordeal.

On the following day, the third since the hand appeared, the eagle was
still present and still foreboding; it was a cause of growing concern to me.
But she brought a dream from the night before:

Figure Two   Figure Three

There is a caterpillar with specks of green and red crawling up my arm. I am kind of scared. But someone urges me to let it be, just as I want to give it to someone else and it is crawling toward my back. Then it turns into a yellow butterfly (Figure Four).

This was a good prognostic sign. The butterfly is a symbol of psyche and heralded the emergence of new psychic structure. The yellow color showed it carried with it a new consciousness. As a Self symbol it signified a very positive process occurring alongside the threatening hallucination of the eagle. The eagle itself was a forerunner of a more gentle process as indicated by the dream. It was remarkably like the phoenix that rises out of the egg in alchemy.

In the days that followed, the eagle, a spiritual form of her animus, gradually lost its threatening and ever-present quality. By the fifth day it was somewhat smaller and described by A. as "cuddly" (Figure Five). Unlike the previous drawings, in this one she is wearing shoes, indicating a return to a reality standpoint. On this day she had a conversation with a young man she had recently met. He was an artist and had been urging her to accompany him on a trip to another continent to aid the poor there. For the first time in her life she had not jumped at a man's fantasy and had felt some reluctance at such a sudden and extreme move. On this day he had been especially insistent. As he became more and more

Figure Four

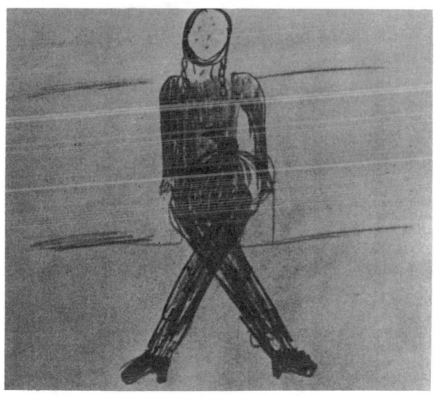

Figure Five

demanding in his argument with her, she began to feel the eagle behind her, only now it was protecting her and ready to spring at him. With this she could suddenly see that the young man was not at all sure of himself. His confidence wilted and she had been saved from another fantasy flight. At last, she had gained a positive animus, a "good inner object."

Near the end of the ninth month she left analysis: she felt prepared to get on with her life in a more conscious way. I saw her ten months later and the experience of the eagle was still very real to her. At that time the animus development that had occurred, in terms of the transformation of the grandiose-exhibitionistic self, was stable. No doubt much more material would later have to be worked through. For instance, the issue of the "blackness" that tended to fill her had not really been dealt with. This is shadow material, principally envy. But at this stage it was more important that she continue to consolidate the gains of a positive animus development.

The eagle represents an archetypal content, a healing factor that cannot be attributed to personal material except at the risk of destroying it. Reductive, psychoanalytic interpretations might have understood being eaten by the eagle as a symptom of masochism. But this emphasis, based on personal guilt, would have been repressive in terms of her emerging impersonal spirit.

The transference-countertransference union, initially in the form of the mirror transference and later shifting to idealization, served as a containing vessel for the unconscious process, the transformation of the self in its exhibitionistic-grandiose form. The case illustrates the catalytic nature of envy and rage, and especially how an archetypal content, here symbolized by the eagle, can emerge during the process of transformation.

Although the transformation of A.'s narcissistic character was by no means complete, the elements noted here would still be fundamental in a more lengthy, comprehensive analysis. Later one could expect the feminine realm of *being* to gain more prominence, and the ego might better assimilate the emotions of envy and rage. When this does occur, the transformation process may be described according to the model at the end of this chapter.

8   Exhibitionism and Its Transformation

The following clinical material highlights aspects of the transformation process in a narcissistic character disorder where the *prima materia* is exhibitionistic fantasies. It concerns a woman in her late thirties; I shall call her D. Her case illustrates:

1) The importance of revealing exhibitionistic fantasies of grandeur for the transformation of narcissistic structures.
2) How working at too deep a level, prematurely, can result in an envious rage.

3) How the catalytic nature of this rage may be incorporated into a gradual transformation of the grandiose-exhibitionistic self.
4) How the formation and stabilization of the transference-countertransference process is for the narcissistic personality analogous to the motif of the "suitor test" in fairytales.
5) How the transformed, exhibitionistic-grandiose self can become a positive animus in the form of an internal mirror.

I am taking the case up after approximately a year of analytical work, at a stage where a mild mirror transference was dominant. At that point exhibitionistic material—stories told with a feeling of shame, and dream imagery of being naked—began to appear. D.'s exhibitionistic needs were the needs of the Self to be gently mirrored rather than, as had been the case, psychically raped by her mother's perfectionist demands and depressions, which had left D. with a great fear of expressing herself. Mother had to be mirrored first, while D. got the leftovers—which were far too meager to encourage an ego-Self differentiation. The only safety was in retaining a state of merger of the ego and the Self.

The term *exhibitionism* is usually considered a pejorative one. This is, however, dependent on the empathy of the observer. To someone aware of the extreme pain involved, the level of despair of a Self that has not been seen, and of an ego imprisoned in this field of despair, the term is very apt to the phenomenology, and in no way pejorative. There is a prime need to be seen as the absolute center of the world. This need must be accepted as healthy and functional, or there can be no development.

While the mirror transference was intact, and her exhibitionistic fantasies were starting to appear, D. had the following dream:

I found a large outdoor amphitheater, where there was a living prehistoric animal on display. It was enormous, filling the whole center of the amphitheater. It had wings and feathers like a bird, but the body was extremely heavy and it was clear that the animal could not fly.

The bird is a good image of the fantasies she would languish in, for long periods- fantasies of achievement, fame, power, money, etc. But just like the bird with small wings, these fantasies could never get off the ground. They could not sublimate into any form that was commensurate with the size of her ego; they could not become ego-syntonic. Rather they stayed filled with an archaic energy. If this approached her ego, her real life in time and space, it would result in a great fear of being emotionally flooded.

The small wings were reflected in a minor idealized transference. This would be the result of a spiritual dimension which she did have to a large degree, yet in an impersonal way. She was very attuned to transcendent levels, aware of these energies, but had rarely been able to extend such an idealization to another person without its being misused. If the dimension of idealization is only experienced archetypally, a fine spiritual connection can exist—no small achievement—but there is always a nagging fear of hubris, due to the untransformed exhibitionistic needs of the Self, which require an interpersonally transformative dimension. Also, in this state of affairs, there is little sense of the embodied Self, and hence little or no sense of personal identity. D. had a very strong transcendent spirit, a close kinship with archetypal realms, but little sense of her own unique "experiment in life."

In order to avoid the misuse of her idealizations—which she had experienced in the past, including several analytic relationships—she employed a very common defense: She idealized men while accepting the role of their anima.[82] This kind of idealizing process is a holding pattern, but it does not allow integration. One is forever in thrall to the idealized person. It is a way of gaining some feminine identity, through identification with the man's feminine side, but in terms of psychological development it can only be temporary, and must eventually be replaced by a less seductively-controlling idealization, and later, one hopes, by a positive animus that can help realize the feminine Self.

It was only through being an "anima woman" that D. could participate in her father's spirit; it was her habitual way of relating to men, she knew no other. It was a positive sign that a mirror transference had developed; this indicated a healthy concern for herself. Later, the idealized mode emerged more strongly, but not until she was able to disengage from being the anima woman, and not until the mirror transference transformed. This helped her gain the necessary strength to make the separation.

The transformation of D.'s archaic Self structure was, as I have said, initiated by the emergence of exhibitionistic fantasies; I shall capsulize these events in what follows. With expressed fear and reserve, she got up the courage to tell me that she had fantasies of having to be the best in whatever she attempted. She gave me numerous examples from her past. At first I could not understand why they were so traumatic. She spoke of her child-prodigy years and how she gave up certain endeavors, such as mathematics, whenever she came only second. She was especially gifted, but had to be first in everything. As I continued to listen to her examples, I felt a deep stirring within me, a keen sense of how much her soul had suffered in the past by not having realized these gifts. And I shared this with her, believing that I was being empathetic with what she was presenting.

That evening I received an angry telephone call. She was furious with me for what she expressed as "patronizing" her, and feeding her "poor me" ego. I was surprised, as I had felt so moved and connected to her story. This was the first time any anger with me had been expressed; I told her I would think about what she had said and discuss it with her next time. The mild mirror transference had been long established at this point, and our analytical container was able to stand this emergence of anger.

In reflecting upon her complaint I realized I had made an error. I had heard her stories as if she were telling me about old fantasies of childhood, and failed to realize that she was attempting to tell me that she still suffered from these same, inflated preoccupations. Anything less than being the best, at anything, was still impossible, leading to a state of psychological paralysis. By empathizing with her past condition, I overlooked her present, ego situation. If I had properly related to her, I would have said how difficult it was for me to share these embarrassing, exhibitionistic fantasies.

I had also failed to respect her need for distance; I had overempathized, worked on too deep a level, and as a result had become intrusive. While in subsequent stages of transformation of the narcissistic character (which shall later be discussed, and which did occur with D.), this depth penetration is necessary, at this stage it was inappropriate. It stirred up an inner envy reaction, a deep-seated belief that I was only teasing her, and would assuredly abandon her later. It is the emotion of envy that translates into the "poor me" feeling.

The result was that she needed to stop sharing her exhibitionistic fantasies for several months; they were "put on the back burner." Two weeks after the session in which I had made the error in overempathizing, she had the following dream:

> I am riding a horse in a castle, up and down stairs. Another man is there and he rides on the horse behind me. It is a test of sorts, as I am thinking about whether or not I will marry him. He must stand up to the test of staying on the horse behind me. But he falls off. He says that he can ride his own horse, but this doesn't interest me. I don't think I'll marry him.

D. readily understood this as a transference dream, and she was quite cognizant of one possible interpretation, that she *should* allow the man (me) to ride his own horse. But interpreting it this way was not to the point. It was much more relevant to see that I had failed the "suitor test," which was to ride behind her—a variant of the fairytale motif in which the hero wins the princess only by being able to hide from her.[83]

This pattern is often dominant in dealing with the narcissistic character disorder: the analyst's countertransference response—in this case my overempathy—must be contained, else *he* is seen, and fails to function in the necessary, mirroring role.

Gradually, after this realization, a healthy transference union was reestablished; eventually she decided to "marry" me. But in the meantime there was an extremely important dream, showing how the rage that was mobilized by my error in turn became creative.

> I am in a large house. A child has just arrived who is like a wolf-child, biologically human but animal in her behavior. The adults are running around rather frantically, trying to make arrangements to get the other children out of the way—or at least to protect them from her, since they see this half-animal little girl as threatening. I think they were also frightened

for themselves. However, she was "ours"; she had been found and somehow it was known that she belonged to our household, so we couldn't turn her away. I begin to search for the little Negro girl of recent dreams, who is also a party of the household, because I sense that she will know how to interact with this half-wild being. I am calling her name, which seems to be Kore or Kora. I wake up and think of the wolf-child as my rage, which perhaps can only be approached wisely by the black child, who may be a growing Earth self.

It was clear to both of us that the "wolf-child" was the new rage that had entered as a result of my error. It appears as a threat to the family, indicating her family's repression of any negative affects, and D.'s experience that these emotions were dangerous. Yet the analytical relationship could contain them, and that is probably why the wolf-girl was claimed, a very positive sign.

The little black girl, the one she called Kore (the other name for Persephone, the divine maiden in Greek mythology), had in previous dreams represented a growing, instinctively feminine capacity for *being*. Now, with the wolf-girl, another shadow side, envy and rage, entered the picture.

As I have noted, one major form envy takes is a "poor me" attitude. It reflects the position that "I have nothing and I will get nothing." But it splits off from rage, from the felt desire to "spoil" the withholding object. Instead, this rage is turned back onto oneself, resulting in the "poor me" reaction. D. was angry with me for apparently encouraging her "poor me" attitude, that is for bringing up and exacerbating her envy. Her "strategic retreat" for several months from intense analytical interaction was a necessary measure for her, but also represented an attempt to somewhat spoil the analytical process. It was of major importance not to analyze this side issue, but rather to focus on the remarkable transformative effect that her rage had. The wolf-girl was indeed taken in by her inner family, the rest of her complexes, and showed up in the following active imagination.

> In my mind's eye I can see the prehistoric bird monster and attacks on him, not only by me but by wolf-girl and the young, black child. I think it would be impossible for me to paint what I see, because the flesh of the huge animal is now shiny (liverlike, and reflecting light off the surface), and there are less defined but nevertheless distinct scenes all over the surface of the huge body. Perhaps later I shall be able to describe in words what these are. The wolf-girl has a tiny hatchet, and the Kore figure a sharp knife. I am at its head, also holding a swordlike knife, but not using it. . . . In a while, black Kore brings me a piece of the bird's flesh, which I try to swallow.

The expression of rage thus initiated a transformation in the archaic ego-Self structure. Her rage, as the wolf-girl, is surely crude, working with a hatchet, while the more refined and cultured sides of her personality, the Kore and D., use knives, symbolic of logos. But the narcissistic character must learn to allow his or her rage to be crude and undifferentiated, for it represents the result of early wounds that are often preverbal. They must learn to be able to be angry even if they are not "right," that is, even if the emotion does not have a logical context. This, too, is necessary in the transformation process.

In other active imaginations the bird became smaller and stayed reflective, like a mirror and liver surface. It became an animus that could *contain* anger. This again points to the creative function of her anger, for the liver has long been thought of as the seat of anger. And a later active imagination revealed one of the "distinct scenes" on the bird's body: the image of a magician.

The magician is a dominant image in the psychology of the narcissistic character, an apt form for the masculine power drive of omnipotence through which "the word is the deed." D. could thus begin to reflect, through the medium of the animus as the new bird, on her own grandiosity which had paralyzed her through its totally unrealizable nature and magical pressure. Gaining this vantage point, she could begin to be objective about this power drive and see its connection with her exhibitionistic needs (to be the best in everything). This "masculine" capacity for internal mirroring complemented her emerging feminine sides, characterized as Kore and the wolf-girl.

Concerning the wolf-girl, personification of D.'s envy and rage, one further note is in order. These affects, when accepted as part of the transformation process—which may mean being interpreted in a correct manner or simply being recognized (so they can eventually be felt as shadow qualities)—in effect *become* the capacity to have needs. The patient, often for the first time in his or her life, begins to feel entitled to something. Changes followed in D.'s life along this line, changes concerning her greater independence and consolidation of a reality-oriented personality through which her creative gifts could gradually be realized.

9   The Narcissistic Character's Fear of the Unconscious

Two dreams follow, both from women at crucial stages of life. The first was about to separate from a very destructive marriage after twenty years. The second woman had made difficult and important separations before; now she was confronted with another, and needed the guiding wisdom of her unconscious.

Both women were training as therapists and both were well-versed in the literature of narcissism; consequently the dreams are unusually explicit in their language. Nonetheless they exemplify a central fear of the narcissistic character: that allowing the unconscious to interact with the conscious personality *inevitably leads to death and nothing more.*

1)   I am with K., who says that when Narcissus falls into the pool, all he does is drown. I say that a flower grows. Then she goes and gets some small books and tells me with the same despondent tone that she's been reading Shakespeare's tragedies lately.

2)   I could not find a cab to take me home and stood in front of a synagogue for hours. They closed the place. I started walking and came to a highway or main road. Some commotion went on and workmen with strong lights were trying to lighten up a pond or surface of water. After a lot of searching they brought up the stiff body of a boy. He seemed dead. But to my surprise as I looked again, even though I was horrified, I saw that the body was very much alive. He had curly hair and was vibrant.

In the first dream, K. was a younger friend, a woman terrified of separations and abandonment. The dreamer herself, however, after a great deal of work over many months, was handling these emotions very well; consequently in the dream she can oppose a positive attitude to that of her despondent, regressive shadow. Such a shadow carries the basic belief system of many narcissistic personalities. The belief is that entering the unconscious, losing one's usual structure and attitudes, leads to absolutely nothing; there is no regeneration, no rebirth, just death. Here the dreamer herself personifies the opposite view, that something new can come; the flower that Narcissus is transformed into is seen as a symbol of new life. (I will return to this dream in chapter four, when discussing the significance of the narcissus flower.)

The second dream illustrates the same narcissistic fear. The dreamer associated the pool and the feeling of the dream setting to a postcard she had of Narcissus looking into a pool. The synagogue, according to her specific associations, represents the collective life she had lived for many years, a life dominated by the attitude that one must not express anger or any strong, negative emotions. They were absolutely unacceptable. At the time of the dream she was approaching this most difficult area. The previous day she had risked expressing her true, feminine feelings in a confrontation with a very unrelated, male friend. The result, as the dream shows, is that rather than death and decay, there is new life.

The narcissistic character is thus dominated by the great fear of entering the unconscious, in terms of any emotional interaction with it. This situation can arise, and the fear be constellated, in an introverted or extroverted manner—alone or with another person. But, and this is what often distinguishes the narcissistic character disorder from the psychoses, if the plunge into these feared emotional depths is taken, the belief that no rebirth can occur is often proven wrong. Rather than death or eternal chaos, one finds just the opposite: a true meeting with the Self, an inner reality that is dependable. That is my experience, and it is why I continue to be optimistic when dealing with the narcissistic character.

10   Transformation of the Narcissistic Self

The Self in the narcissistic character disorder is an amalgam of autonomous elements, a "false uroboros." There is an absence of the tension between opposites that characterizes a healthy psychological structure. When one of the elements is dominant, it has no connection with any of the others. Instead, it takes over and triggers the ego's defensive system, making consciousness difficult and limited. When transformed—which happens when they are recognized and assimilated by consciousness— these amalgam elements form a differentiated structure with an inherent tension between opposites. Then the ego can begin to function in a stable manner.

Within the undifferentiated amalgam four primary elements can be recognized. They may be approximated as follows:

shadow
black magician
ego-persona identity
false bride

1) The *black magician,* a term borrowed from folklore, represents that factor in the psyche that drives for control and exhibits extreme grandiosity. It insists upon total determinacy of events, so that spontaneity and chance are defended against. Rather, reality is equated with *its* thoughts and needs, and the power to "know" and control is continually exhibited. This omnipotence simultaneously demands mirroring, without which its very existence is threatened. A good example of this quality is the dark side of the Old Testament Yahweh.

2) The partner of the black magician in the amalgam may be called the *false bride.* This represents a wrong connection to the Self in terms of concern with power, and it manifests in the identification with appearance. Just as the witch in "Snow White and the Seven Dwarfs" has a magic mirror that she consults to assure herself of her beauty over all others, so too the bewitched feminine side of the narcissistic character (whether male or female), rather than relating the ego to the Self, turns psychic energy back onto the ego. Hence the person is always referring internal and external events to his or her own ego.

The false bride is the enemy of the true bride, who represents the proper soul connection to the Self and functions in part as the capacity for *being.* The dominance of the false bride leads rather to continual thinking and fantasy, and especially *doing,* usually concerned with gaining self-esteem.

A prime feature of the false bride, often united with the black magi-cian, is the refusal to show suffering. This would reflect a weakness that would endanger their drive for power. Instead, they present a façade of well-being: "I'm okay, I can handle everything." Analogously, the bride of Yahweh during the exile was said, in Kabbalistic tradition, to be the witch Lilith.[84] Yahweh was separated from his true soul, the Shekinah, who suffered along with the children of Israel until her reunion with Yahweh.

3) *Ego-persona identity* is characterized by undifferentiated social com-pliance and adaptability. Social acceptability is so dominant a need for the narcissistic character that the ego cannot separate from the persona, which in this case becomes a rigid mask carrying the inner false bride attitude that paradoxically denies the need for another person. The per-sona ego is not individual; it demands omnipotence and perfection ac-cording to collective values. It continually strives to meet these impossible demands, often collapsing under the strain, manifesting as energy loss and depression.

4) The *shadow* is the fourth element. Its primary characteristic is envy and an associated rage. Narcissistic rage, with its unforgiving quality for wounds to the ego's self-esteem, colors much of the individual's sense of history. Envy, the recurrent conviction that "nothing will ever be there for me, only for others, so I'll spoil any potentially giving object," chronically inhibits change and the integration of anima or animus.

In the unconscious, untransformed state of the Self, these elements are not separate, they are parts of a homogeneous amalgam. This mixture is often created by the ego's regressive fusion with the Self, a result, perhaps, of improper handling by parental figures of the emerging exhibitionism and idealization during childhood. Usually this exhibitionism is carried by instinctual and aggressive energies. In its regressive flight, the ego at-tempts to recreate the original paradise or uroboric condition. But it is a "false uroboros" in which needs are repressed rather than automatically filled by a positive parental experience.

In psychotherapy the transformation of the amalgam takes place in a manner analogous to the ascent and descent of energy known to the alchemists.[85] It is a circular process by which "matter is spiritualized and spirit materialized." But the alchemists' projections reflected the transfor-mative dynamic *within* the Self, while in the psychotherapy of narcissistic character disorders, the ascent and descent of libido unfolds through the transference-countertransference process. This is the vessel to contain the "circular movement," inhibited by the regressive ego-Self merger.

The ascent of libido is analogous to the idealized transference, while the descent of libido corresponds to the mirror transference. The spiritual "ascent," through the patient's idealization, in turn "descends" through the analyst's proper relationship to the induced mirror transference; for example, by containing while experiencing his own exhibitionism.

Equally, the mirror transference and its exhibitionistic energy is caused to "ascend" by the analyst's induced idealized response, and the proper processing of these energies. In this manner, the ascent and descent of libido is mutually experienced through the analytical vessel.

Although a general topic of chapter two of this study, it is worth noting here that the mirror was taken by the Neo-Platonists in their commentaries on the Narcissus myth as having the effect of drawing the soul down into matter and bodily life. Mirroring does have just this function. In distinction to the Neo-Platonic dread of matter, modern man should welcome this descent when there is a concomitant spiritual awareness.

When the elements in the narcissistic character disorder begin to transform through the constellation of the transference-countertransference process, they begin to be experienced as separate aspects of a totality. With this new Self structure, ego and unconscious exist in a relationship of consciously realized mirror symmetry, each influencing the other.

The quaternity structure that appears as a result of the transformation can be represented and characterized in the following way:

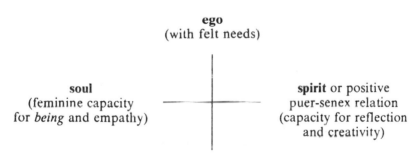

ego
(with felt needs)

soul
(feminine capacity
for *being* and empathy)

spirit or positive
puer-senex relation
(capacity for reflection
and creativity)

shadow
(old narcissistic character disorder)

1) The *black magician* gives way to a positive spirit; the Self is felt as a "content of the ego" and as its source, both "father" and "son." The positive puer-senex constellation emerges. An embodied awareness becomes possible for the ego. Compulsive *doing* becomes reflection.

2) The *false bride* gives way to the true soul. The positive value of suffering emerges. Psychic energy is channeled toward the Self and away from its excess investment in the previous ego-Self merger. The capacity to *be* appears as a positive value. Relatedness, as opposed to being right, becomes a primary value. Generally, the care for one's soul becomes meaningful and represents the transformation of the previous attitude in which appearances were the dominant factor. A capacity for empathy develops.

3) The *ego* disengages from the persona and becomes a carrier of personal identity. The capacity to feel and express needs for another person emerges. An awareness of rage at not being mirrored or at one's idealizations being improperly treated is more conscious, and gradually becomes a capacity to express anger in a related manner. The ego also becomes aware of its "pettiness" and becomes chagrined at the experience of envy, which it gradually recognizes to be a common, all-too-human psychic experience.

4) The *shadow* of the new quaternity structure becomes the old narcissistic character disorder. That is, the narcissistic character disorder in its exhibitionistic-grandiose form does not simply disappear. Rather it becomes the substantial shadow side, always potentially regressive, of the new personality structure.

The narcissistic character disorder does not only result from insufficient maternal empathy. It is also an archetypal pattern and constellates to protect a new Self structure from invasion from other archetypal contents, as this aspect of the Old Testament Yahweh protected the monotheistic vision from the mother archetype. Equally, it exists as a resistance to change, and then it functions just as a narcissistic character formation stemming from early infantile deprivations. It then causes a merger with the Self, and all the old symptoms of exhibitionism and grandiose control tend to appear. Hence, the duplex nature of narcissism stays as the shadow side of a Self constellation, either protecting its integrity, or else resisting its transformation, whence different archetypal centers would become dominant.

Jung's general attitude toward neuroses was that in the long run they have a positive purpose. He believed that those who become neurotic are also in a sense chosen—because they are then forced to deal with the unconscious. Narcissistic characters may be carrying the seeds of a new conscious experience of the Self in which both matter and spirit, both ascent and descent, have equal value. As such, they would be heralding a change in the collective unconscious Self image.

The uroborus, symbol for both narcissistic self-absorption and individuation as a circular, self-contained process. (Eleazar, *Uraltes chymisches Werk,* 1760)

II

The Mythology of Stage One:
Transformation of the Masculine

1 Introduction

The Narcissus myth is an image of psychic existence that is between the personal and archetypal polarities, partaking of each and separate from neither. Narcissus is a figure representing the pattern of existence in transit toward or from archetypal reality, clinging to the archetypal world or straining to separate from it, scorning personal relationships that would separate from the eternal, and equally rejecting the otherness of the divine realm which would place him closer to the human.

The more conscious aspect of the Narcissus image is akin to what Erich Neumann describes as the "magic-phallic" phase of ego development.[86] The more unconscious aspect is a fusion of masculine and feminine elements, which in chapter one I called the black magician and the false bride. This fusion of opposites has been long observed in mythology and art. Thus the decorations of the Mirror Room of the Chateau d'Anet, as noted by F.A. Yates in *The French Academies of the Sixteenth Century,* were designed in pairs of opposites—Sobriety and Inebriation, Love Extinguished and Love Returned, Virginity Tested and Protected, Narcissus opposed to Hermaphroditus, etc.[87]

This mythological awareness—if at this point we stress the "monstrous" nature of the hermaphrodite, as a premature or forced union of opposites—recognizes the fusion of opposites in the realm of Narcissus. But equally it represents the fact that the realm from which Narcissus attempts to separate is *not yet* differentiated into opposites. And, as the archetype points to the future, the hermaphrodite foretells of a potential new union of opposites in which masculine and feminine creatively reciprocate—with *doing* and *being,* for example, having equal value. But in the fusion of opposites (either as regression or as a stage toward progression), the "world parents" have not yet separated,[88] the clinical notion of projection is not yet meaningful, and earlier, archaic forms such as projective and introjective identification dominate.[89] The world of the mother is neither all-encompassing nor yet releasing, and the elements of masculine existence are bound with the maternal, existing as a "patriarchal uroboros,"[90] and awaiting a human spiritual relationship for their further separation.

Because it is intermediate, neither personal nor archetypal but a combination of both, the myth of Narcissus is a drama that concerns Narcissus' relationship with a nymph, Echo. His mother Liriope was also a nymph, a creature in mythology who partakes of an existence that is neither fully

71

godlike nor merely human; it represents a middle ground, the ground of the Narcissus story. And this story occurs as an eternal possibility in the human soul, not only at approximately six months of age, when the infant begins to enter the so-called mirror phase, nor only as a result of being stuck there through poor maternal empathy, but equally at any time an ego meets its archetypal source and then must separate into relatedness and time and spatial realities.

The Narcissus myth is especially significant for our present historical time, as it has been in other transitional epochs, for the archetypal world is no longer held in tension by collectively valid religious forms, and thus has begun to constellate strongly in the human soul, acting like a magnet drawing consciousness back toward the archetypal realm. Then egos may seem to be narcissistic, but actually are being drawn back into a realm of "not-yet existence." They may become stuck, yielding the pattern known as the narcissistic character disorder, or they may become reborn to inner and outer object relations, relationships to other people as separate and distinct, and to the Self as the transpersonal other. A new Self structure may arise which is hermaphroditic in the positive sense: not a fusion of male and female elements with which the ego merges (with a consequent gender confusion), but a union of opposites that allows for an equality between doing and being, and a conscious eros union with others and with the unconscious.

But in transition or in "stuckness," the narcissistic ego is in a middle domain, a realm of nymphs and—in clinical terms—a domain of self-objects and mirror or idealized transferences. These transferences—energized, structural propensities that bind people when the narcissistic realm is constellated—are neither personal nor archetypal; they are a fusion of both, and equally transitional between the capacity to see people as real, with human qualities and dimension, and the awareness of the archetypal as non-ego.

It is usually possible to tell if the narcissistic condition in an individual is a protective defense for an emerging ego-Self relationship, or if it is a stuck pattern, a character disorder. But this cannot be known through a catalogue of symptoms, only through directly experiencing the person.[91] For the narcissistic character can have great power over another person, the power of the magic-phallic phase in the frame of the adult. This is not unlike the power of the magician who identifies with the archetype, the essential difference being that the magical practice involves consciousness and ritual, so the magician is aware of his power and effectiveness, while the narcissistic character is not. But the unconscious, narcissistic power leaves the object or "target" feeling controlled, forced to fight for its own existence or else to echo back thinly what streams out and controls it. Such power is not uplifting, not restoring and spiritualizing as is that of someone connected to, but not identified with, the Self.

This chapter is not primarily clinical, although we shall rediscover many of the clinical facts that were described in chapter one. Rather it focuses on the Narcissus myth itself, first recorded by Ovid in his *Metamorphoses* in 8 A.D., and recounted, changed and commented upon in the ensuing centuries. In this literature we shall find much that now has a place in the clinical notions of modern psychotherapy. But further, we shall find a true focus for the phenomenology of narcissism, one that recognizes the archetypal and human dimensions of existence, and sees the Narcissus image within them.

Without understanding the link of Narcissus to the archetypal world, one cannot gain any sense of the purpose or meaning of the so-called narcissistic character disorders; one is then obliged to consign them to the barren heap of pathology. And that they can just remain there during the course of an individual's life is indeed the most tragic aspect of the stuck narcissistic condition. But this too is nothing new, nothing specific to our times. In varying degrees, it has always been the case, and we shall witness this observation, along with others, as we survey interpretations of the Narcissus myth through the ages.

2 Ovid's Myth of Narcissus

The following translation of the myth is by Louise Vinge.[92] I include it here in its entirety because we shall be concerned with most of its elements. It begins with praise for the blind seer Tiresias:

> He, famed far and near through all the Boeotian towns, gave answers that none could censure to those who sought his aid. The first to make trial of his truth and assured utterances was the nymph, Liriope, who once the river-god, Cephisus, embraced in his winding stream and ravished, while imprisoned in his waters. When her time came the beauteous nymph brought forth a child, whom a nymph might love even as a child, and named him Narcissus. When asked whether this child would live to reach a well-ripened age, the seer replied: "If he ne'er knows himself." Long did the saying of the prophet seem but empty words. But what befell proved its truth — the event, the manner of his death, the strangeness of his infatuation. For Narcissus had reached his sixteenth year and might seem either boy or man. Many youths and many maidens sought his love; but in that slender form was pride so cold that no youth, no maiden touched his heart. Once as he was driving the frightened deer into his nets, a certain nymph of strange speech beheld him, resounding Echo, who could neither hold her peace when others spoke, nor yet begin to speak till others had addressed her.
>
> Up to this time Echo had form and was not a voice alone; and yet, though talkative, she had no other use of speech than now — only the power out of many words to repeat the last she heard. Juno had made her thus; for often when she might have surprised the nymphs in company with her lord upon the mountain sides, Echo would cunningly hold the goddess in long talk until the nymphs were fled. When Saturnia realized this, she said to her: "That tongue of thine, by which I have been tricked, shall have its power curtailed and enjoy the briefest use of speech." The event confirmed

her threat. Nevertheless she does repeat the last phrases of a speech and returns the words she hears.

Now when she saw Narcissus wandering through the fields, she was enflamed with love and followed him by stealth; and the more she followed, the more she burned by a nearer flame; as when quick-burning sulphur, smeared around the tops of torches, catches fire from another fire brought near. Oh, how often does she long to approach him with alluring words and make soft prayers to him! But her nature forbids this, nor does it permit her to begin; but as it allows, she is ready to await the sounds to which she may give back her own words.

By chance the boy, separated from his faithful companions, had cried: "Is anyone here?" and "Here!" cried Echo back. Amazed, he looks around in all directions and with loud voice cries "Come!"; and "Come!" she calls him calling. He looks behind him and, seeing no one coming, calls again: "Why do you run from me?" and hears in answer his own words again. He stands still, deceived by the answering voice, and "Here let us meet," he cries. Echo, never to answer another sound more gladly, cries: "Let us meet"; and to help her own words she comes forth from the woods that she may throw her arms around the neck she longs to clasp. But he flees at her approach and, fleeing, says: "Hands off! Embrace me not! May I die before I give you power o'er me!" "I give you power o'er me!" she says, and nothing more.

Thus spurned, she lurks in the woods, hides her shamed face among the foliage, and lives from that time on in lonely caves. But still, though spurned, her love remains and grows on grief; her sleepless cares waste away her wrteched form; she becomes gaunt and wrinkled and all moisture fades from her body into the air. Only her voice and her bones remain: then, only voice; for they say that her bones were turned to stone. She hides in woods and is seen no more upon the mountainsides; but all may hear her, for voice, and voice alone, still lives in her.

Thus has Narcissus mocked her, thus has he mocked other nymphs of the waves or mountains; thus has he mocked the companies of men. At least one of these scorned youth, lifting up his hands to heaven, prayed: "So may he himself love, and not gain the thing he loves!" The goddess, Nemesis, heard his righteous prayer. There was a clear pool with silvery bright water, to which no shepherds ever came, or she-goats feeding on the mountain side or any other cattle; whose smooth surface neither bird nor beast nor falling bough ever ruffled. Grass grew all around its edge, fed by the water near, and a coppice that would never suffer the sun to warm the spot. Here the youth, worn by the chase and the heat, lies down, attracted thither by the appearance of the place and by the spring.

While he seeks to slake his thirst another thirst springs up, and while he drinks he is smitten by the sight of the beautiful form he sees. He loves an unsubstantial hope and thinks that substance which is only shadow. He looks in speechless wonder at himself and hangs there motionless in the same expression, like a statue carved from Parian marble. Prone on the ground, he gazes at his eyes, twin stars, and his locks, worthy of Bacchus, worthy of Apollo; on his smooth cheeks, his ivory neck, the glorious beauty of his face, the blush mingled with snowy white: all things, in short, he admires for which he is himself admired.

Unwittingly he desires himself; he praises, and is himself what he praises; and while he seeks, is sought; equally he kindles love and burns with love. How often did he offer vain kisses on the elusive pool? How often did he plunge his arms into the water seeking to clasp the neck he sees there, but did not clasp himself in them? What he sees he knows not; but that which he sees he burns for, and the same delusion mocks and allures his eyes. O fondly foolish boy, why vainly seek to clasp a fleeing image? What you seek is nowhere; but turn yourself away, and the object of your love will be no more. That which you behold is but the shadow of a reflected image and has no substance of its own. With you it comes, with you it stays, and it will go with you—if you can go.

No thought of food or rest can draw him from the spot; but, stretched on the shaded grass, he gazes on that false image with eyes that cannot look their fill and through his own eyes perishes. Raising himself a little, and stretching his arms to the trees, he cries: "Did anyone, O ye woods, ever love more cruelly than I? You know, for you have been the convenient haunts of many lovers. Do you in the ages past, for your life is one of centuries, remember anyone who has pined away like this? I am charmed and I see; but what I see and what charms me I cannot find—so great a delusion holds my love. And, to make me grieve the more, no mighty ocean separates us, no long road, no mountain ranges, no city walls with close-shut gates; by a thin barrier of water we are kept apart.

"He himself is eager to be embraced. For, often as I stretch my lips towards the lucent wave, so often with upturned face he strives to lift his lips to mine. You would think he could be touched—so small a thing it is that separates our loving hearts. Whoever you are, come forth hither! Why, O peerless youth, do you elude me? Or whither do you go when I strive to reach you? Surely my form and age are not such that you should shun them, and me too the nymphs have loved. Some ground for hope you offer with your friendly looks, and when I have stretched out my arms to you, you stretch yours too. When I have smiled, you smile back; and I have often seen tears, when I weep, on your cheeks. My becks you answer with your nod; and I suspect from the movement of your sweet lips, you answer my words as well, but words which do not reach my ears.—Oh, I am he! I have felt it, I know now my own image. I burn with love of my own self; I both kindle the flames and suffer them. What shall I do? Shall I be wooed or woo? Why woo at all? What I desire, I have; the very abundance of my riches beggars me. Oh, that I might be parted from my own body! And, strange prayer for a lover, I would that what I love were absent from me! And now grief is sapping my strength; but a brief space of life remains to me and I am cut off in my life's prime. Death is nothing to me, for in death I shall leave my troubles; I would he that is loved might live longer; but as it is, we two shall die together in one breath."

He spoke and, half distraught, turned again to the same image. His tears ruffled the water, and dimly the image came back from the troubled pool. As he saw it thus depart, he cried: "Oh, whither do you flee? Stay here, and desert not him who loves thee, cruel one! Still may it be mine to gaze on what I may not touch, and by that gaze feel my unhappy passion."

While he thus grieves, he plucks away his tunic at its upper fold and beats his bare breast with pallid hands. His breast when it is struck takes on a delicate glow; just as apples sometimes, though white in part, flush red in the other part, or as grapes hanging in clusters take on a purple hue when not yet ripe. As soon as he sees this, when the water has become clear again, he can bear no more; but, as the yellow wax melts before a gentle heat, as hoar frost melts before the warm morning sun, so does he, wasted with love, pine away, and is slowly consumed by its hidden fire. No longer has he that ruddy colour mingling with the white, no longer that strength and vigour, and all that lately was so pleasing to behold; scarce does his form remain which once Echo had loved so well. But when she saw it, though still angry and unforgetful, she felt pity; and as often as the poor boy says "Alas!" and his hands beat his shoulders she gives back the same sounds of woe. His last words as he gazed into the familiar spring were these: "Alas, dear boy, vainly beloved!" and the place gave back his words. And when he said "Farewell!" "Farewell!" said Echo too.

He dropped his weary head on the green grass and death sealed the eyes that marveled at their master's beauty. And even when he had been received into the infernal abodes, he kept on gazing at his image in the Stygian pool. His naiad-sisters beat their breasts and shore their locks in sign of grief for their dead brother; the dryads, too, lamented, and Echo gave back their sounds of woe. And now they were preparing the funeral pyre, the brandished torches and the bier; but his body was nowhere to be found. In place of his body they find a flower, its yellow centre girt with white petals.

When this story was noised abroad it spread the well-deserved fame of the seer throughout the cities of Greece, and great was the name of Tiresias.

3   The Initial Structure of the Myth

The background to Narcissus' birth is a violent one, a forced union: Liriope is raped by the river-god Cephisus. Structurally, this points to a problem in the area of the archetype of the *coniunctio,* the union of opposites. As is well known clinically, the treatment of narcissistic disorders is mainly concerned with the extreme defenses against relatedness, both to others and to the unconscious. Union is greatly feared ("Hands off! Embrace me not! May I die before I give you power o'er me!" well images the attitude of the narcissistic character), therefore much of the healing process in therapy centers upon the formation and handling of the transference-countertransference union. The Narcissus myth and its explications illustrate the *coniunctio* problem, especially in the Echo and reflection episodes.

But can we first gain some understanding of the character of Narcissus —whose myth images the aetiology and possible transformation of the clinical narcissistic character—from the image of rape which describes the union yielding his birth? Is there anything to be gleaned, for example, from the negative quality of the male force, Cephisus, or perhaps from Liriope's passivity and her questioning of Tiresias?

First, consider Cephisus, described as a river-god and hence larger in stature, more "archetypal," than Liriope, a nymph. The masculine force is clearly dominant and overwhelming, a form of power that Neumann calls the "patriarchal uroboros":

> The figure of the patriarchal uroboros borders on the formless. It belongs to the deepest archetypal stratum of . . . forces at work in woman and is closely bound up with nature. But this nature-spirit takes on cosmic dimensions. In its lower aspect it can assume the form of an animal—snake, bird, bull or ram. However, as a demonic or divine spirit which bursts in upon woman and inwardly fertilizes her, it usually takes wind and storm, rain, thunder and lightning as its symbols. . . . Despite this masculine-patriarchal aspect, the symbolism of the patriarchal uroboros transcends the polarity of sexual symbolism and encompasses the opposites in a single totality.[93]

Cephisus was the river associated with the Shrine of Apollo at Delphi,[94] and thus could be seen, in relation to Apollo, as the overwhelming force of inspiration that invaded his priestess. But here, as the rapist of Liriope, the negative aspect of the patriarchal uroboros is emphasized.

A Swedish fairytale illuminates the relationship between the overwhelming masculine force and the narcissistic formation. It is called "Leap the Elk and Little Princess Cottongrass":

> Princess Cottongrass was full of love: "I am young and warm. I have warmth enough for everyone and I want to share the good I have." She wishes to leave Dream Castle, where she lives with her mother and father.
>
> She sees an elk, Long Leg Leap, and asks him to take her out into the world. He cautions her of the difficulties, but she insists and, on his back, rides away from Dream Castle. Long Leg Leap cautions her not to let go of his horns and not to speak to a band of elves that will attempt to confuse her. But as they are asking her numerous questions, her crown starts to slip away and she lets go with one hand to grab it. That is enough for the elves to snatch away her crown. The elk warns her again, and tells her that she was lucky that time. At night he watches over her as she sleeps, but he is "seized by a longing to do battle and a desire not to be alone anymore."
>
> The next day, with the princess on his back, he races into the forest, but manages to restrain himself and slow down. Again he cautions her not to let go of his horns, this time when a witch questions her. But as her dress begins to slip away, she reaches for it and the witch grabs it. He tells her how lucky she is; if she had let go with both hands she would have had to go with the witch.
>
> All along, the elk is getting wilder and wanting to run and mate without restraint. He manages to control himself, with difficulty, and soon carries the princess to his very special place, a pool. He cautions her not to allow the heart she wears around her neck to fall off, but sure enough, she looks into the pool, and the gold heart her mother had given to her falls into the water's depths and she cannot retrieve it. She insists upon staying at the

pool, even though he asks her to leave. She is enchanted now, and stays, gazing into the water, searching for her heart.

Many years have passed. Still Princess Cottongrass sits and looks wonderingly into the water for her heart. She is no longer a little girl. Instead, a slender plant, crowned with white cotton, stands leaning over the edge of the pool.[95]

In this tale the princess has a good, initial maternal bond, symbolized by her mother's gift of the golden heart, but a great deal of naiveté. She has a positive mother complex; she is like a newborn child, living in a dream world. But she knows she must depart, and the necessary separating happens, as always, through a masculine force, here through Leap the Elk. The princess would eventually have to pass through the stage of narcissism, representative of the emerging capacity for internal mirroring of her Self structure, and consequently of identity formation. This stage follows her separation from the uroboric oneness of the castle; the ensuing negative mother imagery, the evil dwarfs and the witch, represent the forces of regression which attempt to hold her back. But, while getting past the witch and the dwarfs, she gets stuck at the pool, fixated on the heart she has lost, the gift from her mother, symbolic of an eros connection to the Self. Like Narcissus, she is enchanted, regressively fused with the unconscious, cut off from the possibility of consciously mirroring the Self.

A positive, initial Self connection was lost *because* the male force was too primitive, too untamed and compulsive. The elk is symbolic of the patriarchal uroboros, the male-accented force deeply embedded in nature which works toward individuation, leading a person out of the unconscious life of merger and innocence. But here it is too wild to be a successful guide; rather than a prince who might have married the princess, he remains an observer and moreover retains an inhuman form. Hence the development of the feminine is thwarted: the princess regresses, turns into a plant, just as Echo turned into stone.

The overwhelming male force, characterized as Cephisus or the elk, is an essential attribute of the narcissistic condition. Even with an initially positive maternal bond, the wildness and overwhelming fusion needs of the patriarchal uroboros render the initial Self formation powerless in terms of continued psychological growth and identity formation. The masculine power drive crushes the feminine—in both men and women—and the capacity for *being,* essential for the "I am" awareness that is central to identity formation, is absent; in its place is compulsive *doing.* (Ask the narcissistic character who he is, and he will usually tell you what he does.)

The Cephisus-like force is experienced, to various degrees, whenever we are the target for the controlling energies that dominate the narcissistic side of a personality. In their positive, purposeful nature they are a demand to "shut up and listen!" and to "be with me!" They are the energies which tend to flood the ego, but which could become a sense of felt power, real and valid effectiveness. In their negative form they are sadistic and ruthlessly controlling, senselessly destructive of relatedness, while they are fueled by an envious underside which insists that no positive mirroring relationship will ever exist.

Within the individual, the patriarchal uroboros is responsible for the fear of being flooded by exhibitionistic energies and envy, a fear that leads to both strong defenses and unconscious pressure. The ego is then either periodically crushed—enfeebled by the inner pressure to perform, unable to value simply *being,* the joy of existing—or else is driven to more and more, often senseless, achievements.

The rape of Liriope by the river-god Cephisus illustrates this archetypal issue at work in the formation of the narcissistic character disorder. Even if there is a high degree of maternal warmth, the disorder may develop as a result of problems with the archetypal, masculine realm. It is facile to overestimate the role of the maternal in early character formations, while underestimating the negative effects of masculine, archetypal factors. Both are crucial.

As an intrusive power into a woman, or as a power tending to over-whelm a man, the patriarchal uroboric aspect of the collective uncon-scious is nowadays no longer held in check by projection onto religious forms (such as the Old Testament Yahweh), and so appears in a particu-larly immediate manner. Men have long defended against it through identification with what is popularly known as the male-chauvinist atti-tude; it remains deeply rooted as an unconscious attitude of depreciation and often hatred of women. Women, meanwhile, somewhat like Liriope, have defended against its invasive power through masochistic attitudes.

As these defenses increasingly wear thin, the challenge to consciousness is clear. The sadistic, controlling power, represented by Cephisus in the Narcissus tale, must be confronted with individual consciousness. Men and women must do this not only individually but also together. Men are just as responsible for the patriarchal uroboric invasions in their partners —the "irrational unreasonableness," hysteria and fear, long dumped onto women—as are women for the positive animus development that would be a bulwark against emotional flooding. For a man's lack of awareness, and usually his defensiveness against his unconscious deprecation of women, is a channel for the very forces that lead to emotional flooding. His denial of his shadow qualities, for instance, is often just as determin-ing a factor, in the constellation of the negative patriarchal uroboric force that overwhelms his partner, as anything that might be active in her alone.

The factor imaged as Cephisus is an aspect of the overall structure of narcissism. In chapter one I noted the analogy between the alchemical god Mercurius and the phenomenology of narcissism as described in psychoanalytical literature. The patriarchal uroboros is a quality of Mercurius, an aspect of his untransformed nature in which the opposites are merged but which can nonetheless lead to a new Self development. The archetypal nature of the forces at work in narcissistic character formations points to the fact that a newly emerging Self may be behind narcissistic symptoms. This development would be more than personal. It would point to a change in the collective unconscious, a change that was perhaps first imaged in alchemical speculations, but had to await the objectivity and ego-development of scientific thought before it could fully root.

Given its archetypal nature, a spiritual attitude toward the Cephisus-like force is necessary. The problem is not only one of personal related-ness. Rather there is a religious problem embedded in the issues of narcissism, one that can become accessible through creativity, introversion and meditation, acts that can constellate the positive, archetypal psyche (a quality hinted at in the figure of Tiresias). An attitude that respects archetypal dominants, while paying due regard to issues of relatedness and transference problems, is essential in the therapy of narcissistic character disorders. The growing awareness of this may account for the current upsurge of interest in the Jungian approach.

There is an important phenomenon in the treatment of narcissistic character disorders that exemplifies the workings of the negative patriarchal uroboric force. This is the countertransference response that commonly is induced by the idealized transference. Unfortunately, it often repeats what once happened between parent and child, the destruction of the healthy ego-Self connection while it was attempting to develop through idealization.

Idealization, the process by which an individual or collective image is seen as perfect, omnipotent and wise, is a necessary avenue along which the energy of the Self unfolds. Kohut and Neumann, although from very different perspectives, have made this clear.[96] But the person stuck at a narcissistic level, merged with the Self and severely defended against inner rage and outer relationships, has suffered from never being able to extend an idealization to another significant person and have that idealization properly received. The proper reception of idealization involves knowing, instinctively if not consciously, that this energy belongs to the young child: the object of the idealization is not godlike but the energy is, and that energy belongs to the child's emerging Self structure. The adult must be able to allow the idealization in such a way that later the energy can be integrated back into the child's psychic structure. This process was never successful for the narcissistic character, and its difficulties are re-peated in the transference-countertransference process in psychotherapy.

Through countertransference reactions to being idealized, we can gain a sense of the force of the patriarchal uroboros. For the therapist feels "seen," recognized as important, a source of wisdom and value, and then tends to identify with this emotional response. It can be difficult not to, for the thrust of the reaction is compulsive. Naturally it hooks onto the analyst's own unintegrated exhibitionism, his frustrated needs to be seen as a unique person. But even if these needs are somewhat integrated, the strength of the idealization may lead the analyst to take control of the session with self-aggrandizing anecdotes, personal stories, mythological amplifications, etc. The result is that the patient's own process is once again crushed, symbolically raped by the analyst's nonmirroring exhibitionism.

The negative aspects of the energy stemming from the patriarchal uroboros provide a clear image of what is met clinically in the treatment of the narcissistic character disorder. Through the mythical background it is possible to gain an overview of this force, as is very hard to come by from a purely clinical viewpoint. For example, its positive, transformative nature can easily be missed, leading to a very pessimistic view of narcissistic formations. An overly positive attitude can be equally illusory. But in the clinical material presented in chapter one (section seven) we saw a positive aspect of the patriarchal uroboros, an eagle which first appeared as overwhelming, devouring the patient, but eventually transformed into a positive, spiritual guide.

Interpersonal relatedness, especially as it develops in the transference-countertransference process, is essential for the transformation of the patriarchal uroboric force, so that its positive, spiritual significance may emerge. But, to reiterate, the power is transpersonal in origin; it is not an introject from interpersonal relations, even though these may transform it for good or ill. And being transpersonal, its constellation can depend upon irrational factors as much as interpersonal issues, upon introverted activities, such as active imagination and meditation, as much as on any outer, object-related involvements.

Now consider Liriope, Narcissus' mother. She seems to play a minor role, but is there anything in her behavior that is helpful toward understanding the development of Narcissus? Commentators upon the myth have noted a "narcissistic" quality in his mother. For instance, Robert de Blois' *Floris et Liriope,* which appeared about 1250, describes Liriope as a lovely princess in Thebes who will not hear of any suitor. Through duplicity, Floris approaches the proud maiden and seduces her. When she becomes pregnant he must flee. And even though he later gains distinction and honor as a knight, their marriage when he returns after twelve years is regarded as dishonorable for Liriope. The story, as Vinge tells us, then centers upon Narcissus, who is "as proud and unapproachable as his mother was."[97]

But is there not something suspect about Liriope in the Ovidian tale itself? After all, why all the concern about the life span of her son? In answer to the question about Narcissus' long life, Tiresias replies that his life will be long "if he ne'er know himself." But to know himself would mean a knowledge of self in distinction to others, and that means separation from the mother world. Do we thus not see, in Liriope's concern for her son, the fear that he would separate from her?

Liriope, as she appears in *Floris et Liriope,* has qualities of the "false bride." She is concerned with herself and is nonmirroring of the male. This aspect of the feminine is also emphasized in some later discussions of the figure of Echo, where she is seen negatively as a simple creature of gossip (others, as we shall see, envision her positive potential). Perhaps the nonmirroring quality of Liriope accounts for her having to be raped by Cephisus. This would be in accord with clinical knowledge, that often the overwhelming Cephisus-like response is constellated by poor mirroring from the therapist. It may show the desire to break through to a personal *eros* reaction which would take the patient more into consideration.

Internally, Liriope would point to a lack of internal reflection in Narcissus, a lack of the quality of mirroring which would bring him a sense of his own uniqueness. Externally, on an object level, she has qualities commonly found in the mother of the narcissistic character, self-involved and totally unmirroring.

We now come to Tiresias, the last figure in the quaternity structure with which the tale begins. Tiresias is the archetypal wise old man. He would have special knowledge of the *coniunctio* problem, especially since he lost his sight as a result of one himself: He was asked to arbitrate a quarrel between Hera and Zeus as to whether male or female enjoyed sex more. "Often," he answered, "the man enjoyeth but one part. Nine parts the woman fills, with joyful heart." Hera was furious at this reply and blinded him, but Zeus gave him the gift of prophecy as a compensation. In other tales Tiresias is also involved in problems with the *coniunctio,* for example when he saw snakes coupling, and killed the female. He was then turned into a woman for seven years. When he later saw two snakes coupling and killed the male, he was turned back into a man.[98]

Tiresias' life is thus conditioned by his involvement in the central issue of the Narcissus tale. His sight is lost as a result of a power battle between male and female, Hera and Zeus. But as a consequence, he gains inner sight, sight into the unconscious. (Tiresias was said to have been the only one to maintain his *thymos,* the organ of consciousness, in Hades.) Tiresias represents the possibility of transformation through introversion, through connection to the inner world. We shall come to this positive potential in later versions of the Narcissus myth, and through an analysis of the reflection episode. If Narcissus could delve into his inner world, and know himself *as the Self,* he would die, meaning that the vanity-ridden Narcissus, like that behavior in the narcissistic character, would disappear.

But the child of the union of Cephisus and Liriope is aloof, rejecting any intimacies, with others or with himself. No wonder, with his background. And no wonder the aloofness and chronic identity diffusion of the narcissistic character, with the overwhelming, internal power-drive of the Cephisus-like force, tending to flood the ego with exhibitionistic energies, and the nonmirroring, internal state symbolized by Liriope. Yet the tale shows a way of possible development, remarkably close to the modern clinical approach, in the figure of Echo.

4   Narcissus and Echo

It has been said that the Echo episode was added by Ovid to a prior version of the myth; if this is so it only more attests to Ovid's genius, for Echo admirably represents the feminine counterpart of Narcissus. And she also represents what is found clinically when facing narcissistic attitudes of extreme defensive control. Then the demand for mirroring, the demand that we "shut up and listen!"—respect the meaning of this control—indeed reduces us to an echo, unless, that is, we blunder and break through, ourselves identifying with the negative, Cephisus-like force. But otherwise we are indeed controlled, by the patient's mirror transference, and we have little voice of our own.

Now the main question becomes one of *how* we echo what we are being told. Should we merely babble in return, mirror in the way of yea-saying? Or is there a possibility to be an echo in a deeper, more meaningful sense?

In early treatments of the myth, perhaps up to the twelfth century, Narcissus is the main concern, and Echo is secondary. But gradually she becomes important in her own right, treated with compassion as an example of unrequited love. This may indicate a development in collective consciousness. Similarly, echoing as a mode of empathetic mirroring (in distinction to interpretation) has become more widespread in therapy over the last decade. It has become more and more clear that how we echo is a major factor in the healing of the narcissistic character disorder.

If we are shallow in our replies, our echo will be like the Echo of Berchorius' fourteenth-century moralization: "Echo signifies flatterers who surround the mountains, that is to say the men of high station.... If it happens that something is uttered by someone they will answer his words at once and throw back the words like a blessing."[99] And previously, in the twelfth century, Alexander Neckham wrote: "By echo is meant those who are too inclined to talk; indeed they want the last word, these great conquerors."[100]

In the psychotherapy of the narcissistic character, it is possible to succumb to the desire to talk too much, to having the last word—if we identify with the grandiose pressure dominating the patient. Also there is a tendency to mirror in a shallow way, giving the impression that we are bored and do not care enough to try to penetrate the meaning of the narcissistic defenses. It is common, as well, to feel that no matter what we do, or how we try to reach the patient, it is not enough. Like Echo, we can feel our love unrequited, our interest ineffective; generally we may feel scorned.

And yet, to only echo can have an extremely positive outcome, if we understand its meaning. An intriguing explication of Echo illuminates this. As Vinge tells us, the Pythagorean "symbolic dicta" were an enigmatic collection of sentences considered to be Pythagoras' message to his disciples, which the Neo-Platonists and their successors of the sixteenth and seventeenth centuries racked their brains trying to interpret. Among them is a sentence that Marsilio Ficino translated into Latin and Gyraldus reworded to read: "One should pray to Echo when the winds are blowing."[101]

Gyraldus says that he knows of no interpretation of that dictum, though he does refer to the Neo-Platonist philosopher Iamblichus from the early fourth century: "He said that [Pythagoras] suggested that one should love the image of nature and the power of the devine."[102] But the dicta became an object of interest in the early sixteenth century, through the publication of Gyraldus' work, and in *The Seven Days,* the Italian lawyer Alexander Farra gives a description of the path to peace in God according to the doctrines of Renaissance Platonism, commenting on the "wind and echo" dictum:

> *Pray to Echo while the winds are blowing.* The wind is the symbol of God's spirit. . . . It moves the mind, and then the reason is set in motion, and when it has been moved, the image or form is reflected and returns by the same path to intellectual unity, enlightening, exciting and raising to God all the parts of the soul, so that it makes them one spirit with him. This reflex is by the symbolic theologians called *Echo.* . . . it is the daughter of the voice, and since it sends out a divine and blessed splendour over the entire spiritual realm, it deserves to be worshipped and respected without any hardening of the heart, so that it does not happen as it did for Narcissus who, in his ingratitude escaping from the enamoured Echo, fell in love with his own reflection. . . . Echo signifies the divine spirit which descends to enlighten our souls. . . . Narcissus, escaping, signifies the impure and vicious person who does not obey the divine voice.[103]

Echo, the nymph, seems to be understood here as an allegorical representation of the relationship between God and man. That relationship is compared to reflected light or sound.

Echo would thus represent, psychologically speaking, the connection between the ego and the archetypal world. In clinical work this is also the case. When the analyst echoes back the patient's controlling comments, he must do so with an implicit understanding of the archetypal (sometimes called metapsychological) background. This understanding requires that what is offered by the patient not stop short at the analyst's ego, but be taken into his unconscious and then allowed to return to the patient, not carrying anything new except an awareness of what has transpired. It is a circular process, one that depends on hearing the archetypal meaning in

what se ... recognizes the workings of ... is an unusually close
The ... parallel ... e, the Tukano Indians
of the I ... ca. The Tukanos have
a sophi ... evelopment, cast into
four ca ... udes only about three
per cen ... s. They are exception-
ally gif

know ... anism of the *echo* by
whic ... f its Creator
Th ... . To perceive is to *see*
and ... be classified. But to
conc ... In perceiving, the eye
sees ... and reflects, and what
is he ... ' one knows what is
symb ... c thought is expressed
in th [04]

This ... w; both recognize that
the ech ... the archetypal significance ... cchoing in the divine
and no ... ledge of the archetypal
forces ... ' from the destructive
counter ... eness of the profound
workin ... the most boring, meaningless,
The ... way from the Echo of
the Py ... m the Tukano Indian
concep ... copy of the psyche's
reflective capacities, and this accounts, perhaps, for her failure to connect
to Narcissus and her eventual tragic ending.

But we must recall the circumstances of her being reduced to an echo.
Hera was responsible, just as Hera was the one who blinded Tiresias. And
in both instances there was a power problem, a battle between Hera and
Zeus. So along with the strong negative mother constellation in the unconscious background of Narcissus, there is a similar background to the
affliction of Echo.

In a sense, Echo becomes an "anything but mother" kind of daughter.
She is in service to the Father, and alienated from the mother archetype.
Her final condition as a voice without body is characteristic of this mater-
nal alienation, and is one reason for her echo being ineffective.

The male-female conflict, which so dominates the aetiology of Narcissus, also dominates that of Echo. Not only is there a severe wounding of
ego development in the narcissistic condition, but also the contrasexual
dominant is always disordered, either rendered ineffectual or power-

driven. It is this poor structural development in the anima/animus that requires mending through the analytical process with a more deeply rooted echo, mirroring that reflects the depth of psyche. It might be added, in connection with Echo's sad ending, that the analyst's mirroring is most effective when it is *embodied.* In other words, it requires a sense of body experience and reality; not a flighty connection to symbols, but an awareness and communication of their power in the context of the patient's life.

But is the process of echoing, being an empathetic mirror, even in real, psychic depth, enough for the transformation of the narcissistic character disorder? Surely, without sensitive and effective mirroring there is little chance of penetrating the narcissistic defenses. Like Narcissus, narcissistic characters are terrified of being controlled, for they have so little sense of personal power. Hence the sadism and extreme cruelty that dominates their behavior when in any way pressed, just as "Hands Off! Embrace me not! May I die before I give you power o'er me!" is Narcissus' reply to Echo's advances. But while a meaningful echoing response is necessary, there is reason to doubt its transformative effectiveness even when it exists with great psychic depth.

To use a mathematical simile, the echo, clinically the way of empathy, may be necessary but not sufficient. And as the Narcissus tale suggests, there is more involved in the transformation of the narcissistic character, and especially more if the dimension of the *descent,* the embodiment of Self in distinction to a solely spiritualized solution, is desired. Beyond the echo are the substantial problems of rage and envy, and later, the introverted experience of the Self.

5   The Curse of Envy

Various commentators on the Narcissus myth have noted the role of envy in Narcissus, an observation supported by modern clinical understanding of narcissism.

For example, the seventeenth-century lyrical poet Marino, in his epic *L'Adone,* likens the lover to Narcissus, and speaks about his punishment: "He looks at [his reflection] and greets it—Alas the fool!—derives a true pain from the false image. As lover and beloved he is now freezing, now boiling, he has become both arrow and target, both bow and shot. He envies the soft flowing water its transient figure."[105] And before this, in the sixteenth century, one of Spenser's sonnets, combining the motif of the eye perceiving beauty with the Narcissus theme, portrays the emotion of envy:

> My hungry eyes through greedy couetize,
>   still to behold the object of their paine:
>   with no contentment can themselves suffize,
>   but hauing pine and hauing not complaine.

> For lacking it they cannot lyfe sustayne,
> and hauing it they gaze on it the more:
> in their amazement lykc *Narcissus* vaine
> whose eyes him staru'd: so plenty makes
> me poor.[106]

Phrases such as "hauing pine and hauing not complaine," and "so plenty makes me poore," carry the sense of envy, just as does Narcissus' lamcnt, "What I desire I have; the very abundance of my riches beggars me." The feeling conveyed is that there will never be enough; the more there is for others only shows how little there is for me.

The dominant role of envy is apparent in the interaction between Narcissus and his suitors. They experience envy, since he represents an object both desired and completely unobtainable. And just as this emotion can, in severe cases, lead to suicide, so in a retelling of the myth by an ancient author, Canon, one of Narcissus' suitors is so pained that he threatens to kill himself. And Narcissus sends him a sword![107]

If we look at the curse uttered by the suitor in Ovid's tale—"So may he himself love, and not gain the thing he loves!"—we see the dynamics of envy. For the curse is that Narcissus should feel the same envious emptiness that his suitors do, never able to attain what he desires, though the object of satisfaction is so near. This is implicit in the statement that the goddess Nemesis hears the suitor's plea, for according to Helmut Schoeck's comprehensive sociological analysis, Nemesis and envy are closely connected. He tells us that "the classical conception of a divine power that represents the principle of envy is linked most often with the word 'nemesis,'" adding that "in Herodotus, Nilsson discovers a tendency to call the divinity [Nemesis] 'envious.'"[108]

In other retellings of the myth, other divinities are often responsible for carrying out the curse of envy. Amor and Venus are commonly mentioned. In all cases, the archetypal principle of eros is violated by Narcissus, and in his state of hubris he is a target for the curse, as if he had to experience the envy he fears most. And in this, he is exactly like the narcissistic character, fearful of any intimacy and especially any feeling of need, lest envy be evoked and felt. It would seem that the dreaded emotion of envy, first met by narcissistic characters most commonly in their own narcissistic mothers, must eventually be faced.

It is my clinical experience that the dynamics of envy enter the transformation process of the narcissistic character disorder after the defensiveness of the mirror transference has dissolved. Or it enters initially, when the narcissistic transferences are primarily defensive formations against envy, against the unconscious belief that no object will be willing to accept the energies of the transference, to be idealized or controlled for the patient's benefit. Instead, the belief is the opposite—no one would ever care enough. This leads to hatred of the object of the transference energy, that is, a negative transference. What shows then is the hatred aspect of envy that is usually turned back onto the Self, manifesting as intense self-hatred. Indeed, as has commonly been observed, the problem with the narcissistic character, like Narcissus, is not self-love but self-hate. A sixteenth-century poem by Maurice Sceve, for example, compares the lover to Narcissus: "I endure without complaint that love consumes me like Narcissus, although I have not offended against Amor. Amor kills me by kindling within me love for an unattainable object, but at the same time he wants to keep me alive through love."[109] This state of tortuous envy leads inevitably to self-hate, mournfully expressed at the end of the poem: "Why must I be killed with self-hate since he dies enough who loves in vain?"

The problem of envy, as it afflicts the inner condition of Narcissus, is especially apparent in his state at the pool after he recognizes himself. In examining various interpretations of this, we shall see not only the problem of envy but its possible resolution. The scene of Narcissus at the pool, the so-called reflection episode, has always been by far the most popular element of the tale. Let us keep in mind that it was the curse of envy that led him to the pool, and to the degree that redemption can be found in the reflection or shadow Narcissus sees, envy itself has a positive potential.

6 Narcissus and His Reflection

An important key to understanding the reflection episode is found in the meaning of the words *imago* and *umbra,* reflection and shadow. They are used together in the narrator's apostrophe to Narcissus: "That which you behold is but the shadow of a reflected image." Since the words *imago* and *umbra* were generally interchangeable, Vinge mentions that it is not clear what the expression means; but she finds it unsatisfactory to explain it away as a tautology, especially in view of the linguistic precision of Ovid's text.[110] And also, why an apostrophe at all, why the need to step back and comment upon Narcissus at the pool, when his condition is so self-evident?

Clearly, the narrator is equating reflection with shadow and underscoring its meaning. This meaning is clear if we recall the manner in which traditional, so-called primitive cultures viewed a person's shadow.

In *The Golden Bough,* under the subtitle *Taboo and the Perils of the Soul,* Frazer gives ample material to show that among primitives the shadow or reflection was taken as the soul, and consequently was a subject of great concern and importance. His amplifications of this theme cover twenty-three pages; here are some brief examples:

> He regards his shadow or reflection as his soul, or at all events as a vital part of himself, and as such it is necessarily a source of danger to him. For if it is trampled upon, struck, or stabbed, he will feel the injury as if it were done to his person. . . . In the island of Wetar there are magicians who can

make a man ill by stabbing his shadow with a pike or hacking it with a sword.... The Baganda of central Africa regarded a man's shadow as his ghost; hence they used to kill or injure their enemies by stabbing or treading upon their shadows.... An ancient Chinese writer observes: "I have heard that, if the shadow of a bird is hit with a piece of wood that was struck by thunder, the bird falls to the ground immediately. I never tried it . . . but I consider the thing certain." . . . The natives of Nias tremble at the sight of a rainbow, because they think it is a net spread by a powerful spirit to catch their shadows....

If the shadow is a vital part of a man or an animal, it may under certain circumstances be as hazardous to be touched by it as it would be to come into contact with the person or animal.... The Kaitish of central Australia hold that if a woman who is suckling falls under the shadow of a brown hawk, the breast will swell up and burst.... The savage makes it a rule to shun the shadow of certain persons . . . he regards as sources of dangerous influences.[111]

All the examples found in Frazer's study show that the reflection or shadow is an object of *mana,* power that is transpersonal, the godlike or soul-quality of a person. When Narcissus sees his reflection, he is looking at his soul, his vital center.

An important example of the identity between the mirror image and the Self is found in the early Greek Dionysian mysteries. This is worth noting for its intrinsic, amplificatory value, and also because in antiquity parallels were sometimes drawn between Dionysos and Narcissus.

In the mysteries of Dionysos, the mirror played a role in the rite of initiation. Its significance in the myth of Dionysos is also relevant to

Frieze in the Villa of Mysteries, Pompeii, showing the use of the mirror in the Dionysian initiation ceremony (see page 90).

Narcissus, for the death or attempted killing of Dionysos happens while he looks in a mirror. As Kerényi tells us:

> According to the Orphic history of the world, Dionysos was no sooner born to Persephone daughter of Rhea than he was enthroned king of the world— ruler of our era—in the birth cave itself. . . . The nude boy (as shown on an ivory pyxis, ca. fifth century A.D.) raises both hands, as though saying delightedly, "Here I am!" Beside him two armed Kouretes are seen. One is performing a knife dance; the other, drawing his knife, is about to take part. The child will be stabbed while looking at himself in the mirror. Nonnos provides the text to the pictures. The mirror, which catches the soul along with the image, gives promise that the murdered god will not pass away entirely.[112]

In the initiation rituals, as depicted on painted walls in the Villa of Mysteries in Pompei, part of the imagery, as described by Kerényi, is of

> two aged sileni instructing young satyrs and initiating them into satyr man- hood. One silenus is their teacher in lyre playing and song; the other is performing the initiation ceremony. *The content of the ceremony is that in a silver bowl, serving as a concave mirror, the boy to be initiated sees a reflection not of his own face but of a crude silenus mask which is being held aloft by another boy, probably already initiated. The initiate is being prepared for the* thiasos *with Dionysian women.*[113]

Thus the mirror image shows *not* his own face, but his Dionysian soul, making ritual use of the fact that the mirror can reflect an experience not of the ego, but of its archetypal roots. Also, in these initiation ceremonies, there were some in which mutilation, perhaps circumcision, was involved, along with the initiate looking in the mirror.[114] Clearly, this would be a rite in which identity with the god Dionysos, stabbed while himself look- ing in a mirror, was achieved.

The negative aspect of Dionysos has affinities with the Cephisus-like force. As we shall see in chapter four, Dionysos was a central figure of the Eleusinian Mysteries, and the river Kephisos was said to run near Eleusis. In Dionysos comes the possibility of redemption from the impact of his negatively intrusive, Cephisus aspect.

Psychologically, the shadow or reflection carries the image of the Self, not the ego. It is interesting and even psychotherapeutically useful to have persons suffering from narcissistic character disorders study their face in a mirror. Often they will see someone of great power and effectiveness, precisely the qualities they feel a lack of. For even though they may overwhelm others with their energy and personality qualities, they them- selves feel ineffective.

I recall encouraging one such man to look into a mirror in my pres- ence; I told him to relax, breathe and study the object in the mirror. The person he saw had so much strength that he could barely look. This man, in fact, had a strong religious quality and a personality that overwhelmed others in his executive capacity, a situation they continually complained about. He himself was always surprised at his effect on others. His mirror reflection gave him a sense of his real power, the power of the Self. But in the state of fusion with the Self he could feel little of its strength, and was frequently overwhelmed by inferiority feelings. If he could separate from the Self and respect its will rather than identify with his power drive, he would be able to feel his true effectiveness, and know that it didn't belong to him, but stemmed from the archetypal energy of the Self.

This is, of course, just what the narcissistic character has the most difficulty doing, and it is also the problem for Narcissus when he recognizes his image: "Why, O peerless youth," says Narcissus, staring at his reflection,

> do you elude me. . . . When I have smiled you smile back. . . . My becks you answer with your nod; and, as I suspect from the movement of your sweet lips, you answer my words as well, but words which do not reach my ears.—
> *O, I am he! I have felt it, I know now my own image. I burn with love of my own self; I both kindle the flames and suffer them. What shall I do? Shall I be wooed or woo? Why woo at all? What I desire, I have; the very abundance of my riches beggars me. Oh, that I might be parted from my own body! And, strange prayer for a lover, I would that what I love were absent from me!*

Narcissus cannot separate from his archetypal core, and this tormenting fact leads to wanting such a "strange prayer for a lover . . . that what I love were absent from me!"

Ultimately, it is Narcissus' refusal to separate, his need to possess the Self and its archetypal potency and beauty that leads to his tragic ending. He recognizes the otherness of the Self when he recognizes his reflection— "Oh, I am he!"—but he can do little with this other than again become ego-centered—"Shall I be wooed or woo?"—and again identify with the Self: "What I desire I have; the very abundance of my riches beggars me." Narcissus' momentary recognition is thus quickly drowned in self-pity, a hint of the envious and exhibitionistic interior that torments him and is actually responsible for his inability to separate from the Self and allow its otherness.

Narcissus must possess his idealized image; he cannot allow its otherness for that would be too threatening to his basic design, to be mirrored himself. Hence the sudden switch: "Shall I be wooed or woo?" Narcissus' libido quickly changes from an idealization into a mirror form, showing how his unredeemed inflation, in psychoanalytic terms his grandiose-exhibitionistic self, gains control.

7   Historical Interpretations of the Reflection Episode

The theme of Narcissus and his reflection has received much attention in retellings of the myth. Some are true to Ovid's version, but many depart from it in significant ways, with important psychological implications. They reveal the same phenomenology of narcissism that we meet nowadays in clinical practice, showing the myth to represent a basic structural propensity of the psyche. But attitudes toward the myth, and especially toward Narcissus' interest in his image, also change, showing that changes in ego consciousness and the cultural Self image warrant different attitudes toward Narcissus.

In early classical literature after Ovid there are some brief versions of the myth, sometimes with an interesting twist. For instance, the poet Pentadius wrote: "The boy whose father was a river, worshipped springs and praised waves, he whose father was a river. The boy sees himself when he looks for his father in the river, and in the clear lake the boy sees himself."[115] This is a unique rendering, as far as I know, perhaps showing insight into the fact that the missing father can be just as crucial an aspect of the narcissistic character as the overwhelming, intrusive father. Both, of course, are examples, psychologically speaking, of the negative father. Clearly, Pentadius' tale derives from the Cephisus incident in the Ovidian myth, with the important awareness that the patriarchal uroboric force can also have a positive aspect, the "good father" the boy longs for.

While there are texts in antiquity that refer to the myth with a moral or psychological bias, as in Lucian or Clement, who stress a vanity motif, the tale is used in an especially interesting way by Plotinus in his discussion of the relationship between spiritual and material beauty. The problem is how a man, living on earth, can reach the beauty hidden in the holy of holies and which can only be seen by the initiated. Plotinus, as Vinge tells us, urges them to enter the holy and leave behind everything the eyes can see:

> When he perceives those shapes of grace that show in body, let him not pursue: he must know them for copies, vestiges, shadows, and hasten away towards that they tell us of. For if anyone follow what is like a beautiful shape playing over water—is there not a myth telling in symbol of such a dupe, how he sank into the depths of the current and was swept away into nothingness? So too, one that is held by material beauty and will not break free shall be precipitated, not in body but in Soul, down to the dark depths loathed of the Intellectual-Being, where, blind even in the Lower World, he shall have commerce only with shadows, there as here.[116]

It is important to note here the extreme emphasis on the "ascent" or spiritual, and the negative bias toward the "descent," which would be body-awareness as well as involvement in life. In Plotinus and his followers descent toward matter is frequently discussed through the metaphor of the mirror, which was said to pull the soul downward from its true source and goal, like the mirror of Dionysos.

As noted in chapter one, the mirror transference, in which the therapist is a mirroring object for the patient, has the effect of embodying mental-spiritual life. The idealized transference tends in the opposite direction, toward the ascent of spirit and its consolidation as a source of value and energy transformation. Both transferences were discussed (in section ten) as part of a single, coupled process, the *ascent ad descensus* of alchemical thought, which is the same as the circular opus of *sublimatio* in which there is as much concern for redeeming body and instinct as for extracting spirit. Thus, within the dynamic pattern set in motion when an emerging consciousness passes through the stage of narcissism—the path along which ego-Self separation occurs together with the capacity for internal mirroring—spirit and matter are transformed.

This pattern can also occur any time the conscious personality meets its archetypal origin, the Self. And this is especially the case as a result of the *unio mystica,* the mystical union with God, which later (perhaps over a number of years) leads to a choice: The experience of the "holy of holies" begins to embody, transforming bodily experience and body-consciousness, while the Light itself dims, and the person may attempt, as was Plotinus' absolute preference, to reconnect, recharge as it were, with the Light it once knew in mystical union. Or, the choice may be to enter bodily life in a transformed body awareness.

Any Self experience eventually leads to the issue of embodiment; there is always an element of choice, even though its strength may be greatly limited by early narcissistic injuries due to poor maternal mirroring. But in the teachings of Plotinus, the descent is to be avoided at all costs.

Plotinus' thought would be consonant with a view that idealization—the way of spiritual ascent and consolidation, leading to goals and structure—is a sufficient passage through the difficulties of the narcissistic constellation. It is true that idealization and a resultant introjection (or constellation) of the spirit archetype as an inner, psychic reality can lead to a separation of the conscious personality from the archetypal realm, an ego-Self separation and a felt connection between the two. But it is not necessarily an embodied ego-Self relationship, nor does it always result in the valuing of outer relationships. And idealization also deflects attention away from the shadow issues of envy and rage.

When these immensely difficult emotions arise, the need for a mirror, for someone to reflect one's identity and its spiritual quality, becomes crucial. For an individual already rooted in spirit, this descent into emotional depths can be dangerous, not only because it poses a threat to the spiritual connection, which yields a sense of identity and purpose, but because a regressive ego-Self merger tends to set in. In reality what occurs is that the part of the personality that has never separated into opposites, the undifferentiated amalgam in which ego elements and archetypal energies still mingle in a core of grandiosity and exhibitionism, constellates and drags down other, more developed ego functions.

The final Neo-Platonic interpretation of the Narcissus myth is attributed to an anonymous mythographer: "For he did not drown in the water, but when he saw his own shadow in the stream of matter . . . which is the ultimate image of the true soul [and he] tried to embrace it as his own."[117] It is this merger, fueled by unconscious mirroring needs that are excited by a glimpse of the Self, that is especially seductive for the narcissistic character.

Mirroring needs can be dangerous needs, and there is thus a great deal, implicit in the dynamics of narcissism and its mythological representative, Narcissus, that must be approached with caution. But Plotinus represents a phobic attitude toward the dangers of mirroring. For him, mirroring caused a descent *away from* the only reality, the spiritual "holy of holies."

*

The Narcissus myth was again taken up with great interest in the twelfth century. As Vinge tells us, the earliest version is in a passage from the *Roman d'Alexander,* written about 1180. In it two ladies sing a song about a youth who "did not deign to love a girl. One day he suffered a misfortune: he came to a well and caught sight of his shadow in the water. . . . He did so lie at the well and suffer his woes the gods turned him into a beautiful flower."[118]

This is true to the Ovidian version, but other retellings change the story, and many are especially significant in terms of the psychology of the narcissistic character.

In the twelfth century narrative poem *Narcissus,* for instance, the central figure is Dané, a princess who falls uncontrollably in love with Narcissus. Dané has full speech and runs to Narcissus, confessing her desire. "I who am speaking to you thus am daughter to your lord, the king." He listens to her and smiles: "Are you out of your mind, maid? You ought to be sleeping in bed, all this is far too imprudent. . . . We are far too young for love, and I cannot help you just because you say that Amor torments you; besides, I know nothing of such troubles as these, nor do I wish to know." She throws herself upon him, naked, and even though he finds her beautiful, he has no mercy and scorns her. She is pained and dejected; "What is it about me that has failed to please him? I am attractive and of noble birth—he is an ill-educated knave. But still I love him; I can never again forget him. And he will not improve, he is evil by nature." And then, noting her now "base life," she appeals to Venus: "Suffer him to know what love is, and in a manner that he may never find aid![119]

Here we have a more substantial "object" than Echo, and in the poem's description of the self-confrontation at the pool this "object-level" of consciousness becomes clearer. After the curse of envy leads Narcissus to his own reflection, which he first thinks is a water nymph or fairy, he recognizes that it is a reflection he loves, and that the beauty he sees can be found in himself:

> He speaks to the meadows and the forest; have you ever witnessed a love such as this? And to the gods: have you no help for me? But of course he does not know what to pray for: naturally they cannot give him what he

already has. Alas, he exclaims, I complain but none hears me. My parents know nothing of this. My friends have lost me. Why does not my mother know anything? If she came and grieved and wept over me it might give me some consolation. But no one has seen me, then, who can bewail my beauty? Yes, he recalls, at least the girl whom I thought so beautiful this morning, and who begged that I should love her. If she would only come, so that I might forget this madness, he sighs.[120]

The poem here pinpoints a psychological reality, and in fact an existential condition. For once a person becomes conscious of being stuck in a narcissistic dilemma—and I emphasize the importance of consciousness, for the narcissistic character is strongly defended against awareness of this level of tortuous merger with the Self and the resultant suffering—a main way out is through outer, object relations. That is to say, an element of choice can exist, but this entails a willingness to sacrifice the merged connection to the archetypal world. The Narcissus figure here is unable to do this; he has stayed too long at the pool. This too is of psychological interest, for the longer a narcissistic character disorder goes on, the more difficult it is to transform. One is not only continually or periodically merged with the Self, but this merger becomes a bad habit. If it has not gone on too long, however, or if the narcissistic character has a special, spiritual quality, there exists the possibility to consciously choose to leave the merger by means of empathetic relatedness.

*

In twelfth-century troubadour poetry we find interesting comparisons with Narcissus, showing awareness of the dangers attending the narcissistic character's need for a mirror reflection. For instance, in a poem of Bernard de Ventadour, "When I See the Lark Flying":

Never have I been in control of myself or even belonged to myself from the hour she let me gaze into her eyes:—that mirror which pleases me so greatly. Mirror, since I saw myself reflected in you, deep sighs have been killing me. I have destroyed myself just as the beautiful Narcissus destroyed himself in the fountain.[121]

Then there is a change of mood, a bitter outburst against the entire female sex, against her who destroyed him and all others who refuse to help him. He has fallen into disgrace, and ends saying that "as my love causes her no joy, I will go into exile, and seek protecting against love and joy." This bitterness and sudden change in mood when one's mirroring needs are not met are exactly what is seen in the narcissistic character. The wounds threaten never to forget, and never to risk another mirroring need. Instead, withdrawal from any love relationships is often the fear-ridden choice.

In another troubadour lyric, an anonymous poem, we can see the important dynamic in the need for an object to be ideal and the refusal to allow this ideal to diminish:

I am like the little child which sees its face in the mirror and presently touches it and fingers it all over so that finally the mirror is broken by the child's folly; thereupon it starts weeping over the harm it has suffered. In like manner a beautiful sight had enriched me, which fault finders have now, however, removed from me by their false villainy.

And therefore, I am sunk in deep distress, and therefore do I fear to lose her love. And I am driven thus to sing with longing. For the fair lady has so defeated me and fettered me that I fear to lose my life through my eyes, just like Narcissus who saw his shadow in the limpid well and loved it to the utmost, and died from the madness of love.[122]

The poet fears the loss of his lady because her ideal quality has been tarnished. Just as the narcissistic character, he can only love an ideal form, for this and this alone can mirror his own needs for an idealized object. To have the object be in any way less than perfect brings a fear of loss.

This poem has been widely commented upon, and there are other models of it in which another stanza is added. Significantly, in one this comes from a dream:

It has given me great agony that her red mouth should blanch. Therefore I have now begun a new lamentation that my eye should see such distress, like a child not yet having derived wisdom from experience, which saw its reflection in a well and had to love it until its death.[123]

Even the poet's dreams attempted to compensate his conscious attitude, showing the lady with imperfections. But he cannot accept this, and thus he remains with his idealizations, and, like Narcissus, stays regressively merged with the image.

Thus the vicissitudes of the need for mirroring (a mirror transference), and the need for an object to be idealized as perfect, are clearly recognized in twelfth-century literature. Narcissistic structuring of psyche is nothing new; only the attitudes toward it may change. Such a possibility emerges in the thirteenth century, an intuition of the value of introversion.

*

The best-known version of the Narcissus myth in the thirteenth century is found in Guillaume de Lorris' *Roman de la Rose*. The tale first closely follows Ovid, and then the author goes on with the story of a lover who "recalls Narcissus' fate [and] allows the beauty of the well to exercise its power of attraction. On its bottom he sees two crystals and from them the rays of the sun are reflected with a peculiar radiance which beautifies the whole of the surrounding landscape."[124]

Going deeper into the well through imagination represents a transition that the narcissistic character generally avoids. For the deep-seated belief is that nothing exists in the inner world, nothing of value, just as there will be no positive outer objects. Consequently, to plunge deeper into the unconscious is a fearful step, but one that must be taken if the blocked narcissistic condition is to transform. In *Roman de la Rose* we see an intuition of what may be found by going deeper into the unconscious instead of staying fascinated on the surface: the true radiance of the Self, here described as sun-crystals.

This would represent a potential introverted resolution to the dilemma of Narcissus. The love of an ego-Self merger is transformed into a love of the Self in its archetypal otherness. But this is only taken up as a successful resolution later in the seventeenth and eighteenth centuries. In the meanwhile, we witness an overriding concern with inflation—identity with the image of the Self.

Marsilio Ficino's handling of the reflection episode is a good example. His fifteenth-century revival of the Neo-Platonic explication was a significant renewal of the meaning and functional possibilities of the character of Narcissus. Ficino's contribution was not in bringing anything new to the understanding of the myth, but in making known the interpretations of antiquity. He told the tale as follows:

> The young Narcissus, that is to say the soul of the daring and inexperienced man, *does not study his own face,* by no means does he regard his own substance and his real essence. But he tries to reach its reflection in the water and embrace it—that is to say he admires the beauty in the body, which is fragile and like running water, and that is the reflection of the soul itself. *But thereby he abandons his own form. The shadow he never reaches.*[125]

The emphasis on the fact that Narcissus "does not study his own face" is important, for it stresses the Neo-Platonic view that while the image carries with it something of its archetypal source, it is not identical with that source. The view here exactly parallels Jung's continual reminder that there is a difference between the archetype and its image. Narcissus would represent the ignorance, for the Neo-Platonists, of this difference, and more: the danger of inflation, of identifying with the image.

Narcissus would be an excellent paradigm for the danger of inflation. For like the narcissistic character, inwardly tormented by envy and exhibitionistic needs, his identity with the image has a compulsive quality. It is not merely the kind of danger that attends any archetypal experience, for example in dream or vision, but it is a heightened quality, a movement best characterized as a *drive* toward regressive fusion. And Ficino, like Plato, Plotinus and other figures of antiquity whose works he translated, represents an acute awareness of how this fusion with the Self disturbs *its* functioning.

This danger is well taken, and it is why Jung cautions that the ego must not identify with the images of the unconscious but must relate to them. But while the danger of inflation is real enough, to shun the image and only center upon the ascending light of the Spirit is totally to lose touch with the body and its positive realities. The image, when reflected upon, just like the process of mirroring, has a tendency to pull consciousness down into the body. The art is to allow the reality of the image to exist without fusing with it. This is precisely what the narcissistic character has great difficulty doing, and why uncovering the underlying issues of envy and frustrated exhibitionism is so important in the transformation process.

For the Neo-Platonists Narcissus thus represents the opposite of self-knowledge. For them, his real misfortune is his lack of awareness of his real Self.[126] And in Ficino's retelling of the myth, as is the case in Plotinus' allusion to Narcissus, *the recognition episode is left out*. Authors who wish to stress Narcissus as representing ignorance of the Self often tell the myth in great detail, but leave out the fact that according to Ovid, Narcissus did recognize himself: "Oh, I am he!" This possibility lies within the narcissistic configuration, and shows why the descent into the body, and the image itself, does not have to lead to a lack of archetypal awareness. It can lead to a new kind of Self awareness, one that includes the body, as in the alchemical *opus* representing the process of individuation.

*

In later times, the possibility of self-knowledge becomes associated with Narcissus. This is especially true in the eighteenth century. But for this potential to be realized requires a capacity to observe images without identifying with them. We begin to see this emphasis in the sixteenth century with Spenser's *The Faerie Queene*.

Spenser uses the comparison between the lover and Narcissus. By gazing into an enchanted mirror, Britomart, representing chastity, has fallen in love with the image of a knight who has shown himself in it. With her nurse, she laments over her distress:

> But wicked fortune mine, though mind be good,
> Can haue no end, nor hope of my desire,
> But feed on shadowes, whiles I die for food,
> And like a shadow wexe, whiles with entire
> Affection, I doe languish and expire.
> I fonder than Cephisus foolish child,
> Who hauing vewed in a fountain shere
> His face, was with the loue thereof beguild;
> I fonder loue a shade, the bodie farre exild.

But the nurse dismisses Britomart's comparison of herself and Narcissus:

> Nought like (quoth she) for that same wretched boy
> Was of himselfe the idel Paramoure;
> . . . .
> But better fortune thine, and better howre,
> Which lou'st the shadow of a warlike knight;
> No shadow, but a bodie hath in power:
> That bodie, wheresoeuer that it light,
> May learned be by cyphers, or by Magicke might.[127]

The nurse thus urges Britomart to seek her internal image in the outer world, if only by magic. The resolution of the potentially stuck, narcissistic condition is therefore to be found, in Spenser's poem, in outer object relations. Psychologically understood, finding the "warlike knight" through "Magicke might" means that the object is to be found through projective identification, yielding an object with an idealized quality. This is a stage toward more realistic object relations in which people gain importance based upon their own reality.

Up to the seventeeth century most of the commentaries on Narcissus saw him as a negative figure. And in this century as well the negative bias is common. Thus in Reynold's "Tale of Narcissus," he "stops his eares to the Diuine voice [Echo], or shuts his harte from diuine Inspirations. . . [He is] an earthly, weake, worthlesse thing, and fit sacrifize for only eternal oblivion."[128]

Many other interpretations are less harsh on Narcissus, but only with the seventeenth century do positive descriptions arise. This is probably due to a transformation of consciousness that occurred then, a change described by Lancelot Law Whyte, who states that in seventeeth-century Europe new words developed which mean "self-consciousness' or "consciousness of one's own self." This first occurred in England in 1620; and in Germany, too, "conscious"—"to know with" (or "to share knowledge with another") in its Latin source came to mean: "to know in oneself alone." According to Lancelot Whyte:

> This was a decisive step in the social development of man . . . taking the form of an individual seeking to impose his personally preferred form of order on the disorder around him, or of the individual seeking to discover a new form of order in himself which could survive in isolation from the environment.[129]

With a new self-awareness, seventeenth-century man could perhaps risk the dangers inherent in the figure of Narcissus, since the growth in ego-strength would lead to less danger of inflation and regressive merger with the Self. Narcissus could thus be recognized as a necessary aspect of creation, symbolizing a healthy movement toward a new consciousness, and not simply a horror of being stuck and eternally worthless. This tendency appears in an embryonic form in a seventeenth-century academic dissertation, where Narcissus' exaggerated self-love is taken as the starting point for a description of true virtue, based upon a just estimation of one's own self and on a noble feeling for oneself. But, for the writer, the *perversa philautia* that Narcissus nurses is the worst of all evils.[130]

Yet even before this, in 1650, there is a remarkably positive slant given to Narcissus by the German Jesuit, Jacobus Masenius. The Narcissus myth is briefly told, and Narcissus himself is described as signifying those who in blind love put their own feats before those of all others, partly those who prefer beauty of the body to divine grace. But then there is a totally different emphasis: He is also a kind of image of God who was seized with love for men and became flesh. The lost human soul and the divine savior could be described in the same symbolic picture—Narcissus in love with his reflection.[131]

Thus the duplex nature of narcissism begins to appear, represented as a process that can lead to a new creation—psychologically an experience of the Self—or to a dead end, a waste of talent and a morbid need for mirroring.

*

Francis Bacon, who represented an essentially new attitude toward science and philosophy—insisting that these disciplines be applied, not speculative but actualized in material output[132]—saw Narcissus in a very negative way. But, incidentally, he is extremely accurate in his description of the paradoxical nature of the narcissistic character.

> Having become depraved and puffed up and finally transported by their self-admiration through this way of living, they succumb to a curious indolence and idleness.... [They] have been endowed with beauty and other precious gifts and for this reason love themselves and perish, so to speak.... They live isolated from the world, withdrawn and surrounded by a little coterie of admirers who listen to them and flatter them and like Echo agree to everything they say.[133]

Bacon sees negative sides of the narcissistic character, their unrealized gifts and their need for constant yea-saying, all getting worse with age. And he sees their collapse under the internal pressure they suffer from, "succumbing to a curious indolence," a description of what is clinically known by Kohut as enfeeblement. But Bacon, in another essay, "Of Wisdom for a Man's Self," displays his awareness of the opposite possibility for the narcissistic character. There, as Vinge tells us, he speaks of self-lovers having a disproportionate zeal for action as long as it is for their own good: "They will set a house on fire, and it were but to roast their eggs."[134] In this essay Bacon sees vanity as positive just because it can spur to action, which was his ideal.

Thus both sides of the narcissistic character, the tendency to collapse under grandiose pressure, or to identify with it in a flood of action, are cogently noted by Bacon. This kind of observation, with its personal flair and ingenuity, is paradigmatic of an emerging new individual consciousness, clearly of an extroverted nature, but akin to the introverted consciousness of Masenius, for both are seeing something positive in Narcissus.

When we come to Milton's *Paradise Lost* (1667) we find the Narcissus theme as part of the process of the creation of the world, just as it represents a stage in the transformation and new-world creation for an individual. Eve, in Milton's poem, is shown as having a choice: Either she can enter creation as the Mother of the human race, or be held back by her own reflection. In Book Four, Milton has Eve herself tell what happened. On first waking to life after her creation she had set out on her way to Adam, but something occurred which hindered her. Not far from her flower-shaded resting place there ran a spring, the water of which widened into a still surface. She went there, she narrates,

> With unexperienc'd thought, and laid me downe
> On the green bank, to look into the cleer
> Smooth Lake, that to me seemd another Skie.
> As I bent down to look, just opposite,
> A Shape within the watry gleam apeerd
> Bending to look on me, I started back,
> It started back, but pleas'd I soon returned,
> Pleas'd it returned as soon with answering looks
> Of sympathie and love; there I had fixt
> Mine eyes till now, and pin'd with vain desire,
> Had not a voice thus warnes me, What thou seest,
> What there thou seest fair Creature is thy self,
> With thee it came and goes: but follow me
> And I will bring thee where no shadow staies
> Thy coming, and thy soft embraces, hee
> Whose image thou art, him thou shalt enjoy
> Inseparable thine, to him shalt beare
> Multitudes like thy self, and thence be call'd
> Mother of human Race: what could I doe,
> But follow strait, invisibly thus led?[135]

Eve goes on, relating with naive frankness that Adam, at first glance, certainly seemed beautiful to her, but yet less soft and attractive than the reflection in the water mirror. She turned around, but was compelled by his calling to stay.

Entering creation in space and time involves a loss, a loss of the fullness of archetypal reality that cannot "fit" into history. But through this sacrifice, creation of the world occurs; in the individual this means the creation of a stable consciousness, connected to its archetypal origins without being identified with them, without being merged through a fear of loss of the Primal Light.

The world of multiplicity, Eve's children, psychologically represents the stage at which complexes and projection come into existence, much as it is represented in the myths that image world creation through the death of a giant or Primal Man. And with projection comes the possibility for integration and further consciousness. But this unfolding of the Self into multiplicity—which Fordham calls deintegration—is blocked to the extent that the psyche is stuck at a narcissistic level of ego-Self fusion. This merger impedes the evolution of the Self as much as it cripples the ego. Giving up the tantalizing merger with the archetypal world is shown in Milton's poem as depending upon a Voice; psychologically, this indicates that the resolution of the stuck narcissistic condition gains as much impetus from the inner, archetypal world, as from outer, object relations.

The narcissistic character disorder is stuck at the point of a new creation of consciousness. And since consciousness always has a transcendent background[136] (for example, the Voice Eve hears), the new creation is also one of a new awareness of the Self. Not only the ego but the Self too is renewed in the successful passage through the pattern of narcissism.

In the course of the sixteenth and seventeenth centuries there had been sufficient ego-Self differentiation, epitomized in Cartesian science and philosophy, so that a positive potential in Narcissus emerges more strongly. The danger of "falling into the unconscious," of an inflated merger with archetypal images, became less severe. Hence, in the eighteenth century the positive evaluation of the Narcissus myth continues, and it is also used in a new way. Narcissus becomes a symbol of conscious self-observation and the adoration of the divine in man. Yet he can still be a symbol of the mistaken confusion of illusion and reality, and the lack of self-knowledge and arrogant self-love.[137] The duplex nature of narcissism is never lost; the seventeenth- and eighteenth-century philosophers foreshadow modern clinical observations, and deepen them. For unlike most modern views, especially those of the schools of object relations and those with Freudian-psychoanalytical orientations, these early observations recognize both the introverted and extroverted aspects of narcissism and its mythological image, Narcissus. They also recognize both the positive and negative potential in the mythical pattern. Narcissus was especially taken as positive by the English poet, Edward Young, who with Rousseau and Shaftesbury recognized the value of introspection in a way that took the images of the unconscious seriously.

Especially significant in this new view of Narcissus was a prior work by Jacques Abbadie, written at the end of the seventeenth century but reprinted well into the eighteenth. It concerns the value of egotism. Abbadie regards self-love as identical with striving for happiness and sees self-interest as the basic impelling force of all man's actions. But he made an important distinction between *amour de soi* and *amour-propre*. The latter is a vicious self-esteem, the former a legitimate and natural guarding of one's self. The two concepts became well known in France, and were important in Rousseau's social and moral system.[138]

Psychologically, Abbadie's differentiation represents a distinction between energy turned onto the ego and energy turned onto the Self. This distinction is the key to the difference between healthy and pathological narcissism, and in the eighteenth century it develops with the growing capacity to differentiate ego and Self, conscious and unconscious. Thus Shaftesbury, in *Soliloquy or Advice to an Author* (1710), stresses the necessity for self-observation and self-criticism: "'Tis the hardest thing in the world to be a good thinker without being a strong self-examiner and thorough-paced dialogist in this solitary way." He also paraphrases the Delphic description as "Divide yourself, or be two."[139] He is positing nothing less than the condition that for true self-knowledge through introspection, there must be a differentiation between consciousness and the unconscious, a structural possibility that then allows for a positive view of Narcissus.

Like Rousseau, Young represents an approach to introversion that is both critical, stressing proper self-esteem, and positive in viewing it as a way to true self-knowledge. Young further represents a remarkable change in the historical view of Narcissus, but a change as we have seen that was being prepared in the previous centuries. Now, Narcissus is used to illustrate true and good self-love. He is not absorbed in an illusion, in Young's view, but in a recognized image: he really does see himself and is aware of it. Not only does this differ from those authors so fearful of getting lost in imagery as to leave out the recognition motif in their retelling of the myth, but it differs from the antique references which differentiate between reality and illusion. Now the image is real, and what matters is the way the ego approaches it. Critical awareness is necessary, and finally esteem for it rather than for one's own ego

In Young's "Virtue's Apology," the eighth book of *The Complaint,* or *Night-Thoughts,* there are the following lines:

> The true is fix'd, and solid as rock;
> Slippery the false, and tossing as the wave.
> This, a wild wanderer on earth, like Cain:
> That, like a fabled self-enamour'd boy.... [140]

Narcissus, the image of introversion and stillness, is compared to the "true," and Cain to the "false." This totally contrasts with the more conventional approach which saw Narcissus as a man who prepares his ruin through self-love.

With Young we come to the real depths of the introverted potential in the Narcissus myth. Vinge points out that "self-knowledge for Young is the way to discovering individual, creative forces. We are ignorant about the dimensions of our soul...."[141] According to Young:

> The writer starts at it, as at a lucid meteor in the
> night, is much suprised, can scarce believe it true.
> During his happy confusion, it may be said to him, as to
> Eve at the lake,
>   "What there thou seest, fair creature,
>   is thyself."—Milton[142]

Vinge notes that Young misrepresents Milton in that Eve left the lake and became the Mother of the human race, but Young's imagery suggests staying with the connotations of the reflection episode. It also throws light on the nature of the situation characterized by Narcissus at the pool: It can lead deeper, into archetypal depths, and equally into the world; in both instances being creative, one of soul-within, and the other of soul-without. No longer is Narcissus a youth in a stupor, fixated and merged with his image: he becomes a way to true Self-knowledge. The introverted way out of the narcissistic dilemma is to go more deeply into it; as Young puts it:

Therefore dive deep into thy bosom; learn the depth, extent, bias, and full fort of thy mind; contract full intimacy with the stranger within thee; excite and cherish every spark of intellectual light and heat, however smothered under former negligence, or scattered through the dull, dark mass of common thoughts; and, collecting them into a body, let thy genius rise (if a genius thou hast) as the sun from chaos; and if I should then say, like an Indian, "Worship it," (thou too bold,) yet should I say little more than my second rule enjoins: namely, "Reverence thyself."[143]

This suggests that it is not a matter of having the light within oneself or of being enfused with it in ecstasy, but rather of actively looking for it and getting to know it.

The positive potential within Narcissus comes to its height with Swedenborg's *De Culta et Amore Dei,* written during a crisis which resulted in his accepting a call to transmit the secrets of the spiritual world to mankind. In this work Swedenborg describes creation and the beginning of Eve's life, probably making use of Milton's *Paradise Lost,* but with exceptional changes. Here is Vinge's translation:

When this wonderfully beautiful girl [Eve] was in her first laughing and playful youth and everything agreeable made her mind joyful, during a walk she happened to turn off to the water of a well which was completely transparent like pure crystal right down to the bottom which was dark. When she cast her eyes into it she was surprised because she saw an image floating below the surface of the water and which as she got closer emerged as if it were alive. But soon, when she noticed that this figure made little movements similar to her own, and that while she looked more closely she recognized her own ivory-coloured bosom with its breasts and her own arms and hands, she returned from petrified amazement to herself, as if from shadow into light, and realized that it was a reflected image of herself. But after she had delighted in this picture of herself, enjoying the strange phenomenon, a new consternation came over her which restrained those thoughts that had already become more and more vivid, an astonishment that she recognized in the countenance everything that was going on in her mind, and rediscovered even the very astonishment and the thoughts circulating around it, and she was amazed that the whole of her secret soul was in this way completely exposed and revealed. Since she could not dispel the cloud induced by her surprise, in the same way as the previous one, she set out with quick steps towards her Celestial beings.[144]

Eve asks an angel to explain the phenomenon and this leads to a long discussion about man as the image of heaven or Order, summarized by Vinge:

The reflection in the well is used both as a real mirror, so that the angel shows Eve how her features carry an image of Order, and also as a simile: man is related to the Highest Order in the same way as the reflection is related to Eve. Eve will be able to find the divine in herself.[145]

The angel thus instructs Eve in the connection between the microcosm and the macrocosm—by getting to know his own nature, man also comes to know the nature of the universe. It is only with Swedenborg, Vinge tells us, that one finds this concept developed with the aid of the Narcissus myth. Psychologically it is associated with a vital ego-Self connection.

Summary

And so we see the broad range of commentaries on the Narcissus myth. There are many more (especially that of Creuzer is noteworthy; it has been treated by Murray Stein in his study of Narcissus),[146] but for our purposes they are not necessary. What we have surveyed runs the gamut, from viewing Narcissus as a severe danger to the soul, to seeing him as a metaphor for grasping the nature of the macrocosm in man himself, the microcosm. From dangerous illusion, as the antique philosophers such as Plotinus would have him, Narcissus becomes elevated to a way toward spiritual illumination.

The great value in scanning the historical views of the Narcissus myth is that it broadens the easily myopic view that clinical approaches can yield. The phenomenology of the narcissistic character disorder, and its intense difficulties in analytical practice, easily hide from view the fact that a world-creating process underlies that clinical world of idealizations, envy, exhibitionism and the transferences. In a sense these disorders are symptoms, in the microcosm of the individual, of the birth pangs of a new collective Self symbol.

As always, everything depends upon the consciousness of the individual, and here the nagging reality of the duplex nature of narcissism is paramount. For the phenomenology of the narcissistic character disorder can lead to dissipation, the waste of talent and the exaggeration with age of symptoms such as exhibitionism and grandiosity. But it can also be the way to a new individual Self, one that is hermaphroditic and consequently a source of value for the feminine and masculine in both men and women, a thrust toward balanced *being* and *doing* and higher values than the power drive of the ego.

For this transformation to occur in the narcissistic character, the compulsive tendency toward inflation, merger with the Self, must be overcome. This means that the difficult emotion of envy and the awareness of frustrated exhibitionistic needs must be dealt with. But if this "shadow" can be felt, then the narcissistic condition indeed can become the *way* toward a new Self-awareness. In the process, the duplex nature of narcissism does not disappear; rather the ego is able to carry both aspects in tension and respond to life in a positive way, buttressed against the demonic power drive of the dark side of the Self.

A further note on envy and its crucial importance: Clinically, I have often had the impression that the torment of envy is a curse of the Self, but a curse stemming from the ego's rejection of the Self. This inner envious condition often projects onto the outer world, and the narcissistic character finds himself the target of the envy of others. The only cure for this situation is to turn to the Self in oneself, initially to "not care" about others while one's attention is directed toward the inner values and goals that define the path of individuation. Thus the "god who wounds is the god who heals"; the envy which so torments Narcissus, and leads the narcissistic character to inner despair, can be crushing and destructive, but it is also a light-bringer, a way out of its own dilemma.

This is the inner way out of the condition of envy, and in the overall healing process of the stuck narcissistic stage it must be combined with a new respect for other people. In risking outer relationships the narcissistic character has to discover that his or her envious expectations are not always met. This can often be at least partly accomplished in psychotherapy. Just as the inner wounding of envy can be healed by inner, archetypal realities, so too the outer wounding, often stemming from early maternal empathetic failures, needs healing by outer, real objects. One does not substitute for the other, and the way through the narcissistic condition is past the terrors of envy and toward inner and outer objects, people as real and the archetypal world as psychic reality.

I want to call attention, finally, to how Jung's work relates to the historical changes in attitude toward the Narcissus myth. When Jung posits the complex as the way to the unconscious, and defines it as having a personal content and an archetypal core, he steps right into centuries of conflict as to the value of imagery, and especially imagery that is not identical with, or even very close to, the Divine Light. Surely Jung's approach would horrify the Neo-Platonist, for to take seriously the personal aspects of the complex would be dangerously close to becoming lost in the life of the body. But Jung indeed takes them seriously, and faithfully believes that they will lead to an archetypal reevaluation of their meaning. To take images seriously, to meditate on and scrutinize their personal meaning, is all in line with the historical development of consciousness, and specifically with respect to the Narcissus myth.

Narcissus represents psychic life in transit to or from the archetypal world. And Jung's view of psychic reality is precisely concerned with this issue. Jung, like the later commentators on the Narcissus myth, recognizes the positive potential in introversion. Like the most astute of them he also recognizes the extremely dangerous possibilities involved in experiencing the Self, the risks of inflation and loss of soul. Over and over again he cautions against identifying the image with the archetype, and cautions against the ego identifying with the image.

The issue of narcissism is the issue of our age, because it is the focal point for a new Self image in transition. Thus Jung, although he rarely used the term, was actually working on narcissistic problems well before the topic became clinically fashionable. This is not to detract in any way from recent psychoanalytical contributions; they are valuable, especially in their study of the transference-countertransference process, and the issues of envy, rage and exhibitionism. But these approaches could benefit by a mythological overview of narcissism, along with Jung's historically syntonic approach.

Within the mythological material, the various conflicting psychoanalytical views toward narcissism are contained. For example, Ovid's myth of Narcissus accords with Kernberg's view of the character disorder forming as a result of a regressive fusion, for Narcissus does recognize himself but then retreats back into merger with the Self. But later seventeenth- and eighteenth-century interpretations, notably that of Milton, represent more of Kohut's view, emphasizing the character structure as a retarded development on the way toward creating the world. Beyond this we have the many explications that see an introverted way out of Narcissus' dilemma, leading to objective self-knowledge, as in Swedenborg.

It is especially the undervaluation of an inner or introverted dimension that limits the healing capacity of the psychoanalytic point of view. Outer object relations alone never resolve the narcissistic condition. Without also reverencing the inner object, the Self, there is no transformation of the stuck, narcissistic state, only repression and eventual pessimism. Jung's approach to the psyche appears to me to be an absolutely necessary way through the problems of narcissism, a way that must be combined with the insights of later psychoanalytic thought.

8 Gains and Deficiencies of Stage One

The transformation process of Stage One largely involves working through the narcissistic transferences, during which the importance of introversion, imagination and the healing function of the archetype is established.[147]

At this point, my experience is that an entirely different clinical picture emerges. It is one that at first looks like a schizoid problem, but as we will see in chapters four and five, what now appears is a part of the Self that was hidden by the previous narcissistic structures. In this context it is appropriate to regard the narcissistic formation as a *defense of the Self*.[148]

This Self image has a largely feminine character; it represents that aspect of the Self that was split off in the narcissistic personality (the union of the black magician and false bride, referred to in chapter one, section ten). Mythologically, a good representation of this is the Greek goddess Persephone. Her redemption requires a kind of Dionysian consciousness, considered in the next chapter. But first, consider the limitations of the transformation process of Stage One.

The feminine and instinct

A lack of a depth transformation in the area of the feminine characterizes Stage One. This is indicated in Ovid's myth by the shallow quality of Echo. In later interpretations and in ethnological parallels, we saw that Echo could assume more significant proportions. But even so, as seen in the Pythagorean dicta and the Tukano Indian myth, she is still a purely psychic creature, a function of relationship to the psychic world of the archetypes, but not to the world of body and instinct.

There is little doubt that a failure to address so-called instinctual processes is for the narcissistic personality a severe limitation. *But how one does this is the key question.* It is a major concern of Stage Two. The instinctual level that arises cannot simply be approached through Freudian conceptions. Rather, it leads us into the archetypal domain portrayed, for example, by the Greek god Dionysos. *Freud's viewpoint of sexuality, and especially infantile sexuality, is a concretization of the particular ordering nature of this archetype.*

What is required in reclaiming instinctual, primarily body, awareness is not a reductive approach which integrates oedipal issues, filled as they are with omnipotent fantasies in the narcissistic character, nor the integration of aggression. These are necessary, but not sufficient. Instead, we are confronted with a far more complex and challenging issue, involving not only instinct or drives but a different kind of consciousness structured along the Dionysian model. Sexuality and aggression are there, but only as the speech of an archetype, the god Dionysos.[149]

The tendency toward rigidity

A major limitation of Stage One, resulting from its limited approach to the feminine, is a residual tendency toward rigidity. As far-reaching as the transformation process of Stage One may be, the narcissistic character still resists change. The new values discovered, such as individuation, creativity and introversion, easily take on the hardened sense of a "way" about them. The change in Stage One to a positive masculine functioning, for example to a sense of spirit not involved in power and overriding ambition, but instead connected to the demands of the Self and its unfolding, is of great value. Soon, however, perhaps after several years, rigidity begins to manifest again. The person doesn't lose what has been gained, but begins either to have all the answers, or else all-too-piously knows that he doesn't. One remains more a creation of spirit than of soul.

In Stage Two, the process of integration or redemption of the emerging, split-off feminine soul requires a kind of masculine. penetrating consciousness that does not follow from the puer-senex pattern of Stage One. The development of this new masculine, Dionysian consciousness is part of Stage Two of transformation, as is its use in the redemption of the split-off Persephone-like soul (see chapter three).

The ego's relationship to the unconscious

For the untransformed narcissistic character the inner world of psychic reality is something not to be trusted; the deep-seated belief is that anything good will vanish. But even the person who has worked through the narcissistic transferences of Stage One still has a limited relationship to the unconscious and its affective power. At least several limitations, all of which change in Stage Two, may be noted.

1) There is a strong tendency to use the unconscious to mirror the ego's constructs. For example, when a creative idea emerges, the unconscious is used, via dreams or fantasies, to fill out the idea or justify its worth, rather than being accepted as a source of consciousness far greater than the ego's. As a result, there is no truly creative dialectic between the ego and the unconscious; one's ideas and fantasies are not modified in the service of an ongoing process of discovery. There remains a need to "tell one's story," often with little concern for clear communication.

Also, there is a bias toward "knowing ahead of time" and then using the unconscious as a support system for one's ideas and their elaboration. The previous fear of object loss now becomes a fear of truly opening to ideas as tools of exploration, rather than as things which merely mirror the ego. To accept *not knowing* as an ongoing reality is still very threatening. Creative work has little in the way of surprise; it becomes dominated by "how to present an idea" in the face of expected rejection.

2) There is a tendency to give too much to others. The unconscious is used as a source of great wealth, in terms of knowledge and energy, and this treasure is given out to other people, but not to oneself. This is an all-too-common situation with psychotherapists, manifesting as *a strong desire to help*. It is another form of the fear of object loss, here appearing as the fear of truly owning one's effectiveness as a separate person. To give to oneself, to care for one's own soul and its needs, often does not even occur to the ego. The fear of not being mirrored is still strong, and the often long-standing pattern of compliance for the sake of survival is not easily given up. As a result, one does not *experience* the unconscious as a personal source of energy and nourishment; one is not *affected* by the unconscious, but uses it to have an effect on others. The gain in self-esteem acquired through being valued by others is seductively satisfying, but sharply called into question in Stage Two of transformation.

3) Connected to the lack of personally experiencing the value of psychic reality is a great difficulty with the reality of psychic *images*. The result of internalizing an idealized transference can lead to a sense of a dependable inner object, but the tendency is then to continuously consult this image as a kind of wisdom figure or spiritual guide. This is quite different from the kind of active imagination advocated by Jung, where the ego meets the affect-laden imagery of the unconscious and reacts just as one would in real life. Meeting a lion results in fear, a spiritual figure in a sense of respect and being uplifted, a snake leads to a kind of horror of the uncanny unknown, a frightening person evokes fear and appropriate reactions, etc. In this process a dialogue develops between ego and unconscious image in which both are affected.

But during Stage One of transformation, and even when its results have been somewhat consolidated, the image does not have this kind of psychic reality for the ego. There is a relative absence of spontaneous images that appear, affect, and are affected. Instead there is a kind of consultation with already established images. While this is quite an advance over the untransformed condition of the narcissistic character, it is still quite limited in terms of a relationship with the unconscious. In Stage Two the appreciation of images and their affective power greatly increases.

9   Feminine Penetrating Power

While the first stage yields a masculine attitude that respects mirroring and can reflect the archetypal background of existence, there is little gained by way of a capacity or desire for *actively penetrating* and being affected by psyche. This limitation exists in an introverted dimension, as well as in relationships. The capacity for what we shall later describe (in chapter three) as imaginal *seeing* is absent, as is a felt, embodied life out of which this imaginal capacity functions. While penetrating in this manner would be much too intrusive in Stage One,[150] depth penetration in an imaginal way that *sees* and is affected by the split-off part is necessary for its integration.

This penetrating capability first existed in the narcissistic personality in a negative way, as the patriarchal uroboros symbolized in Ovid's myth by Cesiphus. Upon transformation, an evolving respect for soul also carries with it a shying away from actively penetrating another's psyche, lest one be intrusive and repeat the assaults inflicted upon others while dominated by the untransformed narcissistic character structure. In Stage Two of transformation the power of an effective penetrating sight can be regained, while power-oriented motives are reduced by the fact that this consciousness must function from an embodied level of awareness. The body is the great limiter, the main assurance we have that we are not inflated and hence unrelated.

As the split-off feminine aspect of the Self begins to be integrated, psychic life gains a different quality. The feminine, best considered now as a new respect and awareness for the realm of the Goddess, gains a value that often exceeds that of masculine ways.[151] When a woman links her own penetrating power to the Goddess, a man feels this as something he must submit to if he is to gain from it. Male strength exists in its own right at this stage, but it does so with full knowledge that it is quite shallow without relationship to a woman.

By the phrase "feminine penetrating power" I am attempting to capture a specific experience I have had of female analysands as they work into Stage Two. A woman's penetrating power is a very different thing from the effectiveness which comes from a well-differentiated animus, and also totally different from the power a woman may exert by identification with a man's anima. It represents, instead, her conscious awareness of the feminine side of the Self, and with this she has an authority based upon a wisdom that is very unlike a man's knowledge. It is as if she had taken hold of the power she once only knew in an unconscious manner by acting out the man's anima. Now, she has an ego grasp on the roots of that power, no longer from being merged with the man's unconscious, but from its feminine archetypal source.

It can be quite shocking to be faced with a woman entering this domain, her natural birthright. From compliance and the readiness to please, albeit with a good deal of guiding helpfulness that many may have wonderfully appreciated, a woman gains an authority that can go against and beyond anything that I as a man can know. I have learned, and continually remind myself, never to take the compliant, anima-woman at face value, nor any woman behaving in a too-submissive manner. Behind this is always the potential for the instinctive feminine Self to appear, and when that happens my male knowledge is cast in the rather small container that suits it. Theories tumble. The woman who has discovered her penetrating power speaks from a source that has an effectiveness, a thrust, that can be felt as an energy different from anything masculine.[152]

The most characteristic quality of this feminine, penetrating power is that when it appears, it is quite obviously not a result of animus development or the integration of life experience. Rather, when it surfaces it is clear that it was always there, only hidden out of great fear. It is the power that Persephone, in the Homeric Hymn to Demeter, reaches for in the giant narcissus, before she is raped by Hades/Dionysos (see chapter four, section three). That is her expectation, and only through the experience of rape is the power ever consolidated. That is part of the Eleusinian Mysteries: The fear of the attacking male force, once endured, turns creative and is a factor which leads to the woman's power. Persephone becomes queen of the underworld, and also has her power in the upper world when she periodically returns there.

Such a woman can constellate in her male partner the recognition that he needs a woman in a way he never imagined. He becomes aware of a feminine power that is at least as penetrating as his own. He opens to its capacity to change him, and becomes open to allowing his masculine spiritual structures to die. His own power becomes in service to the Goddess.

This is a far cry from male passivity, and very different from an archetypal mother-son constellation. (When we turn in chapter four to the Eleusinian Mysteries and the Homeric Hymn to Demeter, we will see that these rites are very different from the son-lover myths of the near East.) A woman would never extend her feminine power, gained through her connection to the Goddess, to a passive man. Either this power would not be constellated and she herself would be unaware of its existence, or she would not show it. But a man can grow into a new awareness of his effectiveness, the value and purpose of his own power, through being affected by this power of the feminine.

On an introverted level, a man becomes connected to his Persephone-like soul as guide. He becomes aware of the reality of the mystery of the soul, of depths unknown, and senses potential visions that could destroy his conscious values and create new ones with demands that tend to frighten. He begins to be able to surrender to the feminine mystery that is also within him. This kind of surrender is the key to change, and it only exists in Stage Two of transformation.

The woman with an awareness of her Goddess-power also experiences a new way of relating to a man. She learns that she too cannot function well without the help of an outer, penetrating force. She needs a real-life partner, else she can never realize herself in the world of space and time. Without one, she can only live as an unpenetrated and consequently unredeemed Persephone; her power remains unconscious, a thing of the underworld, perhaps effective through the role of anima woman, but out of touch with the source of true feminine knowledge and eros that is her birthright. For this she needs a man—one whose own narcissism has been worked through.

If her partner is stuck in narcissistic patterns, however, he cannot be of any help to her in her quest for real feminine identity, linked as it always is to the Goddess. The narcissistic male, indeed, is the greatest obstacle to the development in a woman of real, feminine power.

Ishtar, the Great Goddess. (Terracotta, Sumerian period, Louvre)

III

Modes of Relating:
The Somatic and Psychic Unconscious

I Introduction

In Stage Two of transformation (which again I emphasize intertwines with Stage One), it is especially important that our empathy reach a different kind of depth than was previously demanded. Consequently, it is necessary to consider different modes of relating in the analytical process.

There is much literature which discusses technique, conceptions such as transference resistance, the value of using couch or chair, when and how to deal with rage, the importance of being active or silent, and subtle issues such as how great an analytical depth to work at.[153] But when we come to the question of the analyst's own ontology, not just descriptions of his subjective process but his *way of being in the process,* we have much less to consult. It is much easier to speak about interpretations of our patient's material and of our own countertransference reactions, than it is to attempt to describe the nature of our process along the way. But when we come to issues of the Self and identity, it is this process, the nature of *how* we are in it, rather than the interpretations we come up with, that is the core issue.

As Rosemary Gordon has noted, many clinicians recognize a need for different approaches when the issue is the Self. Discussing, for instance, Kohut and Kahn, she writes:

> There is considerable overlap in the ideas of these two analysts. For Kahn also argues that there is in the psyche an area, the self, which he sees as set apart from the id-ego-superego structures. The analyst, therefore, needs to relate to his patients in two modes: when concerned with the ego-id-super-ego structure, he listens to his patient's verbal communications and attempts to decipher meanings in terms of the structural conflicts—here he offers interpretations. But when he is concerned with the self, his style, so Kahn writes, "is harder to define; it is in the nature of coverage for the patient's self-experience."[154]

Whether it is Kohut defining empathy as "vicarious introspection," or Kahn referring to providing "coverage for the patient's self-experience," we inevitably enter a realm in which different analysts employ their own metaphors. We could add Jung's notion of analysis as a dialectical process.[155]

There can be no doubt that it is necessary to work with an approach of a personal nature. When the Self is the central concern, the analyst's own personality is his major resource. In what follows here, my own subjectivity and choice of metaphor will be only too obvious. But it is also possible to offer a kind of structural analysis for my approach. I believe, for instance, that I am behaving in the analytical process according to a mythical structure. Various amplifications will help to describe this, but the principal ones are the Egyptian myth of Isis gathering up the scattered members of Osiris,[156] and that of the Greek god Dionysos and the nature of his consciousness.[157] The notion of primitive logic, as described by Lévi-Strauss, is also useful.[158] Generally speaking, the quality of consciousness and being that I will be describing follows the alchemical metaphor of extracting the spirit from matter. But in this context matter is best understood as the human body, not as an abstraction for the collective unconscious.

2   Gathering Information Somatically

There is always information to be gathered in the analytical situation, and this of course is not limited to the patient's transmission of dreams or fantasies.[159] For example, the countertransference is a continuous source of potentially objective data, or of a way, for example, to approach resistance. What I want to describe here, however, is how I went about gathering information before I had much working knowledge of the countertransference, and was very dependent upon patient dream and fantasy material. What came out of this—which I now recognize was not at all unique—was an awareness of the value of my own subjective responses, primarily body-experiences. These, as I discovered, are a guide to the patient's process.

It is well known that borderline and narcissistic characters often have great difficulty in associating freely to dream material. With these, and other patients who simply were not bringing dream material to analysis, I devised the following method: First, considering that the dream image of a movie theatre often represents a place for the projection of fantasies, I asked the patient to imagine a blank movie screen. Then I gave a series of instructions such as: 1) Draw a circle in ink on the screen; 2) Allow the ink to flow in toward the center of the circle until you feel a tension near the center, with a white point remaining; 3) Allow the ink to flow back toward the circumference, until there is just a black circle again. Meanwhile I imaginally accompanied the patient's fantasy.

My initial experience of this mutual process was that I had a sense either of being filled or not, a sense that a gestalt was attempting to be closed, and that its lack of closure could be perceived by wanderings of *my* attention, and generally by a sense of looseness in the energy field between us. But primarily, I discovered that this felt sense of closure was most acute if I followed this imaginal process while I was actively aware of being *in my body*. That is, there was a greater difference in my sensitivity to a feeling of completeness—that the act of creating a circle, filling and unraveling it was complete in its own right, a total gestalt—if I was aware of my actual body size and feeling tone, of being embodied, than if I allowed a more mental, detached consciousness.

Once the sense of a full gestalt was achieved, I further asked the patient to draw lines in the circle, dividing it into four quadrants. Once again the sense of fullness of the gestalt was checked by my accompanying the imaginal process. My own consciousness was always "empty"; I maintained a state similar to that at the beginning of an active imagination, and I took my ability to do this (or not) as a sign of the degree of completeness of the gestalt of wholeness between us. When subjective contents did not interfere, and the sense of completeness prevailed, I then asked the patient to see what images spontaneously emerged into the quadrants, guiding them clockwise around the circle.

It was at this stage that I discovered something very new to me at the time. In the state of merger that I had created by the shared imagination technique, I experienced body innervations that went along with the patient's production or resistance to images. For example, a person would see a tree in one quadrant, and I would feel a certain anxiety, perhaps a slight or acute tightening in my jaw. Other images they would produce might result in similar or no body changes. But after they had produced their images, if I went back to the ones that created bodily changes in me, I always found that much more material was nearby. A tree, for example, might have the "strangest image with it," as one person I have in mind said. It had an undershirt near it. In that case we stayed with the image of the undershirt, and eventually uncovered numerous incestuous associations to a prostitute and his mother. But unless I had followed up the clue of my own body response, this "meaningless association" would definitely have been sidestepped. Similarly, it was clear, again by virtue of my own body responses, that when a great deal of time was taken before an image appeared in a quadrant, that too was a sign to follow up this image and what was being withheld.

What impressed me most about this method was the banal nature of the associations that were often suppressed, yet which turned out to be decisive. From a mental point of view, they could be easily dismissed by both of us, if indeed they came up at all. But taking my body as guide, I was surprised to see what lay behind seemingly the most trivial imagery.

(I have often been asked if this approach of listening to the body isn't a matter of typological preference. One might imagine it would be easier for a sensation-feeling type than for an intuitive or thinking type, but I believe a larger issue is involved; namely, the capacity to be embodied in an introverted manner, *in a way that also values the object*—the object here being a combination of the other person, their dream or fantasy and the day's residue they report. For a man this depends on a lunar or anima consciousness, while for a woman it is a consciousness rooted in the feminine Self with its implicit respect for body.)

Another feature emerged: While the patient was in the process of allowing images to appear spontaneously, and while the circle procedure was being followed, random thoughts would at times run through my head, babblings that made no sense. An image of a child, a house, a brook, a battle, a dangerous encounter, etc. As I said, my technique was to allow these and any of my more personal imagery to settle out until my consciousness was emptied. In that way I attempted not to interfere with the patient's imaginal process. But after this was achieved, that is after the imagery was produced and it could be further tracked down by reference to my own body responses—which I might add were quite varied, from random tensions to innervations that were often but not primarily sexual —I then returned to the various images and ideas that had previously floated through my consciousness. And these then made sense in terms of the patient's later productions.

It was clear that in some way a form existed that was being filled, but in a manner very strange to me. For example, in noting these random babblings, and the imagery we came up with, it was often possible to reconstruct the events of the previous day. For example, a series of these images and passing thoughts would begin, in the patient, to take on a life of its own. It was as if they were part of a yet unknown pattern whose effect was making itself felt. It was not just a matter of a gestalt being filled, but a sense of a particular, albeit unknown pattern. But everything said by the patient could be referenced to this pattern. Certain associations or thought processes seemed to click, and others did not fit in at all. In this manner, it often was discovered that there were events of the previous day, events that were imaged in metaphorical form, that were especially painful and in need of remembering.

One patient's imagery, for instance, contained a car, a trunk, a tree, a house and seeds. Among my mental ramblings preceding these images were scenes of violence. Working in the way I am describing, he eventually "remembered" an important experience of the previous day—he had masturbated. The imagery was then helpful in reconstructing the masturbatory fantasy, an anal fantasy involving the sadistic rape of his mother. The seeds were his sperm that readily fit in with the trunk of the car, and my violent imaginings were a clue to the sadistic nature of the fantasy material. This is an example of what I mean by a metaphorical replay of the day's events. In this case it was crucial to discover the masturbatory activity, because it was compulsive, occurring four to five times daily. It was a way of discharging his sadistic feelings, resulting in being very passive and undirected in life.

The structure ordering the method I devised is described by Lévi-Strauss in his book *The Savage Mind.* He calls it primitive logic. He found that primitive thought has its own logic which works through a kind of qualitative method using metaphor, and whose goal is to fit all data into a mythical pattern. Primitive logic has prescribed mythical patterns, whereas I had to discover the pattern.

Another use of primitive logic is in working on dreams. With the ruling idea being to never go beyond the existing dream images, never into a "solution" such as an interpretation, but rather working with the dream as an unfinished gestalt, associations can be elicited and further tracked down in the manner I have been describing. What often then transpires is that the entire dream becomes an image of the previous day's events: The dream is seen as a metaphorical replay of history. Often, the previous day's history is interwoven with conscious or unconscious fantasies that can be discovered and also appear as part of the metaphorically seen dream. In this process the previous day's events and fantasies take on new meaning. While they might previously be part of a relatively unconscious, often compulsive and acting-out life style, they take on the sense of a life being reflected upon through being remembered.

It seems that primitive logic, constrained by the gestalt-filling tendency of a dream, has the capacity to bring life into what was dead matter, bits of discarded history and fantasy. In this "second chance" to be conscious, the rediscovered history always has a tendency to be experienced as if it were happening in the present. Consequently what was once rather totally acted out, without any awareness of being embodied, takes on a conscious, embodied quality. We end with the same dream we started with, not a symbolic interpretation of it. But by then it has taken on meaning in terms of a total pattern.

This kind of logic and constraint to never "problem solve," in the sense of going beyond the given data to something new, is a mainstay of Lévi-Strauss' critique of the difference between primitive and scientific thought:

> The scientist ... whether he be an engineer or physicist, is always on the look-out for *that other message* which might be wrested from an interlocuter in spite of his reticence in pronouncing on questions whose answers have not been rehearsed. Concepts thus appear like operators *opening up* the set being worked with.
> ... Science, "in operation" simply by virtue of coming into being, creates its means and results in the form of events, thanks to the structures which it is constantly elaborating and which are its hypotheses and theories.[160]

He compares the working of primitive logic to the way of the French *bricolleur* or handyman,[161] and describes the "materials" used as

> condensed expressions of necessary relations which impose constraints with various repercussions at each stage of their employment. Their necessity is not simple and univocal. But it is there nevertheless as the invariance of a semantic or aesthetic order, which characterizes the group of transformations to which they lend themselves, which ... are not unlimited.
> ... They must be considered as patterns ... These patterns actualize possibilities whose number, though it may be very great, is not unlimited.[162]

My "materials," my patients' fantasies and my own as well as our body states, all are part of an unknown pattern to be discovered. Yet its constraint can be felt. For example, not working deeply enough, not going after enough associations, has a repercussion on the whole, generally weakening the end result. Each part constrains the other, and the essential constraint is never to "problem solve," never to arrive at an interpretation, never to go beyond the unknown pattern itself.

There is a myth which provides a pattern for working in such a way. It appears in Plutarch's "Concerning the Mysteries of Isis and Osiris," recounted by Mead in *Thrice Greatest Hermes*.[163]

In the myth Osiris has been dismembered by Seth, and Isis is searching for the scattered members. Two aspects of the story are relevant to my method of gathering information: 1) she is helped by babbling children; and 2) she is led by her dog Anubis, the child of Osiris and Nephthys. She thus finds Osiris' parts, puts them together, and eventually he is resurrected.[164]

The babbling children correspond to the kind of aimless chatter that goes through my mind while trying to establish a whole-gestalt quality in the imaginal focusing procedure. Keeping track of this chatter or babbling is nearly impossible in terms of scientific logic attempting to find solutions in the form of interpretations. But mythical or primitive logic is able to follow the trail and put the parts together in a meaningful pattern. Being led by the dog Anubis corresponds to following the instincts, as they manifest in body feelings. The overall result is the renewal of consciousness, represented in the myth by the resurrection of Osiris.

It is not easy to listen to the body, especially when trying simultaneously to be conscious of the reality of the spirit. In Jung's Collected Works there is not very much about the kind of consciousness that includes the awareness of body states—somatic innervations, tensions, etc. Usually, we don't view consciousness in this way; rather we think of it as a mental process of connecting images, ideas and affects to the ego. Or we think in terms of discovering consciousness in the unconscious, establishing a relationship with our affect-laden complexes, and so on. We may even think of levels of consciousness, extending to ecstatic states. But what about maintaining a conscious relationship to the unconscious while also being in the body in a conscious way? And why try to do this at all?

As a matter of fact, Jung did have strong views about "body consciousness," though they are not generally known. We shall now examine them.

3   The Body in Jung's Nietzsche Seminars

The place where Jung deals with the body as such is in the remarkable series of seminars he gave on Nietzsche's *Thus Spake Zarathustra,* already referred to at the beginning of this book.[165]

When the body appears in Jung's Collected Works, say in a dream or an alchemical text, it is commonly seen as a symbol for some psychic reality or complex.[166] Another approach of Jung's is to take the appearance of the body as denoting the need to integrate intuitive perceptions into everyday reality, through "the *fonction du réel,* i.e., sensation, the sensible perception of reality."[167] Or, in his paper "On Psychic Energy," he refers to the psyche as "a relatively closed system,"[168] implying that one can analyze the psyche in terms of its imagery and patterns without reference to the somatic at all. This all sounds quite aloof from the body, and one might be inclined to agree with Norman Brown's rather flippant critique of Jung's attitude as "anti-body."[169]

But this is not true at all. Jung was acutely aware of the great difficulties that the body poses, and in his *Nietzsche Seminars* this is abundantly clear. There he was forced to deal with the body because, for Nietzsche, the Self could not be divorced from the body; in fact at times Nietzsche even identifies the Self and the body—an inflation of the body, as Jung observes.[170] Jung tells us that he doesn't deal with the body per se because it is too difficult to write about. It inevitably leads to a consideration of the so-called subtle body (which he prefers to call the somatic unconscious), a domain in which events are not causal. One would have to postulate acausal processes. He prefers the way of science, the way of description that can be validated, checked and compared. Would he have said this after he published his work on synchronicity in 1951?[171] Perhaps not, but by then he was not inclined to turn to (or was past dealing with) the problem of the body.

Nonetheless, in the *Nietzsche Seminars* Jung offers what I find a remarkable model. He says that we have a conscious-unconscious connection that leads on one side to the purely spiritual or psychic realm, and on the other into the body and matter. As we go toward the domain of the spirit, the unconscious becomes the psychic unconscious, and as we go toward body and matter, it becomes the somatic unconscious.[172]

We are accustomed to a spectrumlike model of the psyche from Jung's published writings, especially his later paper "On the Nature of the Psyche," in which the psyche is portrayed as extending from a red or instinctual pole to a violet or spiritual pole. Both end-points enter the "psychoid realm" which can never become conscious.[173] In the *Nietzsche Seminars* Jung foreshadows this model and goes further into the nature of the experience of the unconscious as the different ends of the spectrum are approached. His later work on the archetype of the *unus mundus,* which

INSTINCTS		ARCHETYPES
infra-red ———————————— experience ———————————— ultra-violet		
(Physiological: body symptoms, instinctual perceptions, etc.)		(Psychological: ideas, conceptions, dreams, images, fantasies, etc.)

The psychoid archetype.

von Franz has done much to elucidate,[174] describes a transcendent level of psychic reality in which *both* aspects of the unconscious are identical, as are matter and psyche. But when the unconscious is approached from the framework of the ego, its psychic and somatic manifestations are a source of very different experiences.

In his Collected Works Jung generally refers imagery to the psychic unconscious. For example, the earth may be taken as a symbol of the mother archetype, while in the *Nietzsche Seminars* it is nearly always representative of the body.[175] Similarly, the motif of descent in the Collected Works is often taken to mean bringing a formulated and stable conscious awareness into actual reality,[176] instead of seeing it as embodying that consciousness. But in the *Nietzsche Seminars* Jung speaks precisely of this—of bringing conscious awareness into the body so that its existence is felt along with the reality of being embodied.

The somatic unconscious, Jung's designation for the subtle body, represents the unconscious as perceived in the body.[177] Further, he tells us that *the unconscious is in the body,*[178] that in fact that is the only way its life can be experienced.

He cautions us not to be thrown by this statement, which contrasts with his more usual one that the unconscious is everywhere; he simply means to emphasize that only in the body can it be *experienced,* much like experiencing the workings of the sympathetic nervous system. Jung speaks of being able to begin to approach a sense of universal sympathy with everything, and how this is an acausal process, not accessible to scientific discourse. But he must enter it here because Nietzsche does.

Jung tells us that the Self is both body and psyche,[179] that body is only its outer manifestation. And further, that the soul is the life of the body. If one does not live in the body, if one does not represent the Self in life in its uniqueness, then the Self rebels.[180]

This is an important notion that Jung underscored: *The Self wants to live its experiment in life,* and if it is not willingly embodied it manifests negatively in somatic symptoms and phobias. In the narcissistic character there is always an aspect of the Self that is not living the experiment of life and has accordingly turned negative. Integration of this quality of the Self can often be achieved through the analyst's body consciousness, as I have described above.

I will refer to these views of Jung's on body and psyche when dealing with the Homeric Hymn to Demeter (chapter four), the mythological analogue of Stage Two of transformation. It is useful to think of Demeter as representing the somatic unconscious, and her daughter Persephone as the lost soul or life of the body, the split-off feminine Self. Within this context, the myth has meaning for both men and women; it is not only a woman's mystery, else the Eleusinian Mysteries would have been celebrated only for women, and we know that this was not the case.

Since body and psyche are two aspects of the same reality, different only because consciousness views them in different ways—from a spir-itual-mental vantage point or from an embodied one—one cannot call Jung anti-body simply because he generally refers the symbolism of the body back to a psychic representation. This spiritual emphasis is often necessary. It is always part of the picture.

The essential issue here in terms of therapy is the role of the archetypal dimension, metaphorically spoken of as an experience of ascent in which the soul meets archetypal energies. In Jung's many years of studying alchemical authors, he gave special attention to Gerhard Dorn's images of the individuation process.[181] There, the first stage is a consolidation on a spiritual level, the creation of the so called *unio mentalis* Only then is there a descent back into matter, whence the body is transformed. This means that *only when* the spirit exists as a reality, when psychic reality is a phrase with *objective meaning*—stemming from a transformation of the psyche such that a felt center exists—then and only then does a descent into the body lead to transformation, and to the experience of the somatic unconscious. Any other kind of descent, such as through body exercises, leads only to temporary changes which must always be repeated, for the lack of the spirit to—as the alchemists would say—"kill and transform the bodies"[182] leads not to transformation, and surely not to the reality Jung knew as the somatic unconscious.

Thus Jung's psychology is not anti-body but rather a proper guide to body. And any way that does not recognize the autonomy of the spirit and the existence of the archetypal realm can only lead to a very concrete view of body, which misses the mystery of the fundamental identity of body and psyche.

In discussing the idealized and mirror transferences in chapter one, the analogy was made between them and the ascent and descent of libido in alchemical thought. The idealized transference corresponds to the ascent of the spirit archetype, and its internalization corresponds to the forma-tion of a spiritual center with a strong unifying and stabilizing power. I say "corresponds to" because there is no reason to assume we are dealing with identical processes. The narcissistic transferences are not archetypal processes; rather they are a kind of hybrid product of personal and archetypal factors, forming a mid-way transference phenomenon. But the idealized transference does achieve results also achieved by the integration of the spirit archetype, and conversely. As already noted, the idealized transference can lead to an integration process oriented more around eros in outer relations than does the introverted experience of the spirit arche-type. The latter in turn can yield a more potent sense of "center" in terms of better contact with an inner, organizing principle. Thus they are differ-ent, but yield results that overlap in important areas.

The existence and integration of the energies of idealization is essen-tial for approaching body in a way that can integrate the split-off Self in the narcissistic character. The *way* one approaches the body is always the central issue, not the particular techniques employed. And just as the alchemical process always specified a spiritual consolidation prior to turning to the problem of the body, the same requirement holds, in my view, in the treatment of the narcissistic character. This is especially true in what I call Stage Two of transformation. Without a consolidated idealization, or an integrated, archetypal experience of the spirit, the body will always be experienced differently from the somatic unconscious. It will be a "thing" with drives and various instinctual processes, but it will not be a live energy process with its own form of consciousness.

4   Psyche-Soma Complementarity

It is not possible to extract information from both the psychic and somatic unconscious simultaneously, with equal amounts from each. Rather, a relationship of complementarity exists: Orienting toward the somatic unconscious limits the information gained from the psychic unconscious, and vice versa.

If one allows consciousness to sink down into the body, which as Jung said is always a defeat for the spirit, the information gained will be different from the connection to the psychic unconscious. The psychic unconscious link—for example, operating through thinking, intuition, or any function which filters data through a theory of the organizing center, the Self—must be sacrificed to get information from the somatic unconscious. Then the primitivelike consciousness I have described can sift and sort data, always within the feeling-sense of a gestalt filling out. Just as Isis in her wanderings is led to Osiris' parts which she must then remember, or Demeter teaches the Eleusinian Mysteries as the procedure for the redemption of Persephone, so the processes of the somatic unconscious can lead to a vision, an emergence of the life of *imaginal sight* which can *see* the split-off Self. What we discover is what we *see*.

This kind of *seeing* is similar to that described by Carlos Castaneda in his don Juan novels.[183] It is a lunar rather than solar vision, a sight based upon imagination that is *real* in the sense of being nearly corporeal, and experienced in a very close relationship to one's body. It corresponds to the distinction the alchemists made between "true" and "fantastic" imagination.[184] It is also a kind of vision or imaginal activity that in the analytical relationship has a mutuality about it, as if its existence depended on the patient-therapist interraction. (It is treated as such when, for example, its contents are shared and their accuracy checked with the patient.) In alchemy, *imaginatio,* the act of imagining, was a major key to the successful completion of the opus. It was a process "half spiritual, half physical,"[185] and is as vital today as then, for we encounter it whenever we link psyches with another person and the unconscious is highly constellated.

The importance the alchemists placed upon the body and the material quality of imagination (stemming from its origin in the body) is also just as necessary today. As Lévi-Strauss points out, we are dealing not with an archaic, prescientific mode of thought in the sense of something that must give way to a more differentiated and abstract, scientific thought, but rather with another, *prior* mode of thinking that still exists in us along with the scientific one.[186]

The sacrifice of spirit for the sake of being in the body can in turn stimulate the unconscious so that imagination appears. This kind of perception is not readily had with less body-reference. It is always interfered with by connections the conscious or unconscious tend to make. The ends of the body-spirit spectrum are in a relationship of complementarity. Operating near to the psychic unconscious limits the kind of information gathered, so to speak, near the somatic unconscious, and conversely. Interpreting, going beyond existing imagery through reduction or amplification to a different level of meaning, is also a vital analytical procedure. For this, the connection to the somatic unconscious must be sacrificed. Both are necessary modes; at times it is even important to switch back and forth during a session. Also, a process can be dominated by either one or the other approach. But always, observing from one vantage point limits observations from the other.

5   Osiris, Dionysos and the Somatic Unconscious

We have discussed an aspect of the Osiris myth, Isis collecting his scattered members, or tracking down the location of his body. (Both versions exist with the motif of children and dogs as helpers.) But then comes the final mystery of the resurrection of Osiris.

In Plutarch's telling of the story he weaves the Egyptian tale in with the Greek myth of Demeter and Persephone, with Hades/Dionysos having the same role as Osiris.[189] Later commentators, such as Otto, have shown that the analogy between the figures of Dionysos and Osiris is only partially correct; their myths are also quite different.[190] But I think there are definite grounds for a close association from the vantage point of the somatic unconscious. Both gods are dismembered, and the process of discovery, of Osiris in the Egyptian myth and Persephone in the Greek, requires the somatic unconscious to a large degree. And the kind of penetration of Persephone by Dionysos is a process which requires a gathering up of the god from his dismembered state. In the figure of Dionysos the erotic element is more apparent than in Osiris. But both figures are helpful in understanding the nature of consciousness, which easily dismembers and must continually be brought together again through connection to the somatic unconscious.

Osiris was Egypt's immanent god, a people's god, worshipped daily with great emotion.[191] But Egypt also had a transcendent solar principle, the god Re. So there was a worship of many gods—the Osirian religion— and at the same time the monotheistic religion of Re.[192]

There are many cultures without an Osiris image. The Hebrew religion had the transcendent Yahweh, while the requirement of immanence only crept back in much later in Kabbalistic thought. Religions can do without Osiris-like gods. The Greek religion as recounted by Homer is very alien from its previous Earth gods and goddesses, notably from Dionysos. Homer hardly mentions him; he is totally alien to the Apollonian spirit that rules the religion of the Olympians.[193] One can thus do quite well with only a more distant, solar principle, while the earthly one is nonexistent or only marginally known. This was not the case in Egypt; if anything, the Osirian religion was dominant.

Osiris is not only, like Dionysos (who is often identified with Hades),[194] a god of the dead, he is a *dead god.*[195] But imagine a dead god that comes back to life: That is a wonderful image of the fact that from the seemingly inert matter of the day's residue, the babblings and random body sensations we experienced, something can resurrect. When sitting "in the body" and doing nothing, knowing nothing—*just being*—we often feel very "dumb." Narcissistic patients can have great difficulty with this, and *our* narcissism is accordingly injured by the feeling of being dumb. Narcissistic psychic structuring leads to a need to know, to glitter and be smart. But we need to be able to be dumb, to have a dead consciousness. That, in part, is the psychological significance of Osiris.

Osiris is distinguished primarily by the passion with which he was worshipped. He was a god approached through emotion, not with a solar consciousness. And he was a god who suffered.

To experience a dismembered state is to suffer, exactly what the narcissistic character avoids.[196] One major effect of an embodied awareness in the presence of a person who is dissociating, for instance entering a kind of withdrawal which makes any sustained consciousness or attention very difficult, is that one feels pain and depression. It is as if, through induction,[197] one felt the distress of the splitting process in the patient—who is meanwhile unconscious of it. Similarly, in the Demeter-Persephone myth and the Eleusinian Mysteries the initiates identified with Demeter—which may be seen as a body-consciousness stemming from the somatic unconscious—experiencing her emotions of grief and rage. Emotional experience dominates the earth religions, and was the key element in the worship of Osiris.

The kind of awareness that Osiris leads to is at first bound up with inertia. It doesn't seem to want to emerge. In the Egyptian myth Osiris is always being thrown "on his side" by Seth, and his worshippers are always bidding him to rise up.[198] He is drowned in water, shut up in a coffin or tree trunk from which he must be rescued. He is dead in the underworld, encompassed by the coils of a serpent, in a state of absolute harmony *until* he attempts to rise up. Then the serpent becomes ferocious[199]—just as unconscious contents "resist" coming to consciousness.

And so it often is with us in analysis. In a state of unconscious, Osirian peace we become sleepy, bored, ready to just allow the hour to pass, hopeful that the regressions we feel will speed the clock along rather than slow it down. But if we recognize that we are experiencing something that has to do with a mutual process it can become interesting.

Awareness of our rage often starts the process of "waking up." Instead of hiding in our own uroboric world (the coiled serpent) as the split-off parts of our patient would prefer, we can become aware of the Sethian forces—rage turned against ourselves, producing dissociation. And then we may reorient toward our bodies, discover it has a life and with that a new kind of being awake. The many babblings, the negative feelings we have for our patient, the boredom and hatred, start to gain meaning, gradually becoming part of a forming whole. Our body reactions aid this if we listen to them and use them to go deeper into the material we hear, rather than ignoring them and grasping for a theory or amplification as a life preserver. We begin to be able to sit and be dumb, to not know, to listen and respect this process. Most of all, we begin to respect silence, for we know that only if something *appears* will it have value. We will find nothing, certainly nothing we look for, through theory or introspection. Only a mutual discovery can be of value.

6 Seeing through the Body

By being close to our body, with psychic awareness relatively low, we are like a measuring instrument in flowing water or a magnetic field; we can use our own reactions to know when the other person's energy is fading and when it is present. But just as in science, where one must know the characteristics of the measuring instrument, whose own nature distorts the results, so too we must be able to filter out our own personal reactions. In fact this is a much easier process working near the somatic unconscious than the psychic unconscious. By not having to *know* we are much less involved in power-motivated countertransference reactions.

The tightening up of our own body, perturbations of sensation in head, chest, belly, sexual organs, throat and so forth, all help track the parts of the patient that attempt to split off, and reveal the fact that the patient is temporarily leaving the here and now. Just as it is possible to walk into a room of people and "pick up" that something is out of order, perhaps dangerous, or that someone is in a complex, so too body consciousness can operate in the here and now, in a more or less continuous way. It is difficult to explain this process causally, except in the unscientific sense that something going on in another person "causes" something to happen in us. In this way, by listening and organizing according to our body consciousness and physical babblings, a new order can appear. It comes up from below, like the resurrection of the dead god Osiris. *The new order is the resurrected Osiris.* And it can be a new dimension of vision, an imaginal seeing, as much as an awareness that suddenly puts order into the previous day's events. Here I must stress that this imaginal seeing is a vague, shadowy vision, not a clear one of solar nature. Trusting it now becomes the cardinal issue. In this state one is often discovering, along with the patient, their split-off parts that begin to feel seen.

Naturally, one never *has* to work in this way. It is possible to be more "objective," to interpret a great range of phenomena, including complicated countertransference issues, while never working through the body. One can do very well with a psychic, more mental, connection, whether one works as a Jungian, Freudian, Reichian, Gestaltist, or out of any other school of thought. And it is so much "cleaner." Unfortunately, it misses a good deal.

The reality is that analytical work from the vantage point of the psychic unconscious is very poor at integrating those aspects of the psyche that are split off and hidden by the narcissistic structuring of the personality. In the underworld of Greek myth, Hades, things are invisible to the eye of solar consciousness. They are visible only to lunar vision, the sight of the blind Tiresias who kept his consciousness in Hades.[200] If we do not make use of imaginal sight, and instead depend solely on the great storehouse of scientific knowledge and the kind of awareness that comes through psychic empathy, then integration of the split-off feminine Self requires considerable regression. Working through the somatic unconscious also involves regression, but often much less and of a more easily controlled kind. *Seeing* can have a strong holding quality, where interpreting may lead to dissociation.

Consequently, especially in Stage Two of transformation, I find it necessary to "work from the underworld," respecting the spirits of the dead, and attempting to "make the dead alive." And so I work with dead matter, inert bits that babble and sensations that randomly afflict. But through this apparently meaningless process meaning can emerge, and that meaning is Osiris. Osiris is the god of yesterday, Re the god of tomorrow, according to the Egyptians.[201] And that corresponds to the fact that much of the previous day's residue is essential in the resurrection of a pattern and perhaps a vision. All the garbage that "doesn't matter" proves to matter indeed, in fact becomes the "matter" of a new consciousness.

The kind of consciousness that Osiris and Dionysos represent is consciousness of an archetype. It is gathered together from the body, and when it comes together in imaginal vision (or structural awareness) it soon dies. It is as if it rises up and then the moment of awareness fades quickly away, and cannot be recalled with anything that resembles its past, momentary reality. It must be rediscovered yet again, and then perhaps let go of forever; a moment not to be regained, but only recovered as another vision.

In the analytic process it is a mutually shared vision, dependent upon both psyches. It is isomorphic to sexuality. Just as consciousness is gathered up from its life in the body, and suddenly comes together as a kind of epiphany, so-called infantile sexuality is gathered up in sexual foreplay until it flows into genital primacy and orgasm. The life that momentarily existed then quickly fades; it will come again, but certainly in its own time.

The analogy of this Dionysian consciousness with sexuality only shows that sexual life exists according to the archetypal model of Dionysos. But so does the quality of consciousness that stems from the somatic unconscious. The Dionysian archetype is responsible for both, and in no way can sexuality or "infantile sexuality" be seen as the cause of the existence of the god Dionysos. The discovery of infantile sexuality is one of Freud's great contributions, and also a back door through which some of what Dionysos stands for entered Freudian thought. But the body is never resurrected from infantile sexuality; its rebirth depends rather upon an archetypal pattern (such as Dionysos or Osiris represents) becoming conscious.

7 Psychic and Somatic Empathy

Empathy, like consciousness in general, has a different quality as it shifts from the psychic to the somatic unconscious as its main reference. When close to the somatic unconscious our empathy is very much a function of a mutual participation in which both psyches operate simultaneously. Each affects the other in a way that makes discovery unique to the moment, not easily repeated. At best what is *seen* can be rediscovered.

Psychic empathy extracts information; for Kohut it is a mode of "knowing":

> Empathy is not a tool in the sense in which the patient's reclining position, the use of free associations, the employment of the structural model, or of the concepts of drive and defense are tools. Empathy does indeed in essence define *the field* of our observations. Empathy is not just a useful way by which we have access to the inner life of man—the idea itself of an inner life of man, and thus of a psychology of complex mental states, is unthinkable without our ability to know via vicarious introspection—my definition of empathy—what the inner life of man is, what we ourselves and what others think and feel.[187]

Empathy is different, of course, from scientifically "operating upon" data and extracting a result; it depends upon being immersed in the field. But there is a vast difference between extracting data within this field, through introspection, and an act of mutual, spontaneous discovery. The former, what I am calling psychic empathy—the kind Jung refers to as introjection or "feeling into"[188]—extracts information and is a process in which there is an observer (the analyst) acting upon a field of information, the patient's psyche. There is little need for a simultaneous embodied consciousness, which in fact would detract from the experience of "vicarious introspection." Somatic empathy, on the other hand, involves a mutual discovery in imagination and embodied consciousness. Other useful differentiations could be Apollonian and Dionysian empathy: The former is more distant and reflective; the latter more enmeshed in the moment and the body.

The more reflective, Apollonian or psychic, empathy is generally appropriate to dealing with the narcissistic transferences. But after they sufficiently transform, the nature of our empathy must shift toward the somatic or Dionysian if we are to successfully penetrate the depths required for the eventual recovery of the split-off Self. While this level of penetration was formerly too intrusive, it now becomes essential.

The following clinical notes are an example of the use of empathy moving back and forth between a somatic and a psychic base. They concern a 35-year-old man whose narcissistic transferences had largely transformed and whose schizoidlike Self had begun to emerge.

I have the same feeling as last time, which I did not analyze: I feel put off by him, a slight sense of disgust. He comments that last time was different from the previous sessions; it felt a little intellectual, like we were analyzing, putting things in place, and then goes on to say how it probably had to do with the fact that previously he had still been turned on by his vacation. I tell him that a feeling is with us, and that it was here last time, but I chose not to bring it out. I mention it is low level, but constant. He knows what I mean, says it's a certain dis-ease. I add that it feels a bit like an expected disapproval, a lack of liking him. He feels that is real, and goes on to say that his greatest fear is of being boring, to be uninteresting to me. I tell him that that feeling of being boring comes from a part of him that easily flees, isn't present, so he isn't all here, like he's not playing with a full deck. I further tell him that this part is sort of on the loose now because the way it had been contained, mostly through power-control of me and others, has dissolved.

He knows what I mean, and sees "it" for an instant, but it then flees away. "Damn, I had it, but it's gone." This happens again. "Why does that happen?" he asks and quickly adds, "It's like being in the woods and watching birds: You don't see them if you walk around looking, you have to stop and wait for them to come." I echo the validity of the analogy, and he quickly notes how his analogy can take him further away—he can get off on it, a bit inflated. "Does it have to be that way?" he wonders, and I tell him that instead he can take the analogy seriously. He can be in the woods, looking, waiting, feeling the metaphor's power. And as he does this, he can then feel its inadequacy, how it doesn't exactly fit the situation of seeing the part of him that flees. This also dawns on him at the time I have noted it.

I tell him how it is impossible to look with his head, but how he needs to be in his body and let it just come. This he understands, and again feels the part come by but flee. I tell him that he needs me to also see it, he cannot do it alone. And when I tell him this, another story jumps into his mind.

He recalls how yesterday he was thinking about watching birds, and that it required two of him to really watch: One to look at the bird, and the other to look at the bird book, pointing out the variations among species essential for identification. I find the analogy illuminating, and he takes it further. I ask,

"Why can't you look at the bird, then the book, and back and forth?" He says, "Because the bird won't cooperate, it doesn't just sit there." And I add an analogy. "The alchemist," I tell him, "is often shown with a library and a laboratory." He wonders how they were connected, by a long hall or by a door? "Mine," he says, "are connected by a hall, while it would be better to have an open door."

I also mention the fact that looking at the book and just being with the bird are complementary. The long hallway would signify a great deal of loss when switching back and forth, while the door that is open indicates easy back and forth access.

By now I am able to *see* the part, as if it is peeking in and out from behind trees. He goes on, and wonders if perhaps at times I have the book, and at other times he does. I agree and tell him that it's like what happened at the beginning of the hour. I felt the induced feelings of disgust, boredom, and then I reflected upon them—I looked in the book. I know that this means that something in him expects this, and also, after a controlling effect has dissolved, that a part like this does expect boredom and general dislike. I used the alchemical analogy of the fixed and volatile Mercury, and how fixing often is aided by earth, the body, and not by the intellect. So, by keeping the book I further help him look into the woods. And as he does this, I see the part again, and as I stay with it he can then reflect—"take the book himself"—on why the boredom feeling exists. He can reflect on the way his creativity, his true Self, was hated in childhood, for instance.

And so we go, back and forth, gradually seeing the part more, but for now it isn't yet fully there. Then he tells stories about photographs, how he works at his art. When he was talking about this creative effort, I could *see* the part stop and become interested. But then he went on to other stories of the day, about how he wanted people to look at his pictures and validate them, and as he begins to note this I *see* the part get frantic again and disappear. I can later recall this for him, and before I get too far he steps in and tells me exactly when it went away, just when he left the creative moment.

And then he speaks of how afraid of this he is, how frightened to take this creative step. He speaks of an old teacher, and tears come to his eyes. He can just "be in the woods" with this teacher; he reminds him of me, and with him/me he can have this creative reach, but alone he is afraid. "Why," he asks? "We'll have to talk about it," he says, noting that somehow he fears attack, but is not quite sure how. I tell him that with the teacher/me he can ward off this attack, but as of yet he doesn't have this internalized.

This is an example of shared, mutually induced vision. My body consciousness and attention to babblings led to it, and then we could discuss it together. Meanwhile, the other kind of awareness, that of the psychic conscious-unconscious relationship, weaved in and out. At the time of this session he was still too frightened to take this kind of process up for himself. For it meant coming into contact with the Self and consequently his own effectiveness, which threatened both great loss ("nobody will be strong enough to be with me") and a fear of envy. So during this period he would attain a Self connection with me in one session, largely lose it during the week, and regain it again the next session.

But through this process he gradually came to be more comfortable with his power. A very important dream brought in the figure of his grandfather, who had a slight association to me. But it was also the beginning of the Self incarnating in him, that is, becoming embodied. With this, he began to help the Self "live its experiment in life."

There were some crucial events over the next few weeks, including the spontaneous imaginal appearance of a four-year-old: once while he was bird watching and in a hypnogogic vision the child was there, pointing to something on the ground; and then while running, trying to "run off" severe anxiety, he got tired and rested, and the child appeared, saying: "Daddy, I'm afraid." This was so intense it brought tears to his eyes.

This contact with not only his own anxiety, but that of the split-off child, all came about after the dissolution of the narcissistic defenses. His defensive rage, his previous controlling pattern, was gone, and he was filled instead with intense fear, now centering upon his job and the relationship with his girlfriend.

In one session, feeling his anxiety and furtiveness—an in-and-out pattern—I suggested he image the child, and try to see how the child felt. This brought an immediate feeling of relief, for it was clear that the child was terrified and needed to be taken care of. The patient was now in the position of being the father he himself had never had at this crucial time, 3 to 4 years of age. Soon after this he dreamed:

> I am in a graveyard, looking at a particular grave that has in some way to do with me. There are three stones placed on a mound that I am looking up at, and I am arguing with someone about a fourth stone. I want it to be a grey color, like the others, but he wants it to be a strange color, like a bright red. It is also not round like the others but has a rectangular shape. Finally, the reddish one is put in, and looking up there are now four stones. The fourth is very strange, not only in the color of red but it has designs on it, and a quadrated intersection of lines.

To the man in the dream he associated: "The guy once worked for me, I didn't like him. He was too much of a business type, too oriented to success in the world."

This is exactly what the dreamer himself had shied away from; he has always been "grey," never really allowing his creativity to work in the world, successful only in spite of himself. The other person is the necessary shadow of ambition he is finally having to integrate.

The child is "the fourth," the unconscious component, as is the graveyard, the connection to the underworld. Notice that the connection to the child slows him down, makes him connect to his body, to an embodied life. The graveyard is the place of the corpse, the dead body. The fourth is the embodied connection to the Self, through the child. It is a connection with passion, a "living of the experiment of the Self," instead of the grey, "poor me," masochistic quality that had ruled his life, destroyed his relationships and generally had him getting older with nothing to show for it that he could respect.

The "grey Self" had given up on the experiment of life. It is the "poor me," masochistically toned identity. As long as this Self-representation dominates the ego, the narcissistic character, even if driven by unconscious power drives, never achieves anything like his potential. There is always a curious lack of depth to his output, a great deal of glitter and talk, often the anticipation of great things, but in fact little that is memorable occurs.

8   The Magical Use of Imagination

The use of imagination has been a subject of much dispute throughout history. It has a special role in the great controversy over magic between the Church and magicians such as Pico, Paracelsus, Ficino and others. D. P. Walker's *Spiritual and Demonic Magic* is a valuable survey of the history of the conflict. Here is one excerpt:

> Erastus gives a detailed refutation of the possibility of producing transitive effects by the power of imagination conveyed in emissions of spirit. He accepts the reality of subjective effects, both psychological ones and the more ordinary psychosomatic ones. But, he says, "certainly no one in their right mind will think that an image fashioned in the spirit of my fantasy can go out of my brain and get into the head of another man."[202]

Clearly, some magicians believed that their spiritual "emissions" could affect the thought and fantasy products of another person.

From our knowledge of the countertransference, and especially the process of projective identification, we know that Erastus is quite wrong. The unconscious emission of spirits by our patients may be a crude way of putting it, but there is no doubt that "psychic infection" is real; what is going on in one person *can* immigrate into another.[203] This is an unconscious process that must be realized and dealt with. But conversely, in working with the somatic unconscious, how do I know that I am not inducing what I think I *see,* and that my patient is not just being suggestible, or perhaps agreeing with me for the sake of maintaining an idealized image?

My experience is that patients have no difficulty at all in correcting my visions, in disputing them, as well as agreeing with them. The wide range of patient responses has convinced me that I am not magically controlling the visions which spontaneously appear. The following brief excerpt from clinical notes illustrates this process:

> I said: "I feel you just went away." She said, "I did, I feel anxious." I ask, "Why?" She says, "I don't know." I said, "That doesn't sound quite on target, it sounds like you are afraid of knowing." I sit with her, gradually gaining her confidence and her ability to be present. As this back and forth

process goes on, I begin to see a child, like an image appearing in active imagination. It seems to me to be happy, and about 5 years old. "Do you feel the presence of a child?" She says, "Yes." "How old is it?" I ask her. "About 3 or 4." "Oh, I thought I saw it as 5.... I see its hair as blond." "No," she says, "it has brown hair." All along I sense the child as if it were in an imagination of my own, yet it is shared, she can make the child flee by going into a head trip. This is visible and when I tell her, she recognizes it and the child returns, again happy rather than withdrawn and depressed, as it gets when she becomes intellectual.

It is especially the role of the body that helps achieve the mutually shared, and easily corrected imaginal happenings. If I am in my body, aware of its size and feeling, then I am completely human. But to the degree that I am not embodied, to that same degree I am a ready hook for idealized and archetypal projections. I am less threatening in my body in the here and now.

Furthermore, by working in an embodied manner one tends to constellate processes in patients that are capable of being consciously integrated as part of their ongoing individuation process. By contrast, when working in a less embodied and interpretive or intuitive mode, or one of psychic empathy, the analyst is often "right" but pulls up contents and images that are not ego-syntonic. Then these contents have a dissociative effect. Strong defensive idealizations often mount up as a result.

Consciousness rooted in the somatic unconscious is always at the limits of what has been integrated. This is a quality of Dionysos too. He represents going beyond existing boundaries.[204] Consequently, working in this way we are often discovering images and even workings of the unconscious that seem very true at the moment but then vanish and are exceedingly difficult to regain. They are like a dream very far from consciousness, and very difficult to bring back to conscious awareness. But they must be allowed to go back into their domain of invisibility.

One must be able to let them go, else the possibility for becoming the "black magician" quickly takes root. If the analyst has to be right, has to be idealized by his patient, the shadow aspect of this method is dangerous. The boundaries that are always tending to be transcended include the analyst's knowledge of his own dark Self. For the Egyptians, Nepthys was associated with Aso, the queen of Ethiopia which was the land (for the Egyptians) of black magic.[205] Nepthys, we recall, was the mother of Anubis, Isis' guide, illustrating the "boundary quality" of this method.

Our integrated consciousness is always being pushed to its outer limits. Therefore we must always be able *not* to know; we must be willing to work on those aspects of ourselves that still need mirroring and consequently demand idealization, else analysis can degenerate into a power position, rather than a creative wrestling with this ever-present reality. While this is a problem in any kind of analytical approach, it is far more manageable in one that incorporates an embodied consciousness.

IV

The Mythology of Stage Two:
Emergence of Feminine Power

1 Introduction

In this chapter my purpose is to show that the Narcissus myth, according to Ovid, has a natural extension in the telling of that story by Pausanius, and especially in the Demeter-Persephone myth which Pausanius includes in his version of Narcissus' fate.

Here and in the next chapter, where clinical issues of Stage Two are the main focus, we will be shifting back and forth between archetypal and developmental-clinical views. This is not a process of convenience, or merely a way of more easily describing a difficult subject. It is necessary because Stage Two concerns the transition from archetypal reality into personal-historical life in a manner that retains some degree of archetypal rootedness, some degree of the original transcendent connection in which every child is a child of God.[206] It is the inevitable and natural loss of the transcendent Self connection that leads to man's constant attempts to regain it in mystical, philosophical, psychological and other endeavors. But too much loss leads to an extreme vulnerability to the negative archetypal emotions, and with it a predisposition to the dissociative states of psychosis and the borderline disorders.

The Eleusinian Lesser and Greater Mysteries, celebrated for well over a thousand years, were an ancient Greek answer to healing the inevitable rift in man's nature as he must shift from childhood immersion in archetypal reality toward life bounded by spatial-temporal limitations, with human objects of real size and affects. As we noted when discussing Ovid's myth, Narcissus represents a stuck condition between the personal and archetypal polarities. The Eleusinian Mysteries, rooted in the Demeter-Persephone mythologem, were an attempt at healing and reapproaching a once-known wholeness, in the face of which our modern psychotherapeutic approaches significantly pale.

A great deal can be learned from the little we know of the Mysteries of Eleusis. *Especially, we can gain an awareness of the value of imaginal seeing in healing.* Our guide for much of this will be Kerényi's masterful work, *Eleusis,* and his earlier study on the Kore or Divine Maiden. I have also found of special value the works of Walter Otto, and Carl Ruck's analysis in the recent study, *The Road to Eleusis.* The latter work is devoted to proving that an hallucinogenic substance was a central feature of the Mysteries.

Ruck's analysis in this context has been illuminating. The fact that the drink the initiates took on the way to the Greater Mysteries at Eleusis, the *kykeon,* seems assuredly to have been an LSD-like mixture,[207] should not be overlooked by a psychological approach. Whatever the importance of the use of drugs may have been, the outcome of the experience was rooted in the archetypal experiences so induced. Our modern experience with hallucinogens should not be sidestepped in helping gain further access to what the *mystes* experienced. This is not a central part, in any way, of the analysis that follows. But my own awareness of the value of the so-called bad trip, *in conjunction with* a powerfully enlightening counterpart, has influenced the way in which I view the great value of the extreme chaos and terror that attended the appearance of the new birth at Eleusis.

The structures defining the narcissistic character defend, as we have often noted, against depression and suffering. Clinically speaking, they represent a withdrawal from fear and depression, but a withdrawal that can have a tactical advantage, as if the personality went on "hold," awaiting the right relationships or experiences through which to unfold.

What we shall discover from Pausanius' story is that there is a feminine soul far deeper and more encompassing that was split off by the massive intrusiveness behind the formation of narcissistic character structures. While Echo was a rather shallow representation of the feminine in the Narcissus myth according to Ovid, it is Persephone that Narcissus seeks in the Pausanius version. Recovering this split-off feminine Self requires more than the Ovidian version tells of: It requires a process analogous to the Eleusinian Mysteries. Part of this is similar to the emotions associated with the depressive position.

Winnicott has called the depressive position Melanie Klein's most important discovery, ranking with the idea of the oedipal complex.[208] The existence of a depressive phase in infant development, around eight to nine months, is not disputed. It corresponds to the infant's growing capacity to see objects as whole, and to integrate the archetypally toned other into a symbolic core of his ego, the Self as a part of the ego. This process depends upon the infant's suffering, especially mourning the results of its fantasized aggression.[209]

The view I want to present here is that this is also a stage in which a certain split generally forms between the psychic and somatic unconscious. The passage is never completely successful. The psychic unconscious then becomes the carrier of imagery and spiritual value, while the somatic unconscious is largely the residue of emotions. The major split is thus into the different aspects of the unconscious. Different archetypes rule these "halves"; in Greek thought they would be the Olympians with their Zeus or Apollo-like religion, as against the former earth deities and their Dionysian/Demetrian-Persephone religion. Healing the split between the somatic and psychic unconscious was, I think, one of the outcomes of the Eleusinian experience.

Demeter can be taken to represent the somatic unconscious, and her reunion with Persephone the recovery of a lost *psychesoma* (Winnicott).[210] But more, it represents the recovery of a *unique* Self, an embodied one.[211] The recovery is not complete—as working through the depressive position never is—for Persephone only returns for part of the year. The initiates of Eleusis identified with Demeter,[212] and thus experienced her emotions of grief and rage, the emotions of the depressive position. But prior to that, in the Lesser Mysteries at Agrai, they identified with Persephone. We shall later discuss this; it was clearly an ancient Greek way of healing, and there is much to learn from it.

So in passing on to Stage Two of transformation we go to a level of development beyond the holding pattern that is Narcissus, into the depths and ecstasy that he fears, lest his fragile identity be devoured. But it must be emphasized that *the death of Narcissus, the transformation of narcissistic structures (such as the transferences we have discussed), is a precondition for successful entrance into this stage.*

In the passage through the depressive position, we all suffer some loss of soul. When we only suffer minor loss, we retain a secret Self, as Winnicott describes it, an energized core of existence and psychic reality. But when the soul loss is extreme, there exists a schizoid state in which our "true" Self is split off and very easily depleted of energy. This part, whether "healthy" or "ill," *wants to embody* as part of the organism's individuation, and the rape and return of Persephone represents the schizoidlike drama in which this true Self is reincarnated.

The Eleusinian Mysteries, which enacted in ritual much of the Homeric Hymn, effectively represent the psychotherapy of man's schizoid soul and its partially successful passage through the depressive position. It may even represent much more, for the ancient Greeks believed the entire cosmos would die if the Mysteries were not enacted. Are we certain that man's individuation doesn't have a vital role in the health of the archetype and the ordering capacity of the Cosmos? In any event, this is a question beyond our concern. We shall be content here if we can shed some light upon the clinical issues of transforming narcissism.

Referring the material of the Homeric Hymn back to infant development has the great disadvantage of distorting its archetypal nature. It also easily causes us to see the mythological material within the typical mother-son mold of near-Eastern myth and ritual. It is very different from this, and our references to early childhood are only made because much of the psychic material that must be entered in the Eleusinian Mysteries appears to also be known from paths traveled by the infant. Elkin, for instance, believes that the infant experiences all the archetypes.[213] I am not quite sure of that, but certainly much that is archetypal is experienced, and definitely the level of transcendent light and joy is known in the first month of life.

But it is quite a different matter to refer these Mysteries back to infancy, than to recognize them as transformation rites for adults who, by necessity, would have had to be rather mature in order to benefit from them. Thus it would be well to bear in mind the following comments by Otto:

> Let us consider the principal goddesses of the Eleusinian cult. They are, as everyone knows, Demeter and her daughter Kore, "the maiden," or Persephone. Here we can disregard the other Eleusinian deities, except for Pluto, king of the underworld, who abducted Persephone and made her his wife. Searching for her vanished daughter, Demeter came to Eleusis; there she found her, there she made peace with the gods and gave to men the holy mysteries and agriculture. This is the narrative of the Homeric Hymn. Despite her Greek name, Demeter is indubitably descended from a pre-hellenic culture, as we can see by many usages and conceptions connected with her religion, particularly her Acadian cults. In Thelpusa, she was called Erinys, "the Angry One": it was believed that, in the form of a mare, she was mounted by the stallion Poseidon, from which union she bore a daughter with a secret name and the accursed steed Areion; and in Phigalia, there was a similar legend concerning Demeter Melaina, whom a wooden statue represented as a woman with the head of a horse, holding in one hand a dolphin, in the other a dove. She was worshipped eminently as the giver of grain, but other fruits and blossoms were considered among her gifts and she was associated also with the growth of man, to whom after death she was a mother, receiving him to her womb, the womb of the earth. In Attica the dead were said to "belong to Demeter." It is easy to understand that women should have played an important part in the cult of this goddess. Persephone, who passes as her daughter, is identified as pre-hellenic by her mere name, which also assigns her unmistakably to the realm of the dead, and Homer has indeed made her known to all as the queen of the dead.
>
> How did Demeter come by this daughter? What does the close bond between her and a daughter signify? For though every god has his father and mother, there is no other example of so close a relation between mother and daughter. Even Athene, who sprang from the head of Zeus, is not so much of a daughter to her father as Persephone to her mother. It seems likely she was regarded as a kind of duplication or continuation of Demeter. But the fervor of their love reminds us of those great nature goddesses who are linked with a beloved: Aphrodite with her Adonis, the Great Mother with her Attis, the Babylonian Ishtar with her Tammuz, the Egyptian Isis with her Osiris. All mourn the sudden death of their beloved, and since his death and resurrection are seen as symbols of the death and reawakening of the earth's vegetation, the analogy to Demeter's adventure seems complete. But this comparison overlooks a difference which increases in importance the more we examine it. The *mater dolorosa,* with whom Demeter has been compared, mourns for her son; Aphrodite, Cybele, Ishtar, Isis and others mourn for their beloved, their husband, their brother. But Demeter mourns for a daughter who resembles her and gives the impression of a double. The character of this relation is very different from that of the others. Despite apparent parallels, it is ultimately unique, requiring a very special explanation.

In [myths that compare] with that of Persephone, the earth loses its fertility when the god descends to the underworld. "Since Queen Ishtar went down to the underworld," says the Babylonian legend, "the bull no longer mounts the cow," etc. The goddess vanishes into the depths, and fertility with her. There is a direct correspondence. But this is by no means the case in the Greek myth. Here, as the Homeric Hymn relates, Demeter wanders about for many days, seeking a trace of her vanished daughter. When finally she learns from Helios that Hades has taken her for his wife with the consent of Zeus, she is consumed with anger against the lord of Olympus. She no longer desires to live among the gods but decides to go among men. In the shape of an old woman, she comes to the palace of the king of Eleusis, where she is received with honor and offered food and drink. She remains silent and refuses all sustenance until Iambe succeeds in making her laugh with her jests. The spell is broken. The queen gives her a potion which Demeter, since her mourning prohibits wine, orders mixed of special ingredients—it is the very same as that later given to the initiates at Eleusis.

Then the queen confides her youngest child to the old woman's care. The boy prospers miraculously in the hands of his divine nurse, who attempts to make him immortal, but her magic is undone by the anxious mother's curiosity. Demeter now gives herself to be recognized as a goddess and demands that a great altar and temple be built for her. No sooner is this done than she hides in her sanctuary, far from all gods, immersed in mourning for her lost daughter. Only then does she cause a terrible drought to descend on the land for a whole year. The human race would have perished, the gods deprived of all offerings, if Zeus had not brought about a reconciliation based on the understanding that Persephone might spend a part of the year with her mother, but that she would remain forever the wife of Pluto. Thus, the disappearance of the earth's fertility does not at all coincide with the disappearance of the goddess who supposedly personified the grain. In fact, it occurs considerably later, induced by the angry mother's vengeance. The same version prevails in the famous chorus of Euripides' *Helena* (1301ff.). Here Demeter, enraged at what has been done to her, withdraws into the mountain wastes and permits nothing to grow on earth, until at last the gods manage to appease her sorrow. In this chorus, Demeter is called the "mountain mother," that is to say, is equated with the "Great Mother," the "mother of the gods."

. . . . Thus we recognize a primeval myth of the earth mother, or mother of the gods, in which, angry, she demands her rights. In Arcadian Thelpusa she is called Erinys, "The Angry One," sharing this name with the terrible goddess of malediction and vengeance. Here her anger is directed primarily at Poseidon, who has ventured too close to her. Another motive for her anger is the rape of her daughter Persephone, and here, as elsewhere, the gods must make a great concession to her. Kore may now spend part of the year with her mother above the earth, but she must return regularly below, and she remains forever the queen of the dead. In this she differs from all those gods who seem to symbolize the flowering and fading of nature. Clearly, her journey to the underworld cannot have reference to the grain, since growth does not cease as a result of her disappearance; rather, it is an act of vengeance on the part of the offended mother.[214]

Otto's remarks well serve to amplify the important role of the goddess's negative emotions (as we shall see in section seven). But they primarily alert us against reducing the Demeter-Persephone mythologem to anything like the near-Eastern cycles of death and rebirth. There is much more involved here, and accordingly more is demanded of both men and women. To begin with the death of the narcissistic structuring is in order. And so we now turn to the meaning of the flower left at Narcissus' death, which relates to the version of the myth according to Pausanius.

2   The Narcissus Flower

What happens after the death of Narcissus? Or, to ask the same question psychologically: What happens after the dissolution of the narcissistic transferences and defenses? Does one's personality then simply begin to unfold, no longer encumbered by such issues as extreme vulnerability to criticism, self-doubt, envy and other affects which once led to chronic states of enfeeblement, or compulsive, power-oriented attitudes toward life?

The answer according to my clinical experience is twofold. On the one hand, there are personalities, often young people, or else extroverted, professionally oriented persons who do begin to develop when their narcissistic structures die. They begin to feel their authority and effectiveness, and gain success based upon talents which had always been there, had shone through, but had never been realized. For such people the "death of Narcissus," what I have called Stage One of transformation, is sufficient in that it is all that is desired.[215]

On the other hand, this stage can be an entrance into another level of transformation, one which concerns, for both men and women, the transformation and redemption of the feminine Self, or soul. As noted in chapter two, there is some transformation of the feminine in Stage One, but it is not in the forefront compared to the spiritual regeneration, a new puer-senex relationship. In Stage Two, this emphasis is reversed.

A dream of the death of Narcissus

The dream which follows is from a woman who had worked through much of the narcissistic structuring of her personality and was at a crossroad of life. She was separating from a marriage of thirty years' duration, a relationship that had been largely based upon narcissistic attitudes of debilitating vulnerability, especially in the area of sexual needs. Her husband was a highly successful politician who had always convinced her (with her all-too-willing compliance) that "things would get better." Life in the present was usually without joy. She always doubted her perceptions, particularly with regard to her husband's covert sadistic attacks which left her feeling emotionally poisoned. But after an idealized transference was successfully integrated, her self-doubts diminished; she began to trust her perceptions, and with this the bonding power of the marriage began to loosen. She then had the following dream:

> I am with K. She says that when Narcissus falls into the pool, all he does is drown. I say that a flower grows. Then she goes and gets some small books and tells me with the same despondent tone that she's been reading Shakespeare's tragedies lately.

This same dream was presented in chapter one (section nine) to illustrate the narcissistic fear of the unconscious. There K. was taken to represent the regressive, shadow side of the dreamer. K. was chronically depressed and had a tragic view of life, a view fueled by unconscious envy that "told" her nothing good could ever exist for her. The dreamer had been separating from this outlook, and had even begun to feel traces of joy and a kind of religious, archetypal dimension to life. Now, then, we need to focus on the significance of the dream-ego's response to her shadow: "A flower grows."

The dreamer had a "good feeling" about the flower, but knew little concerning its symbolism. As a matter of fact, the narcissus, the flower that is all that is left of Narcissus at his death, has generally been viewed through the centuries in an extremely negative way. We will look briefly at the nature of these derogatory views, and then turn to the question of how it can be seen, as it was by this dreamer, in a positive light.

Vinge's study of the Ovidian version of the Narcissus myth provides us with a wealth of examples of the vehemence with which the narcissus was attacked. In the twelfth century, for instance, John of Salisbury, in his condemnation of Narcissus as representing a vain striving for power, glory and praise, tells us that "Narcissus of the fables is transformed into a flower as he is captivated by his empty reflection, and perishes in his youth like a flower without fruit while he, ignorantly, looks at himself."[216] Arnolphe d'Orléans, also in the twelfth century, writes that Narcissus "was transformed into a flower, that is to say into something useless."[217] And around the same time, Alexander Neckham gives a picture of the aging narcissistic character, often all too valid nowadays:

> By Narcissus is meant vainglory which is tricked by its own vanity. . . . When in passing things he admires his shadow-like magnificance and is lost in wonder at the glory, he flames up in a fateful fire because of his undue self-love. Finally, worldly glory vanishing, he is transformed into a flower, and the mere name is all that remains. Where is the glory of the Caesars? Where . . . ?[218]

In the fourteenth century Ovid's *Metamorphoses* was translated into French, but in the *Ovid moralise* there are sections not found in the original. For example: "Narcissus became a flower. What kind of flower? Such of which the Psalmist says that it blooms in the morning but by the evening is faded. . . ."[219] The moralizing tendency continues, and a decade or so later, in *Petrus Berchorius,* we read that Narcissus is like "those who dwell in the well of worldly pleasure [and] see their reflection and their high position, all of which passes away like a shadow (Book of Wisdom V). They love it so ardently and they glory so in this that they lose the life of their souls." This is followed by an attack on spiritual men who reflect upon their own virtue and despise others: "They turn into flowers and end in Hell."[220]

In the same century, Boccaccio's *Genealogia Deorum* appeared, answering the need for a manual of mythology. Referring to Narcissus, he says: "And if perchance something is left of their name, it is transformed into a flower which is red and magnificent in the morning but in the evening droops and dies and dissolves into nothingness."[221]

There are many more examples, but Vinge's summary is concise and sufficient:

> Over the centuries [there] have particularly been speculations, from the Middle Ages till now, about the flower that is made to replace Narcissus' body. Various qualities associated with the concept of flower or with the narcissus have been stressed, varying with the motifs that were regarded as essential to the story or read into it: the flower is beautiful and useless, it withers after a short life, the narcissus flower is late, is sterile, has a soporific perfume, is poisonous, bends over water or grows by it, is visually attractive and isolated—these are some of the explanations.[222]

There is, however, a positive view of the narcissus which corresponds to its implications in the dream quoted above. Note that those who regarded the narcissus as worthless also saw Narcissus himself as purely a negative figure. As we have seen, this corresponds to an attitude of ego-consciousness that is wary of the unconscious in anything but a transcendent, out-of-the-body sense, or, in later times, is suspicious of introspection and anything other than outer reality. But a positive valuation of the narcissus is found not only later, when Narcissus himself could be viewed more positively, but in the telling of the myth in antiquity by Pausanius.

3   Pausanius' Narcissus Myth

The version of the Narcissus myth according to Pausanius was, like Canon's,[223] greatly overshadowed by the Ovidian tale. Canon's Narcissus myth has a much narrower focus on the patterns of narcissism than does Ovid's, but it does capture the aspects of self-hate and sadism, and how these function in the process of transformation, in a way not achieved by Ovid. But transformation was less important to the earlier mythographers than was the moral message of the dangers of narcissism. As we have seen in chapter two (section seven), only in explications and commentaries many centuries after Ovid is there a feeling for the positive potential in Narcissus, a potential stemming from an appreciation of introversion and imagination in depth. And even these say little about the depth of transformation that can arise out of the narcissistic structure. But the Narcissus story that points the way to depth comes from Pausanius. It is from the second century; Ovid's tale and Canon's were written at the beginning of the first century.

Pausanius actually noted two versions of the Narcissus myth; they are usually stated together:

> In the territory of the Thespians is a place called Donacon [*Reedbed*]. Here is the spring of Narcissus. They say that Narcissus looked into this water, and not understanding that he saw his own reflection, unconsciously fell in love with himself, and died of love at the spring. But it is utter stupidity to imagine that a man old enough to fall in love was incapable of distinguishing a man from a man's reflection.
>
> There is another story about Narcissus, less popular indeed than the other, but not without some support. It is said that Narcissus had a twin sister; they were exactly alike in appearance, their hair was the same, they wore similar clothes, and went hunting together. The story goes on that Narcissus fell in love with his sister, and when the girl died, would go to the spring, knowing that it was his reflection that he saw, but in spite of this knowledge, finding some relief for his love in imagining that he saw, not his own reflection, but the likeness of his sister. The flower narcissus grew, in my opinion, before this, if we are to judge by the verses of the poet Pamphos. This poet was born many years before Narcissus the Thespian, and he says that the Maid, the daughter of Demeter, was carried off when she was playing and gathering flowers, and that the flowers by which she was deceived into being carried off were not violets, but the narcissus.[224]

This story is a major source, from antiquity, of the connection between the Narcissus myth and that of Demeter and Persephone. Pausanius insists that the flower picked by Persephone, "the Maid," existed much earlier than the flower into which Narcissus turned upon his death. As we have by now become accustomed in our treatment of the Narcissus theme, this chronology has been reversed by other authors. As Vinge tells us, "In his poem on the rape of the virgin, *De raptu Proserpinae,* produced in the 390's, Claudanius reverses [Pausanius'] chronology. He makes the girls pick the narcissus which once was a young man of extraordinary beauty."[225]

In what follows, it will become apparent that both chronologies are important, for together they help describe depths of the formation and then transformation of the narcissistic structures, depths not readily evident from the outset, nor even well into the clinical treatment of the narcissistic character.

The two narcissi

Why does Pausanius insist that the narcissus flower grew *before* the encounter between Narcissus and his twin sister? He makes this assertion with reference to the Demeter-Persephone myth, so let us turn to their story, told in the Homeric Hymn to Demeter, for now looking especially at the appearance of the narcissus.

Let me tell you the story of Demeter, the holy goddess whose hair grew in rich plaits as only a goddess's does, and of her daughter, whom Hades seized. Zeus, the thunder god, gave her to him. This is how it happened.

She was playing far from Demeter, lady of the harvest who reaps with a golden sickle, gathering flowers with the daughters of Ocean, roses and crocus and beautiful violets, iris, hyacinths, and the narcissus. Earth brought forth the narcissus as a wonderful lure for the blossoming girl according to Zeus's plan to please Hades, who receives all. *It was an object of awe for all to see, both the immortal gods and mortal men. And from its root grew a hundred heads, smelling a smell so sweet that the whole broad sky above and all the earth laughed and the salty swell of the sea. The girl was amazed and stretched out both her hands to take the marvelous bauble.*[226]

There is quite a contrast between this narcissus flower and the one said to have grown in place of Narcissus, a contrast not only in quality but, as we have seen, in attitude. It would seem that they resembled each other in name only: the one sterile, soporific, quickly withering, useless, poisonous, etc., and the other "an object of awe for all to see." What is the connection between the two?

Let us begin by recognizing that the two narcissi can be seen as representing two levels, personal and transpersonal. The narcissus flower would, on the one hand, represent the personality of Narcissus, while on the other, the narcissus of the Homeric Hymn would represent the energies of the Self that he unconsciously fears. The energies symbolized by the flower in the Homeric Hymn would be totally overwhelming to Narcissus. Recall the dream mentioned above, where the dreamer says that a flower grows after Narcissus dies, while her regressive shadow says that nothing happens, he just dies. We wondered then what basis there was for the dreamer's "good feeling."

The Homeric Hymn gives the answer. The flower is connected to the transcendent, archetypal level, the numinous dimension which, as in the Hymn, brings awe and joy, "smelling a smell so sweet that the whole broad sky above and all the earth laughed...." And indeed, several months after the dream, this dimension opened to the dreamer. With it came the fear of being attacked that the Homeric Hymn, as we shall see, goes on to describe. The *fear of joy,* so common in the transformations of narcissism, and the clinging to a morbid, depressed and seemingly masochistic reality (as the dreamer's shadow side represented) has an archetypal root: a fear of psychic rape.

Pausanius, who insists that the flower came before the Narcissus myth, intuits a level of development hidden by the Ovidian version. I do not mean to overlook Claudanius' version, which insists that the Persephone tale came *after* that of Narcissus. This is also valid, for after the death of narcissistic structures, the Persephone soul can be born.

However, if the Persephone-Demeter myth *does* precede the Narcissus story, we are left to consider a possibility that does not readily reveal itself on clinical grounds alone. For it means that a feminine, archetypal quality, Persephone, whom the Orphics called the soul, was split off from conscious life and from the personality symbolized by Narcissus *before that development took place.* In the Homeric Hymn it is taken suddenly, raped by Hades and lost from the view of the upper world, shrouded in the invisibility which is a characteristic of Hades' realm. Persephone in the underworld, invisible to the sight of her mother Demeter and all other gods and mortals, would therefore represent a hidden, split-off feminine side of the narcissistic character.

4 Narcissus and the Dionysian Spirit

In the Homeric Hymn the flower, which I have suggested represents the numinous energies so feared by Narcissus, is placed there by the Earth at the desire of the underworld powers, Hades/Dionysos, and with the knowledge of Zeus. This shows the Dionysian nature of these energies: Dionysos is here the opposite to Narcissus. Just as the hermaphrodite was seen as his opposite, this same motif again appears, for Dionysos is often shown as hermaphroditic, an "effeminate god."[227]

From our knowledge of the narcissistic character it makes absolute sense that Dionysos would be the archetypal power, par excellence, that would characterize the Self he most greatly fears. Even after Stage One of transformation, in which a capacity for reflection and work appears, and structurally a positive senex-puer dynamism functions, there is still a strong fear of everything Dionysian. Empathy may exist, but on a psychic level in which one can reflect from one's own experience upon what the person is feeling. But this is a far cry from the merged, interpenetrating and near-physical states of Dionysian connections. All still goes on with reference to the *psychic unconscious* but not to the *somatic unconscious.*

Persephone would once have known these numinous energies; indeed in some myths she is Dionysos' mother.[228] Here she is shown as being tricked into reaching out for them. This indicates that the Dionysian level is not one she would readily go after. But why not?

The Olympian Zeus religion was a reaction to Dionysian immersion in vision and body that neglected the clarity of spirit known as Apollo, the "most Greek of all the gods."[229] And would not that reaction, as Slater has argued, have a strong, defensive, "narcissistic" element?[230] In the Greek culture the reaction against the older gods of Minoan religion, against the earth deities and Dionysos/Persephone, would certainly have left something behind; it would leave the soul of these depths, Persephone, and her masculine spouse as well, Dionysos. And recovery of this dimension would require a repeat of the trauma of its loss.

But this story is not just Greek; it is also the story of every child. The child is far more Dionysian than Apollonian; it is, in Freud's term, "polymorphous perverse," merged with nature in *participation mystique,* tearing to pieces in its fantasies and resurrecting and being resurrected. And it *sees;* the child sees more than it can bear.

The child's Dionysian foundation is lost as it moves toward an object world, as an I-Thou clarity begins to form. But in this process something tragic happens: Clinically it is known as the depressive position. It is a stage in which there is a consolidation of opposites, but a loss of whole-ness, the Dionysian wholeness of body and mind. To want this again is terrifying because it means loss. The child exchanges its Dionysian roots for a good, mirroring mother, a civilizing of its rage. It is no longer ruthless; it incorporates Apollonian values and acquires a goal-oriented psyche. But it loses something in the process; it loses a part of its soul, and an experience of soma that it was born with. It becomes at least somewhat disembodied, schizoid. It is in a terrible dilemma, for to recover this lost soul now means to risk loss of what was gained. To accept this death, to know that one *can* be reborn, was a goal of the Eleusinian Mysteries.

It is clinically important to have developed narcissistic transferences and worked them through before dropping into Dionysian depths.[231] When this happens without having achieved a narcissistic cohesiveness, we have the so-called borderline, schizoid or psychotic situation. But when this cohesiveness exists and *then can die,* the renewal process that develops is far more predictable and manageable, requiring less depth of regression than is otherwise the case.

The energies of the narcissus flower are not only representative of the erotic, body mystique and merger once known and lost. They are also ecstatic, leading beyond oneself. They are not to be found solely in a return to body, whether that be through exercise or sensitivity to the depths of "infantile sexuality" and the body's erogenous zones. They are also spiritual, but it is a spirit that comes from the depths, from the bottom up. It is a spirit of the body, a spirit in matter that resurrects, has it own numinosity. The Dionysian spirit emerges up and through body no longer defended by rigid body armor. When it begins to rise up, it is especially terrifying to a consciousness rooted in distance and caution.

In the Homeric Hymn the loss of soul to the Dionysian—so that it can regain its roots in these depths—is repeated. But note that it requires a reaching for the flower of joy, excess, awe. Unless we reach out we do not die. Persephone isn't just playing about when she is raped: She is reaching for something ecstatic, transcendent. There is a proper way to enter Hades, the realm of death, a way of transformation. Falling into it, for example in depression, narcissistic injury, psychosis, etc., is not necessarily a way of transformation. Often one just comes back with nothing changed. But there is a way set out, and it involves reaching for the excess of Dionysian spirit, for joy.

The Dionysian energies of joy and ecstasy were probably induced as part of the Eleusinian tradition, most likely in the Lesser Mysteries which had a close link to a former Dionysian mystery. But the newborn infant knows this joy as well: it distinguishes its smile in the first month or two of life.[232] And in the psychotherapy of Stage Two, when the split-off soul returns, it does so filled with both a knowledge of and fear of its own joy.

This is an archetypal dimension (and joy is generally an attribute of Dionysos);[233] the infant is linked to it but so is anyone regaining a link to their split-off feminine Self. The emotion of attack is induced in the analyst, just as exhibitionistic intrusiveness was previously induced through an idealized transference. Whoever the "rapist of Persephone," whether it be Cephisus or Dionysos—and the Eleusinian Mysteries were carried out near the river Kephisos, indicating a link between the two gods—this disordering attack must be reexperienced and lived through, else the further redemption of soul will not progress. The way is as much through chaos and death as it is through ecstasy and joy. It is tragic that so many LSD-induced visions are destroyed by panic and a dose of thorazine, for in the "bad trip" is contained the possibility for the eventual integration of anything transcendent. The Eleusinian priests knew this, and we also must learn the value of chaos, of the disorder that always precedes any new order. Our fixation on order, things Apollonian, is a narcissistic obstacle to the changes that can come from Dionysos

5 The Homeric Hymn to Demeter

The following synopsis of the Homeric Hymn is taken from Kerényi's telling of the myth, interspersed as it is with his commentaries. He precedes his narrative of the mythology of Persephone and Demeter by informing us that

> Demeter differed from Gaia or Ge, the Earth: Earth she was, too; not, however, in its quality of universal mother but as mother of the grain; as mother not of all beings, both gods and men, but of the grain and a mysterious daughter, whom one did not willingly name in the presence of the profane.[234]

This accords, I think, with associating Demeter with the source of the life of the body, with the somatic unconscious. The soul, as Jung tells us, is the life of the body,[235] just as the grain would be an image of the fact that this life and its body were united.

> With great art the Homeric Hymn tells the story of the rape of Persephone. . . . The daughter has gone off to some remote place, where she is playing and picking flowers with the daughters of Okeanos. . . . In accordance with the will of Zeus, Gaia, the Earth has lured her thither and surprised her with a wonderful flower that had never been seen before. . . .
>   It was a dangerous region in which Kore let herself be lured in her search of flowers. . . . Dionysos himself had the strange surname "the gaping one," . . . The notion that the wine god in his quality of Lord of the Underworld was the girl's ravisher does not appear on the surface in the hymn. We should hardly have been able to detect it in the background if an archaic

vase painter had not shown us Persephone with Dionysos. . . . The Homeric poet has Hades, the underworldly brother of Zeus, drive his horses out of the earth in heroic style. He lifts the girl into his chariot and takes his ravished bride on a long journey over the earth before returning to his subterranean realm. The place where this happened was pointed out by the river Kephisos near Eleusis. It was called Erineos after a wild fig tree. . . . In general, there was a close tie between the wild fig tree and the subterranean Dionysos. . . .

The girl's lamentations are heard not by the moon but by Hekate in her cave — but she does not see the ravisher. Helios, the Sun, hears and sees all. The last to hear Persephone's voice is Demeter. She tears her diadem from her head, wraps herself in garments of mourning, and wanders about for nine days, without eating or bathing, bearing two burning torches. On the tenth day she meets Hecate, who also bears a light in her hand, and the two of them go to Helios. From the sun-god they learn who the ravisher was. Demeter's grief turns to anger. She leaves the gods and goes among mankind, taking on an ugly form to avoid being recognized. Thus she comes to Eleusis and sits down by the Virgin's well. . . .

By the well sits Demeter — so the hymn continues — in the form of an old woman . . . [Nearby] is the palace of Keleos. Soon his four daughters come to draw water. At home, with their mother Metaneira, they have left a little brother who still needs a nurse. This the goddess has forseen and offers the girls her services. . . . She is received by Metaneira with her baby at her breast. As the goddess enters, the doorway is filled with divine light. The queen is stricken with awe, although she has not recognized the goddess. She stands up from her easy chair and offers it to the goddess. But Demeter takes only a simple chair and lets her veil fall across her face. . . .

These were the signs of her grief, and all those undergoing initiation had to imitate them. . . . But not every version of the holy story puts Demeter's act of mourning — her sitting in silence — in the palace of Keleos. There was another and perhaps older version according to which the goddess sat on a rock. There she sat "without laughing." This "laughless rock" — *agelastos petra* — was seen only by those who entered the sacred precinct. . . . It was said that Theseus also sat on the *agelastos petra* before descending to the underworld. In various periods the Eleusinians knew of, and pointed out, at least three entrances to Hades: one through the well, a second here, and a third near the wild fig tree by the Kephisos.

As the goddess sat there unlaughing, in Metaneira's quarters or on the rock, Iambe, the hearty serving maid, stepped into her role. . . . Her role was to make Demeter laugh by jests and mockery, to turn her grief into tenderness. This she succeeded in doing by means of obscene gestures. . . .

The blond goddess grows mild and tender . . . But she is not consoled. . . . The queen fills a beaker with sweet wine and offers it to Demeter, who refuses it, saying that for her to partake of the red wine would be contrary to *themis,* the order of nature. We readily understand her words once we know the identity of the ravisher who had snatched her daughter off into the realm of the dead, once we know to whom the cover name of Hades or Pluto refers. According to the hymn, the rape occurred on the Nysan Plain, where the Dionysian ground opened. . . . The subterranean wine god was the ravisher. How could the maiden's mother accept *his* gift? And so she invented another beverage, which was not one of the secrets of the Mysteries but which was drunk before initiation and became a sign of the Mysteries. It was called *kykeon,* "mixture," . . . It was a special brew. Anyone wishing to be initiated at Eleusis had to drink of it. . . . Demeter's mixture was taken after long fasting and was also—as the poet expressly says—compatible with *hosia,* the religious decorum that the mother had to observe in the period of mourning after the rape, an act of violence, an abduction to the realm of the dead. . . .

Demeter takes the little Demophoon under her care. And the child grows and thrives like a god. . . . Each night the goddess lays him in the fire like a log. This she does secretly; the parents notice nothing and can only marvel at their son's godlike appearance. But the queen cannot resist her curiosity. She surprises the strange action of the goddess and cries out in horror: "My son Demophoon, the strange woman is putting you into the fire. I must mourn and lament for you." Demeter turns round in anger. She takes the child out of the hearth fire, lays him on the floor, where he is picked up by his sisters who have rushed into the room, and makes herself known. Her admonition is addressed not only to the queen but to all mankind. . . . "unknowing are ye mortals and thoughtless. ye know not whether good or evil approaches." Metaneira is an example. By her strange action Demeter would have made her son immortal. Now he would remain mortal like all men. For herself the goddess demands a temple above the beautiful well. . . . It is built. Thither Demeter withdraws and lets no plants grow on earth. The gods receive no more sacrifices until Zeus sends Hermes to the underworld to bring the Kore back to her mother.[236]

6   The Depressive Position and Identity with Demeter

What is known as the depressive position is a stage in infant development in which the opposite qualities of the mother, perceived by the infant as good and bad, merciful, diabolical, etc., combine into a whole object.[237] This process occurs through the dynamic of the infant's mourning for the lost "good object" which it believes its own rage has destroyed. Concern for the object develops, and its wholeness can be maintained.

Previously, there was—if development was successful to this point— only a state in which the good object was more powerful than the bad object. The child's ego was based upon the capacity for its belief in the saving capacity of the good object. Also, the good object at the earlier stage is close to the archetypal first object, the energy of the Self out of which the child was born. As the child's object world differentiates out from its divine objects into mother, and then father, as whole objects with good and bad qualities, the initial energy of the transcendent other introjects as a symbolic sense of the Self.

This is an observable process in infant development. Seen from the point of view of the ego, from the vantage point of life developing in time, it is a causal series of events. But the depressive position is, I believe, also a symptom of a separation of the unconscious into a somatic and psychic nature, a separation incurred by the ego's emergence into space/time. From this vantage point, the psychic and somatic unconscious suffer a loss of each other. The emotions of Demeter, her grief and rage, are the affects of the depressive position, but they are also the emotions of the somatic unconscious split from its own completeness. The developing child becomes identified with these emotions; that is the depressive position.

All the archetypes intermingle, they contaminate each other. We are well aware of this in Jungian psychology, and know that to a large extent the feeling-tone distinguishes one archetypal pattern from another.[238] Otherwise, every archetype merges into another, and each one loses its uniqueness. But Persephone, as Kerényi tells us, *is* uniqueness.[239] In the individual this sense of uniqueness comes from embodiment: Unless the Self lives an embodied life it has no uniqueness, its experiment is not lived. The archetype too wants to develop, and this development is dependent upon its uniqueness being experienced. Without her daughter, Persephone, Demeter's uniqueness is lost. Perhaps that is one reason she separates from the gods and lives among men, disguised.

We may choose to see the depressive position in terms of infant development, but that is a scientific-causal approach and one that favors the psychic unconscious. Or, we may choose to look at the depressive position from the vantage point of the somatic unconscious, and of its loss. In this approach, as Eleusinian initiates, we identify with Demeter, with her suffering and rage.

This is the position the analyst is faced with when these emotions surface in his patient. If one works from the somatic unconscious, as I have described in chapter three, then the person's schizoid "in-and-out" program (see chapter five, section one) induces depression. The attempt to stay with the part of the person that is splitting away, pulled away as Persephone was by Hades, results in a feeling of being depressed. And the induced expectancy that we will attack if that part shows its joy leads to an induced rage.

In working with the split-off Self through an embodied consciousness, we suffer the emotions of Demeter. We need a Helios, an observing consciousness to orient us, but after that we suffer them, preferably with a lunar consciousness, as symbolized by Demeter's two torches.

7 The Return of Persephone

The Eleusinian initiates, sitting passively and in silence, having experienced Demeter's emotions of grief and rage, *see* the return of Persephone. This *beatific vision,* lesser than the light of mystical union, was the goal of the Eleusinian experience.

The testimonies of the Eleusinian experience show, as Kerényi tells us, that

the great vision, the *visio beatifica* of Eleusis, was seen with open, corporeal eyes: No distinction was made between the light of the Mysteries and the light of the sun. For the devout such a seeing was important. It was a different matter in the philosophical myth of the soul, which spoke of a *visio beatifica* in a bodiless state, before birth. But such a vision was also described in the terminology of the Eleusinian Mysteries. Sokrates does so in Plato's *Phaedrus,* in such a way as to disparage the Eleusinian vision but at the same time to attest to its existence. . . .

"But then," we read in the *Phaedrus,* "there was beauty to be seen, brightly shining, when with the blessed choir . . . the souls beheld the beatific spectacle and vision. . . . This did we celebrate in our true and perfect selves when we were yet untouched by all the evils in time to come. . . ." In his account of the higher *visio beatifica* beheld by the disembodied souls, Sokrates confirms that visions were seen in the Telesterion of Eleusis, even if they were not "perfect" and "simple" and "still" enough.

They did not satisfy the philosopher, and in this way he indicated their spectral, fluttering character.[240]

The way of a higher ascent, the vision of ideas of the disembodied soul described in the *Phaedrus,* is the mystic's way of gaining a source of transcendent order that overcomes evil and generally has the centering power to subdue all disorder. It is akin to the child's experience *before* the depressive position in which the terrifying emotions of the negative mother are overcome by recovering the experience of the positive mother. The Eleusinian experience was different. Its path was one that would unify the two aspects of the Great Goddess, but only at the willing expense of sacrificing the "greater light" so exclusively revered by Sokrates and all who look down upon the Goddess. Thus the priestess Diotima explains to Sokrates: "These are the Lesser Mysteries of Love, the *myesis* into which even you, Sokrates, may enter; but as to the greater and more hidden ones, the *epoptika.* . . . "[241] The implication was that a person would have to be willing to follow the lunar light of the Goddess, rather than the bright, solar vision of transcendence; clearly Sokrates was not open to that.

The specific Eleusinian way is often told with reference to Heracles for whom, as Ruck tells us, the "failure of the immortal solution is emphasized, for he too through his initiation learns that dying is a higher art than eternal life."[242] Further:

The meaning of the initiation of Heracles [into the Lesser and Greater Mysteries of Eleusis] is clear from Euripides' *Heracles* tragedy, where two versions of the Heracles persona, the heroic and the anti-heroic, are portrayed in conflict. The heroic Heracles has just ascended from Hades, having brought back from there the dog Cerberus, the last of his series of labors; the anti-heroic Heracles, however, in the person of the "wolf-man" Lycus, moves back toward the chthonic realm of his origin, the tomb and death. The heroic Heracles metamorphoses into the anti-heroic when he becomes intoxicated by the toxins he had subdued in his heroic phase, the aconite that came up from Hades with the dog Cerberus and the she-wolf "rabies," the madness that changes dogs into wolves. The play presents this metamorphosis as the paradoxical complement to Heracles' heroic persona and gives it an ethical value, showing that the love of humans for each other in the unbroken chain of mortal generations is a higher art than the loveless eternity that would unite Heracles with his immortal father Zeus.[243]

The toxins that subdue Heracles would be that aspect of the Goddess that lead to the so-called bad trip in hallucinogenic drug use. They are the terrors the child knows, which he attempts to subdue with reference to the positive love of his mother. That there is value in these dark emotions is an essential point of the Eleusinian way. Only through these dissolving energies is an embodied soul gained. Otherwise we are left with the disembodied way of mystical ascent.

Through the power of Persephone, notes Kerényi, "the evil element was transformed into a kindly one."[244] This way of Eleusis differs not only from that of mystical transcendence, but also from the narcissistic "solutions" of idealization and grandiose control. It is a way that sacrifices power and a lofty notion of spirit for the sake of its Dionysian embodiment, hence a vision of lesser light. It is a way that values depression and rage—the emotions of the depressive position—and also terror and chaos. But most of all *it is a way that knows vision* and regenerates in its comings and goings. The constancy of certainty gained from the transcendent solution, or its narcissistic caricature which often manifests as a striving for perfection, is sacrificed for approximate wholeness in body and soul.

The Eleusinian initiate had to be passive. "A state of peculiar passivity," writes Kerényi, "had to be attained if the venture was to succeed. . . . The phenomena to which the passive state leads were called *ellampsis,* 'flaring up,' and *autopsia,* a term for divine apparition. . . ."[245]

The Mysteries could not have existed without the mysterious birth in Hades—the result of the union of Persephone and Dionysos. The offspring, which was announced in the Mysteries as: "Brimo has borne Brimos,"[246] shows that the newly born child, who was closely associated with Pluto and Dionysos, was born out of the matrix of terrifying emotions symbolized by the dark aspect of Persephone. A new male consciousness was born out of the experience of terror. Brimo means "the power to arouse terror . . . to rage."[247] One of the births at Eleusis was a Dionysian consciousness conceived in terror, the terrifying aspect of Persephone. The other was the Goddess herself.

The terrifying emotions experienced in Eleusis would be the same ones that followed upon Persephone's reaching for the giant narcissus flower. But in Eleusis they became integrated into an aspect of the Goddess herself.

In Otto's remarks on Demeter presented at the beginning of this chapter, we saw her characterized as "the Angry One." But also recall Otto's clarity about Persephone and Demeter being doubles of each other. Persephone acquires the dimension of terror as part of her rebirth. She has been penetrated by Dionysos/Hades, taken his seed before returning to her mother, and in this Dionysian penetration she not only gains her power as queen of the underworld, but also she gains it, part of the year, in the upper world.

The feminine that is reborn and embodied is one that is closely connected to its dark aspect. It does not forget its rape. The rape of Persephone follows the general pattern of the "reluctant goddess."

> The best known variation of it came at the beginning of the cyclical epic, *Cypria*. Here the bride—the original Kore—was called *Nemesis;* the bridegroom and seducer Zeus. . . . This marriage was and remained a rape. . . . The goddess was not to be softened by love; she succumbed to violence and therefore became the eternal avenger-Nemesis. The Kore to whom she gave birth was called *Helen.* . . . Helen is the eternally youthful Nemesis, spoiling for a rape and always wreaking her vengeance afterwards.[248]

A similar story, Kerényi goes on to say, was told of Demeter, and it also applies to her daughter Persephone. The Goddess suffers rape, for only in that way does she become transformed by her own mysteries.

A woman connecting to her inner Persephone gains her penetrating power. Her male companion is now Dionysos far more than Apollo, and her existence is rooted in the feminine archetypal depths of the Goddess. A man sheds the burden of the heroic and can become antiheroic in the manner of Heracles. Rigidity is cast away, change welcomed. He can enter the precinct of the Goddess and partake of her mystery and identify with Dionysian vision. He is now both active and passive, male and female, different from a woman, but not a stranger to her mystery.

It is of interest that Hermes is the one who brings Persephone back to the upper world. By looking to Hermes we will again come to that consciousness, so totally opposite to the causal-scientific approach, that we previously discussed as stemming from the somatic unconscious. But in Hermes it gains a marvelous focus.

8   Hermes, Persephone and the Analytical Relationship

In working from the somatic unconscious we experience much that proves to be a guide to the patient's process, and eventually to a proper, "passive stance" from which to *see*. Why should our reactions be helpful? Why should our so-called countertransference have a potential dimension of objectivity? And we may further, and especially, ask why this helpful situation may occur in apparent uniqueness, unbound by causality, and be so much a function of the moment. To the Homeric Greek mind the answer would most likely be that it is all the working of Hermes.

Hermes, writes Otto, is "the gay master of happy chance, never at a loss, who is little troubled by standards of pride and dignity, but who despite all remains lovable. . . . the friendliest of gods to men."[249] And is it not a friendly act of our unconscious that anything like our subjectivity, unmeasured by causal critique or order, could be of value? Hermes guides us here, but only if we allow ourselves to be untroubled by standards of pride and dignity. We can be easily wrong, because whatever we know or say is a gift, and all we can be responsible for is properly understanding it. It is a great relief to be able to see how foolishly we may have processed a countertransference reaction, but in the spirit of Hermes this may be accepted with a light heart, for it was not with evil intent.

Otto asks, "What is the underlying thought in the concept of Hermes?" —and he proceeds to give us a wonderful profile of the god:

> He is the friendliest of gods to men and the most generous giver. But *how* does he bestow his gifts? To understand this we need only think of his magic wand. . . . He is the bearer of the magic wand. . . .
>
> From him comes gain, cleverly calculated or wholly unexpected, but mostly the latter. That is his true characterization. . . .
>
> This then is the "good" in Hermes' manner of giving it. A number of gods are expressly called "givers of joy" . . . but what it means in his case we can see from the festival of Hermes Charidotes in Samos, where thievery and robbery were permissible. But Hermes protects not only palpable knavery but also every kind of craftiness and deception. . . . The mysterious god who suddenly puts a treasure trove in a needy man's way, as suddenly makes the treasure vanish.[250]

Hermes is the archetypal background for the *imaginal.* It comes as a gift, and in the process of gaining access to it, we indeed are very dependent upon craftiness, especially in an analytical relationship. Let the therapist try to explain the way in which he or she makes use of a subjective reaction. For example, it is difficult to explain how one deals with a feeling of hating a patient. "Do you just say you hate him?" one is often asked. "Do you repress it?" What do you do in a way that helps you to understand how he hates himself, and furthermore how it can be freeing for him to know that you too can hate? And how do you do this with love, as part of a joyful discovery? That truly is a gift of Hermes; it may appear, and the next moment be gone, leaving us in the most awful subjective countertransference muddle.

> Hermes [is] the kindly spirit who leads the flocks from their folds in the morning and faithfully guides them on their way.
>
> But here too this kindly service is only one side of his activity. The guide can also lead astray; the watcher can also allow treasures to vanish and be lost.[251]

Hermes is the spirit that rules the transference-countertransference reactions and the dynamics of their interpenetration, out of which the treasure, a vision, may emerge. But just as suddenly, we may find ourselves on another path, and we follow it up, perhaps for weeks at a time, before finding again what we once were granted, and again see that we had had a treasure easily lost. This treasure is often the child of joy that can be *seen,* the Persephone child—but easily lost to sight as we get sidetracked in other issues. Hermes takes us along many dead ends. But through him we can accept this as part of the work.

I have a patient who complains about "time lost" as a result of my poor interpretations and my sadistic countertransference that has "held him down for so long." He is quite correct, from his Apollonian viewpoint. But I also *see* him; I *see* a young, split-off child who is gradually appearing and then retreating. I *see* because of Hermes' gift, and through him I also err. That is the reality I must learn to accept. Hermes may lead one astray, but he also gives the healing, light hearted grace with which we can laugh at ourselves, rather than fall into a grandiose seriousness. And in this spirit, my errors can be acknowledged and perhaps be useful. But *I* do not know. That will be a gift of Hermes.

> In the realm of love too Hermes is at home.... To connect his eroticism with that of the true gods of love involves a basic misunderstanding. Love too has its share in luck; indeed, it may entirely hinge on the favor of the moment.... [252]

Love in the analytical relationship is not ruled by the "true gods of love." It is love that comes and goes, totally dependent upon the moment. Misunderstanding this causes the awful misfire of concretizations—but that too can be a trick of Hermes. His kind of love is dependent upon chance; one could say it is a synchronistic occurrence and not the love that develops from a real relationship. The analytical relationship of course has this, but it is never its primary feature. Knowing this allows us to willingly let go of a felt love-reaction at any time, to let every session be the first, and to welcome hate as openly as love itself.

Otto underlines that "it is always uncanny guidance that constitutes the essence of [Hermes'] activity."[253] Our involvement in the transference-countertransference process, especially in its mutually penetrating forms of imaginal consciousness, is always dependent upon an "uncanny guidance." It is never led by an Apollonian spirit of clarity.

Hermes is also distinguished by speed:

> The speed which distinguishes him is indicated by the wings on his hat. He possesses "golden" sandals "with which he could fly like the wind over land and sea." This is an apt picture of his nature.[254]

The speed of Hermes is the power by which the multiplicity of images, the psychic babblings and somatic feelings we experience, are linked together. He connects them all, well beyond our conscious capacity. He is a master *bricolleur.*

> [The] mystery of night seen by day, this magic darkness in bright sunlight, is the realm of Hermes.... In popular feeling this makes itself felt in the remarkable silence that may intervene in the midst of the liveliest conversations; it was said, at such times, that Hermes had entered the room.[255]

Silence is a vital part of *seeing.* Being able to be silent and wait until something of the night appears in daylight, that is a metaphor for the appearance of the Eleusinian-like visionary state. It is Hermes that brings Persephone back to the upper world, and this generally happens when we are silent, rarely ever when we are talking or thinking.

Hermes, then, is a spirit of gain but also of loss. We always lose our vision of the returning soul, that is in its nature and in the nature of the vision which sees it, guided as it is by Hermes. He is the archetypal power, par excellence, of acausal order or synchronicity. We learn to lose and gain. That is Hermes' way, and it was the experience of the initiates at Eleusis.

It is Hermes and our Hermetic consciousness that can help Persephone in returning to the upper world. This kind of consciousness is rooted in body awareness, in matter. It is consciousness that stems from the somatic unconscious, whose processes, like Demeter, were imitated by the Eleusinian initiates.

> To enter into the figure of Demeter means to be pursued, to be robbed, raped, to fail to understand, to rage and grieve, but then to get everything back and be born again.... What, then, is left over for the figure of Persephone? Beyond question, that which constitutes the structure of the living creature *apart from* this endlessly repeated drama of coming-to-be and passing-away, namely the *uniqueness* of the individual and its *enthralment to non-being.*[256]

The individual gains uniqueness by taking part in the process of the healing of the split between the somatic and psychic unconscious. The guide here is Hermes and his peculiar consciousness; the way is through imaginal sight, a vision of the queen of the underworld, the archetype of everyone's departed or lost soul.

Hermes conjuring the winged soul out of an urn. (Attic funeral vessel)

V

Stage Two of Transformation:
Clinical Issues

1 Introduction

The split-off feminine Self of the narcissistic character returns in Stage Two, much along the lines of the mythical pattern discussed in the last chapter. A Persephone-Demeter mythologem appears as if it were always operative, only sheltered from view by the holding and defending power of the narcissistic transferences. Once these sufficiently lose their once-needed function—just as in the Homeric Hymn Persephone loses the protection of her idealized father Zeus—an entirely new dimension opens up.

This is experienced as a sharp change in the transference-countertransference energy field. From one that had been relatively stable in its controlling/idealizing dynamics, suddenly it becomes extremely difficult to concentrate upon the person or the process. There are shifts, a kind of random coming and going of attention and the capacity to attend. We can eventually learn that we are experiencing, along with the patient, the archetypal dynamics of the rape of Persephone and her return, but at first it looks as if all the working-through of the narcissistic structure only led to a deeper, schizoid or borderline personality disorder.

In fact we *are* reaching a schizoid level of the individual, but its nature is very different from that of the schizoid personality. In the latter case, the split-off Self (which is called the "regressed ego" by Guntrip) [257] is passive. It has withdrawn into a deathlike sleep, wholly without heart, and when it appears at all its energy content is easily drained. But there are schizoid dynamics, such as the "fleeing in-and-out" quality of the schizoid individual,[258] that are symptomatic of a different kind of split-off Self. Eigen refers to such a case as follows:

> The regressed ego, as Guntrip describes it, is wholly passive. It seeks the womb. [But] the ego structure [here]...is intensely alive and active in its compressed density. It is experienced in an aura of power—it exudes a sense of power. The respite here is not passivity in the womb, not a sleep, but an active seeing stillness, compact and electrifying. It does not appear that Guntrip's schema has a term which aptly describes this ego realm.[259]

Eigen is using psychoanalytic terminology in speaking of an ego structure that is intensely alive and exudes a sense of power. In our framework

155

we would speak of the split-off Self reconnecting with the ego, gaining ego-quality. This it does, but it also remains eternally connected to that greater archetypal dimension of the Goddess. That accounts for it being "intensely alive," and for the "aura of power" it exudes. And it also accounts for its having an "active seeing stillness." It *sees* because it is linked to that archetypal power that leads to *imaginal vision,* and it is silent because only in silence does it *see,* and in silence can it be *seen.*

The central clinical issue that unfolds in Stage Two is parallel to the structure of the Homeric Hymn: The split-off Self reaches out to archetypal energies of joy; it is infused with joy, and then, just as quickly, comes a massive expectation of attack.[260] This all goes on as a drama in the patient's unconscious, of which he or she would often rather stay unaware. But at this stage his own awareness is kindled, and if his inner world can be *seen,* he too will *see.*

It is possible to mistake the schizoid quality that manifests at this point as a transference resistance, for in Stage One it is commonly indicative of a resistance to the formation of a narcissistic, and especially idealized, transference. The major difference, however, is that narcissistic transferences have already formed and been worked through, with viable behavioral changes and new psychic structure. Furthermore, the nature of the new transference that attempts to form is the major issue in the "in-and-out" quality we perceive—it does not have the induced features of a narcissistic transference.

What we are dealing with is an archetypal dynamic which only looks schizoid. It would be more valid to speak of a further manifestation of Mercurius, with special attention to its phenomenology as the *fugitive stag,* darting here and there, in and out of the forest (the unconscious).[261] In alchemical terms it is in an "unfixed," volatile condition; it requires the fixing capacity of consciousness and body, and its containment in a vessel —the analytical transference relationship.

To aid the return of the individual's Persephone-like soul requires that we take the passive role of the Eleusinian initiate, and like Demeter experience the emotions of grief and rage as we are embedded in the schizoid dynamic. We feel grief as our energies are carried along by the withdrawing soul, and we feel rage over being abandoned ourselves. Almost inevitably we become mixed in and identify with the rapist, for the patient's expectancy of sadistic attack is so strong as to easily induce this emotion in us; thus we tend to become the parental figure that once attacked in his or her own envious need for a Self.

At other times, this envious attack is purely a subjective matter: The patient's joy is a marvelous thing, and at times it is difficult not to want it, and in the process tend to repeat the role of the rapist in our own envious excitement. But there is always a mixture of subjective and objective factors; their separation is the work and art of analysis.

2   The Doubling Motif and the Emerging Self

There was a doubling of the principal deities at Eleusis. Kerényi tells us:

> The student of Eleusinian mythology must acquire a kind of double sight if he wishes to do justice to the entire tradition—the literary and the pictorial—with all their contradictory statements side by side.
>
> The double vision I have in mind was not subjective: the two simultaneous visions have their mythological counterpart in two mythological stages on which the same divine person appears in different roles and sometimes even simultaneously. This is the case above all with Persephone, who appears as queen of the underworld and as the daughter of her mother.... "Go thou only," says Hades ... "to thy mother.... But when thou are *here* [in the underworld] thou will rule over all that lives and crawls on earth! Thou will be honored above all the immortals.[262]

This doubling of the Eleusinian deities, and primarily Persephone, is represented in a clinical aspect of the phenomenology of the returning, once-split-off soul. When the schizoid dynamic appears, indicating a new level of transformation, it often does so in the form of two children. They are not equal, exact doubles, but rather one is more potent than the other, far more "archetypal," the true child of joy, while the other is more passive, easily depressed and generally masochistic. As we shall see, the "masochistic child" has actually created a safe territory in which to live, a territory that is a substitute mother.

The deeper child image, the child infused with joy, comes forth much less than does the other, usually slightly older child. It is much like the Homeric Hymn's pattern: One Persephone is queen of the underworld, and *there* she has dominion over "all that lives and crawls on earth." The other Persephone, the one that returns to her mother, while being more potent than prior to her rape and return, still is much less the Goddess than in her underworld, background numinosity. What can be seen with the usual, nonimaginal sight is always less potent than what reveals itself to the kind of imaginal vision of depth that was known at Eleusis and through Demeter. While the Eleusinian experience is certainly dealing with phenomena of far greater scale than what we meet clinically, there appears to be a definite correspondence between the two, perhaps not unlike a relationship between macrocosm and microcosm. The Eleusinian experience did not derive from personal psychodynamics, but it definitely speaks to them and they both follow similar patterns.

Before going on with the phenomenology of the two inner children, it is important to further reflect upon the nature of the changes that occur in the transference-countertransference energy field.

Imaginal penetration

A primary experience that attends the dissolution, in a positive sense, of the narcissistic structures is a growing awareness of *not* penetrating the person. One begins to become aware of not feeling into them in the here and now, and especially of the tendency to lose body awareness.

While this also happened during the period of the narcissistic transferences, it was easily lost sight of in the course of struggling with the psychic control and other induced reactions from the transference. Often, when these are strong, it is difficult to feel related—at best it may be possible to empathetically reflect upon what is happening to the person, why he or she needs such and such a transference, and out of this kind of reflection present an understanding and nonreductive approach to their material. But it is another matter to actively experience the person's depths in the moment. We are kept away from this by the narcissistic defense, and must respect this distancing. Anything less is felt as a kind of psychic rape, as getting too close to a precious part.

This is not the case once the transferences have sufficiently dissolved. Instead, there is not just an awareness of not being really present in depth, but that one could be. *At this point, not penetrating actively, and not working carefully in the moment and with a presence that only felt embodiedness can bring, is a kind of withdrawal that is sadistic.* While a distanced, reflective point of view was absolutely necessary in Stage One of transformation, and too much penetration was destructive, now the situation reverses: Distance, reflection, and a lack of being very present in a manner that "feels into" in an imaginal way that has substance, are now felt as sadistic withholding.

Suspiciousness diminishes

During the narcissistic transferences, a patient always has a parallel set of negative feelings toward the analyst. These are screened away by the idealizing process, but they always intrude occasionally, and then hostility and envy enter in the form of doubt: "Does he really know what he is doing?" Or, "Does he really care about me?" But these are usually not verbalized; they are the dark, doubting side of the narcissistic transferences. *When these transferences dissolve sufficiently, this form of envious doubt leaves.* For the patient now has sufficient ego strength, but especially an emerging Self connection that allows the courage to see for himself. Now he can take enough of his own power to see and know, so that the paranoid defensive process becomes unnecessary. This is a crucial subjective change in the patient that changes the nature of the transference. *However, it does not mean there is less dependency.*

The new transference is in no way one of less need; rather it is one in which need is intensely experienced. It is the kind of transference union that calls up archetypal elements in both analyst and patient. I hesitate to call it an archetypal transference, for such pure forms do not exist. But it has an archetypal aspect in the sense that the dependency that develops is a need for the analyst's own Self connection.

The analyst's ability to relate to the Self in the here and now becomes the central issue, for without this level of depth the patient knows he cannot develop. It differs from a narcissistic transference in that the analyst is a real "other" for the patient; his or her reality—especially assets and deficiencies—is seen. Consequently, at this stage, patients will often say they know they are not only involved in a transference; they know they are seeing the analyst as he is, not only as a replay of early introjects or as an idealized projection. They insist they are seeing his actual worth, and this centers upon his values and especially archetypal connection. Clearly, there is always a degree of projection involved, and there is always some idealization. But there is also accuracy, and at this stage, in distinction to the stage of the narcissistic transferences, this level of accuracy is felt.

As a result of growing ego-strength and archetypal connection, and the lessening of the protective use of paranoid defenses, the patient is able to "look and see," and recognize if the analyst really has a Self connection or not. The patient can begin to trust his own sight, at first very marginally, but in time more and more. At this stage the analytical situation moves into the kind of dialectical relationship that Jung describes,[263] one which could have been quite destructive in the earlier stages of transformation.

The patient's emerging capacity for *seeing* is nothing too mysterious. It is only what every young child has: The child *sees* its parents' psyches, it *sees* "where they are coming from." It often *sees* a psychotic element, which it then attempts to heal at the cost of giving up its own Self. And it *sees* if it is hated because it has a Self. All this sight is often too much for a child, and its imaginal vision is cut off.

3   The Joyful Child and the Masochistic Child

The major quality of the split-off Self that appears with the dissolution of the narcissistic and primarily idealized transference is joy. It is the "child of God" that defines every newborn child. But the early experience of the narcissistic character—and this is true to some degree for everyone—is that this Self was psychically attacked. As a consequence, the child's Self withdrew, and instead a more compliant and masochistic attitude developed. That is the causal process behind the phenomenology of the "two children," corresponding to the archetypal doubling at Eleusis.

But it is important not to reduce the archetypal level to the personal aetiology. We are dealing with two ways of viewing the psyche, and the Eleusinian way cannot be reduced to a causal pattern. The "two Persephones" are the way the soul appears as it is regained. The fact that we experience these aspects in a causal frame is only because we experience them in historical time, rather than timelessly, which is a quality of the archetype. There is a great mystery to the appearance of the "two children," but the psychic rape experienced by the child of joy is transmitted most commonly through the parental unconscious.

An example of psychic attack

The following clinical example illustrates the nature of this interaction, and while it comes from two adults, it is the same dynamic that afflicts the infant-parent relationship.

A man came to his therapy hour complaining of how strangely his wife had acted the day before. He simply could not understand why she got so upset at minor things. She told him about major psychic changes she was going through, but wouldn't talk about it much. She was somewhat depressed and very agitated. He asked her to do an errand for him, and then was upset because she wouldn't just say that she didn't want to do it, but instead seemed ambivalent. He complained: "I can speak up when I have to, why can't she?"

In the evening of the day's events I have partially described his wife had the following dream, which he related to me. "I am with a woman who is my husband's assistant. She is burning my arm with a cigarette." The wife, in reality, was not acquainted with her husband's assistant at work. The dream shows how her husband's unconscious, symbolized by the unknown woman, sadistically attacks his wife. That was what he was doing unconsciously, while "consciously" he felt put-upon by her "craziness," as he described it.

It was to understand his wife's mood that he had come to his session that day, but the meaning of his wife's dream became quite clear to him: His refusal to penetrate her psychic condition empathetically, a process he was quite capable of, while instead being rational and aloof, was actually an unconscious sadistic attack, manoeuvered by his impersonal attitude.

This is the nature of the attack a young child, often at the age of a month or two, feels when its connection to joy, its true parent, is met with nonrecognition, nonrelatedness. Only it is not just its arm that is burned; rather it feels a massive attack on its Self-hood. Such a child will later go to almost any extreme to avoid repeating early psychic rape traumas. A major one is to retreat and show only a pale copy of itself, one with a strong masochistic feeling-tone.

The masochistic child

Relating to the masochistic child aspect of the emerging Self is a matter of some difficulty, on account of the strong sadistic feelings it induces in the analyst.

It is essential *not* to interpret this dynamic, at least at the outset and often not for some time after its appearance. Rather one must *become the parent,* which means to relate as a parent to this child-quality of the patient. Being the parent does not mean giving advice. It represents a feeling state that is unconsciously communicated to the patient. It shows that the analyst is willing to get close in a kinship sense, to *see* and understand within that emotional framework. One incarnates the identity of the positive, nurturing mother or father that the patient had so little of. One does not interpret the ever-present sado-masochistic dynamics, even though there is a strong tendency to do this.

By being the parent, we allow a controlled regression. The patient often feels younger, perhaps seven or eight years old, and even looks this way. It is not a severe regression, it is one that is largely containable by the holding power of our imaginal sight. We must speak, at this point, to what we *see*, not out of any theory or interpretation.

If we mistakenly diagnose the transformation in the transference-countertransference field as simply uncovering a borderline condition or a new problem, then accepting the parental role might not seem appropriate.[264] Instead, out of concern that this approach would only exacerbate envy, we might take an interpretive stance.[265] That, in my experience, is at this stage extremely detrimental to the transformation process, and especially to the entrance of the divine, joyful child into the transference, from where it can eventually become ego-syntonic in the patient.

At this stage, the patient needs the experience of a parental figure that will not attack but rather be helpful. It is all too easy to interpret expected sadism or inattention as a result of the analyst's boredom reactions, or to interpret a shift in the energy field, which can be felt as being pushed away, as indicative of the patient's rage. An entire range of interpretations on the schizoid or borderline level are possible, especially in terms of fears of abandonment. All of these interpretations are true and must eventually be made. But first the inner child that feels rejected, and hence enraged and hungry, must be fed with caring and attention. This can often mean explaining issues over and over again while wading through a sado-masochistic energy field. It is like dealing with an actual child, without there being a strong regression to child status. The child part can be felt and *seen*, and if we are accurate the patient generally will acknowledge its presence. I must add that the continual need to go over the same material that is characteristic of the integration process at this new level is, in my experience, quite genuine: There has always been something not really understood.

But as we *see* and care for, and as the patient's suspiciousness begins to diminish, important fantasies about the "two children" are often shared. Just as grandiose-exhibitionistic fantasies, so shame-inducing at a previous stage, had eventually to be shared in the analytical relationship, other fantasies continue to surface at later stages.

The masochistic child as safe territory

When *seeing* and feeling into the patient's masochistic child, it is often difficult to appreciate why a person's ego would cling to an unconscious identity with this part. One patient related the following fantasy he had while doing active imagination with his masochistic inner child, and feeling partially identified with it.

> I am on a sidewalk. I have my own piece of it and nothing anyone does can take it away from me. They can spit on me, throw things at me, do anything they want to me, but the sidewalk is mine. Nobody can take it away. It has a warm feeling.

The masochistic child has its own territory; it is a space that is equivalent to a maternal holding environment. A person identified with this part will generally be extremely compliant in life, unconsciously very much like the patient with the fantasy of being safe on the sidewalk. Indeed, I have found a remarkable capacity in other therapists and patients to appreciate this fantasy. It clearly accords with the schizoid belief system, portrayed by Guntrip, of "better a bad object than no object at all."[266] It also has affinities with the delusionally created "rewarding part object" that Masterson describes in the borderline patient.[267]

It is important not to attempt to drag the ego away from this territory, but rather to allow its existence and recognize its value. For leaving it means not only risking growing up to adult responsibilities, but leads to taking the other side of the child image, the divine child, seriously. That is a great threat, for it means experiencing, as Persephone does in the Homeric Hymn, the attack that was felt when, at a very young age, the energy field surrounding the divine child was disturbed.

That is why leaving the masochistic territory of the compliant child is so frightening. It is necessary for the person to "drink the complex dry"—to stay in it and imaginally feel it, in life as well as in the transference. This must go on as long as necessary.

The masochistic child and the depressive position

Along with recognizing the function of the masochistic territory, it also becomes apparent that the child living there is that part of the personality which is stuck in the depressive position. An important development occurs when the patient can feel the anger of his or her unattended child, and be concerned about that anger rather than withdrawing into depression.

One woman was able to describe her child's anger when she felt it in a session. It was not possible for me to both *see* her inner children and at the same time meet her frequent requests that I explain the meaning of a dream.[268] But interpreting the dream was also often important and valid, and had to be attempted. In the process, however, she would become aware that her child (or children) were angry. She could tell me this and I could feel it. When, at other times, I might feel the needs of her inner child and insist upon just being with her, her child would often become angry because it couldn't control me.

This anger over a loss of omnipotence is, as Elkin has discussed,[269] an aspect of the aetiology of the depressive position. The child's rage, which turns back on the Self into depression, stems from a recognition that its psychic power is now "little" and its parent's physicalness "big," and consequently that its own omnipotence is limited. Passage through the depressive position, as discussed in the last chapter, was always disturbed for the narcissistic character, whose defense especially guards against *feeling* depressed. As Klein describes, a successful passage through the depressive position is necessary for the introjection of Self projections.[270] While Kohut appears to pay this little mind, I find it an essential aspect of the process of integration, but one that occurs in Stage Two of transformation.

The experienced loss of omnipotence—which is by no means complete after the transformation of the grandiose-exhibitionistic self—continues in Stage Two with the depressive position and, as we shall see, working through the oedipal complex. But first consider another important feeling that surfaces as trust grows in the analytical relationship.

The hatred of the divine child

A feeling patients often become aware of is their hatred of the younger, divine child that first makes its appearance in the "in-and-out" dynamic described above.

When I asked one woman why she hated this child, she replied: "It gets me into trouble." It exposed her too much to painful attacks of envy. Another patient (the same man who had the sidewalk fantasy) met this child in a dream: "I am walking across a street and a little boy approaches me. He has a glass of water. But I start to torment him, splashing water at him. He becomes enraged and hysterical and smashes the glass onto the street." When he first described this dream he was aloof from it, with little awareness of how awful an inner condition this described. As he entered more deeply into Stage Two of transformation, the dream image of the enraged child became a painful reminder of his sadistic attitude toward that side of himself.

Avoiding the "evil eye," the massive envious attack that usually dominated the narcissistic character's childhood environment, results in abandoning even one's most precious part. Feeling this, a reality of Stage Two, leads to a felt suffering, precisely what is most completely rejected by the narcissistic character, and even the person who has gone through the changes in Stage One.

It is as if one has to hide one's most precious part but does it so successfully and for so long that one either loses the way to it, forgets it, or finds that one's fortress is so strongly defended, so locked up, that even oneself cannot get in.

I often encourage patients at this stage to look at me, to become very centered in their body and to trust what they *see* in me at the time. Often this brings fear. One patient, a therapist himself, looked slowly and carefully and told me he saw a four-year-old boy. He was quite right—I was aware of this image from a dream I had had the previous night. But the next time he saw me he confessed that he hadn't told the whole story. What he had seen was that my child was depressed, as indeed it was! But the patient was afraid to say this. Why? Because, as it turned out, this would have given him a feeling of power, which in the context meant that he himself would have had to grow up, be his own adult and responsible self, and take care of *his* child. Rather than do this, he hid his vision, still needing to idealize me, while he stayed merged with his own masochistic child. At the bottom of this there was a replaying of his need to heal his depressed mother. He gave up his *sight* to this end; it could gradually begin to be recovered with the aid of this kind of analytical exercise.

4   Dionysos and the Erotic Transference

Another important change in the transference that goes with a growing capacity for trust and vision, is the appearance of a strong erotic energy. This can be misunderstood—as an eroticization of a narcissistic transference[271]—or it can be used to buttress another common viewpoint which would have it that the narcissistic structures only defend against oedipal anxieties and a too-harsh superego.

Just as there is some truth to seeing a schizoid or borderline element in the emerging Self structure, so too there is validity in the observation of oedipal material. It is not its existence that is at issue, but rather the reduction of the emerging phenomenology of the Self to personal, oedipal conflicts. Just as the shadow side of the Self has attributes that can be justifiably called borderline and schizoid, so too it has a strong oedipal quality. Often, this is in the form of an oedipal complex that was only barely able to form, if at all. The patient is frightened of these energies out of a fear of acting out, a fear based upon the fact that the oedipal sexuality is in an omnipotent reference frame. The patient believes that if he dares to feel these energies they will be irresistible.

Often there is much personal history to support this fear, at times a history of early sexual abuse, and more often a series of experiences in which people were quickly attracted by the patient's sexual energies. But the omnipotent belief system does not even require this kind of reinforcement; it exists even with patients who have never had any adult or childhood experience in which acting-out or their attractiveness was a reality issue.

It is unfortunately easy to identify the energies of the deeper Self—the emerging child that often appears as younger and as skittish, actually frightened of its archetypal connection to joy—with this untransformed oedipal sexuality. Strictly speaking, this is a level that belongs to the shadow of the emerging Self, and eventually must be analyzed on the oedipal level. This means a recovery in the transference of the repressed or never previously existing oedipal conflict. It does not mean treating the conflict symbolically, as a drive for rebirth.

It is important that any interpreting on the oedipal level be done with the shared awareness of *which* child's fantasies are being explored. Otherwise the deeper Self, represented by the divine child, feels crushed.

The two parts of the emerging Self, the part with an archetypal link and the older part, carrying all the residual elements of a process that has never successfully unfolded, *unify in the analytical vessel through dealing with the erotic energies of the transference.* But this means that these energies are eventually experienced as archetypal, as representative of the quality known in Greek myth as Dionysos. And with this, what appears as a strong erotic attraction can be recognized as *the archetype of coniunctio on the level of penetrating through vision.* It is an energy field that binds, but one whose goal is an imaginal connection, not a physical one. The Dionysian religion, probably stemming from ancient Crete, was a religion of vision.[272]

Dionysian concerns become a therapeutic reality at this stage. Previously, prior to the formation and integration of the narcissistic transference energies and structure, sexuality could be a seductive element of control, whereas now it is part of an archetypal constellation. The Dionysian energies of this pattern are usually known at the earlier stage in only a negative way. The narcissistic defense rejects intimacy and anything like the kind of penetration demanded by this archetypal power, for positive structures necessary to help contain the Dionysian energies do not exist; the person only experiences, at times of narcissistic injury, the "mad god" side of Dionysos that gave him such a bad reputation.[273]

Dionysus as a negative force strikes in dismembered, depersonalized states, delusion, paranoid feelings, etc. What Kohut describes as the near-psychotic levels that the narcissistic character falls into, but which he can ascend out of through properly addressing the narcissistic injury in question, are the domain long ascribed to Dionysos. Perhaps the one-sided, negative view of Dionysos is a result of the god's appearance in psyches—and in societies—ridden with untransformed, narcissistic problems. But when he appears *after* narcissistic transferences have formed and transformed, the experience of Dionysos is quite another matter.[274] His energy field may be highly erotic, but his import is equally spiritual and visionary.

In Stage Two it is possible for patient and analyst to allow these Dionysian energies to enter the analytical vessel without the danger of acting out. For there is now enough internal structure so that there is a natural, inhibiting factor. This is not to say that emotional flooding may not still happen, threatening loss of control, but it is now not a pathological process to be feared, but rather an experience of archetypal energies which are, as Jung points out, always a defeat for the ego.[275]

The imaginal as mutually shared vision is the greatest aid in not falling into identification with the seductive energies of this level. Knowing that we do not know anything that we do not *see,* and waiting, with respect, for a mutually known vision, often results in the sense that an archetypal image, a Goddess, rules this encounter. When this is *seen,* acting out the strongly erotic energies is quickly recognized for what it would be—an act in the service of shadow aspects of the personality.

Dionysos and his queen, Persephone, are the powers that rule Stage Two of transformation. Any attempts to fit these energies into a personalistic vessel, no matter how far-reaching, is doomed to failure.

In the kind of shared energy field I have been describing, what often develops is a transformation of the transference into a sense of kinship.[276] Analyst and patient are together on a path of discovery, with neither having more nor less effectiveness. This may not diminish the patient's need—he feels this acutely—but the analyst too can marvel at how his growth is so tied to that of his patient.

5   Integrating the Two Inner Children

A patient's creativity can help in forming a positive transference union with the split-off child. It would seem that if the person can gain the strength that his own creative efforts yield, he also can gain the courage to share and risk more. A woman whose split-off child was in a very skittish transference relationship with me had the following dream:

> A very bright and creative young boy enters a room and begins to touch a seemingly useless pile of clothing on the floor. But as he touched it, it began to stir and become a pregnant woman's stomach. It was actually hiding the woman. I am frightened to enter the room and hasten to call many other children to enter.

Pregnancy is often symbolic of a forming transference relationship. This patient needed to finish some creative work, but she was reluctant to take on this task. It would have made her "too well," she said, and then she was certain she would be attacked by everyone's envy, certainly by mine. So the transference union was eluded through disseminating her gifts in an ineffectual multiplicity of concerns—the many children she calls into the room.

Another woman, whose transference was at a similar stage, had numerous dreams of a child or children outside a room. Sometimes this was explicitly my office. There were two dreams over a one-year period that were nearly identical: Two children, dressed in red, were perched on a windowsill outside a room. Eventually other dreams appeared in which the children were inside a room, and then inside the analytical office. With this, their presence was very real, felt by the patient and myself alike. The masochistic child could be imaginally experienced as a third party, and if it wasn't attended to, its energies of withdrawal, depression and rage could often be felt. Sometimes both children could be noticed, with the luminous joy of one flittering in the background, and the other hapless and depressed, stuck in fear of change.

This woman wondered: "How do I distinguish the children from me?" This was initially helped during the analytical hours by my *seeing* the child and calling her attention to it, so that she could gain a sense of its feeling-tone. Eventually she could operate, first along with me and then when alone, in the following way: To begin with she might feel anxious. She would objectify the anxiety in the sense of just allowing it to exist, without identifying with it. Given her capacity for objectivity—much as is accomplished in active imagination, when for instance one might draw a picture of the anxiety—it was then not too difficult to just wait for the child to appear. Out of the creative tension of the field established by separating from the anxiety—or any other emotion—the awareness of the child would spontaneously appear. And with this, at times, came the recognition that *the child was anxious.*

This could then be further worked with. For example, were both children anxious? Commonly this was the emotion of only one at a time, or of the patient herself. The deeper, more "archetypal" or divine child of joy could be quite content in a silent way, while the more depressed child was terribly anxious over abandonment fears. At other times, when the divine child would come toward her, seeming to want a role in her life, perhaps in terms of a positive, joyful attitude, then the anxiety frequently belonged to the patient herself out of fear of being attacked for having something so good.

6 Transformation and the Individuation Process

An outstanding characteristic of Stage Two of transformation is that the analytical process takes on aspects of the classical individuation pattern described by Jung.[277] In Stage One it is generally not useful to interpret on a subjective level, that is to say, approach dream and fantasy images as aspects of the patient's own personality.[278] Instead, most interpretations have either to be referred to the transference or outer object relations, or perhaps to reflections upon a creative task the person is involved in.

But a central feature of continuing transformation is that the process takes more and more a subjective and classical form. For example, it eventually became possible for the woman referred to in the previous section to consider the image of her mother, which appeared in many dreams, as her own shadow. It was imperative that this be recognized and assimilated, otherwise the woman's inner child of joy would have been persecuted by her own sadistic shadow, as it was in childhood by her mother's lack of empathy.

While dealing with this issue the patient had the following dream: "There are two children lying on a bed, one younger and the other older. A nurse appears and she pours a dark liquid over the older child." The dark liquid represents a kind of baptism in shadow material: The maso-chistic child had to integrate its own sadistic nature which was turned back on itself. The only way this could be done was for the patient to integrate her own sadistic energies, imaged by her mother. The dark liquid is her own sadism, and the dream shows this to have redemptive significance. And it did. For the masochistic child did become assertive and connected with its divine half.[279]

For this woman to allow that the mother image had anything to do with herself was at first quite difficult. It was even a considerable effort in earlier stages for her to see the reality of her mother. This meant seeing that she had been the target of extreme envy; to see how nearly every-thing she had had was spoiled by her mother's envy. She retreated into identity with the masochistic child to avoid the "evil eye." This took many forms, one of which was in giving anything good she had to her older sister. The actual pain of her mother's attack was so severe that it was a number of years before its reality could be seen. To feel hated is a state most of us withdraw from at all costs, and this is especially so if it was chronic in early childhood.

But after the narcissistic transferences had dissolved, along the lines I have been describing, it became possible to directly approach her mother images as representing the patient's own envy and sadism. She generally taped our sessions, and after I first made this interpretation she had a dream in which there was a tape recorder that stopped working! There followed numerous dreams which reflected her strong resistance to seeing her mother as having anything to do with her. It was, she said, "just too awful." Eventually she could accept this, although it took many months. The same was true for another image, that of a very power-oriented man. In real life he was a male friend, and when he had appeared at the beginning of her analysis interpretations had always been made on the objective level, reflecting on their relationship. This too changed; she could deal with her own power-oriented animus that rejected soul.

Another important shift concerned approaches to the persona.[280] Every narcissistic character is strongly identified with the persona, generally a compliant one in the hope of being accepted. At times the other extreme dominates, a stance of aesthetic aloofness and uninvolvement. (The aloof attitude is in fact always the ruling one, unconsciously if not consciously.) It is initially important for the person to separate from the persona, but in Stage Two of transformation it becomes possible to reassimilate it. In the woman's case I have been referring to, she was able to "put on and take off" a persona of grace and charm, and in the process protect herself from an envious environment. Previously, she would have completely identified with that persona and afterwards felt awful about "selling out." What had once been a poison could now become a useful tool. This reconnection to the persona, through being objective about it, is a regular feature of the transformation of the narcissistic character. The central difference is consciousness: the person now knows he is using it instead of being merged with it in a destructive manner.

Another major change is associated with the emergence of oedipal material. Dealing with this level of the psyche is not common in a classical individuation process, but it is absolutely essential in the transformation of the narcissistic character. It must not at first be taken symbolically. Instead, the masochistic child must be allowed to have its oedipal feelings, a stage of mild regression for the ego, and especially to have these in the transference situation.

The main issue here is the transformation of omnipotence. For the oedipal problem, as I have previously noted, is laced through with fantasies of being omnipotent, the deep down feeling that if the patient actually felt his or her sexuality, it would be overwhelming to others This omnipotence fantasy, which is not only confined to sexuality, can then be interpreted symbolically—as representing a drive for rebirth by entering the unconscious.[281]

Emergence of archetypal reality

The numinosity of the Self archetype and its fate-dictating power is, as discussed at the very beginning of this book and throughout, a source of great fear for the narcissistic character. We often find that the positive, joyful connection to the Self—and I emphasize the quality of joy because it is an essence of the recovered, split-off Self—was at an early age lost through magically giving it away to heal a crazy spot in a parent.[282] Patients speak of having sensed in the parent a "black hole" or a "vacuum" that was terrifying and which they tried to fill. Such images are commonly associated with nonmirroring parental figures.

Reconnecting to the "child of joy" is the major analytical path toward archetypal reality in Stage Two. The child's energies infuse the ego with a symbolic sense of wholeness grounded in the Self and through relating to others, and at the same time leads the ego toward archetypal reality as enacted at Eleusis. The ego thus becomes enlivened and joyful in its relationship with people, and at the same time aware of the domain of the Goddess so lost to our culture. Life gains a double reality: On the one hand it begins to reflect the importance of social life and relationships, while on the other it is grounded in the "unseen" world into which initiation has been granted.

The beauty of the power of the Goddess is that she does not value one over the other, nor does she allow either to exist in depth and vitality without the complement of the other. Life and psyche become one.

Notes

CW — *The Collected Works of C.G. Jung*

1. "A Descriptive Catalogue of Pictures," in Geoffrey Keynes, ed., *The Writings of William Blake,* vol. 3, p. 108.
2. See Rosemary Gordon, "Narcissism and the self: Who am I that I love?"
3. Jung, "The Problem of the Attitude-Type," *Two Essays,* CW 7.
4. Harry Guntrip, *Schizoid Phenomena,* pp. 67, 82.
5. See Hyman Spotnitz and Phyllis Meadow, *Narcissistic Neuroses,* p. 99.
6. Harvey Cox, *Turning East,* pp. 81ff.
7. Jung, "Psychology and Religion," *Psychology and Religion,* CW 11, par. 6.
8. H. Schoeck, *Envy,* p. 31.
9. Jung, *Psychology and Alchemy,* CW 12, pars. 247, 249.
10. Jung, "On the Nature of the Psyche," *The Structure and Dynamics of the Psyche,* CW 8, pars. 388f.
11. Donald Winnicott, *The Maturational Process,* p. 185.
12. Jung, *Nietzsche Seminars,* part 3, lecture 5.
13. Jung, *Symbols of Transformation,* CW 5, par. 612.
14. Edith Jacobson, *The Self and the Object World,* p. 22.
15. Winnicott, p. 188.
16. Jung, "Synchronicity: An Acausal Connecting Principle," CW 8, par. 858.
17. See Marie-Louise von Franz, *C.G. Jung: His Myth in Our Time,* chapter 4, for a discussion of the mirror symmetry between conscious and unconscious.
18. Heinz Kohut, *The Restoration of the Self,* pp. 310f.
19. Mario Jacoby, "Reflections on Kohut's Concept of Narcissism."
20. Kohut, "Forms and Transformations of Narcissism," pp. 243ff.
21. Kohut, *Restoration of the Self,* pp. 183f.
22. See James Hillman, *Puer Papers,* and von Franz, *Puer Aeternus.*
23. See Michael Fordham, *The Self and Autism,* pp. 90ff.
24. Edward F. Edinger, *Ego and Archetype,* pp. 6ff.
25. Harold F. Searles, "The Self in the Countertransference."
26. Jung, *Aion,* CW 9ii, par. 76, and CW 8, par. 10.
27. Jung, CW 9ii, par. 75.
28. Jung, *Nietzsche Seminars,* part 6, lecture 2. These seminars took place in Zurich from 1934-1939. Although to date they have not been "officially" published, they were transcribed by participants and may be found in mimeographed form in most C.G. Jung Institute libraries. Since various versions exist, references here will be given to part and lecture, not to page numbers.
29. Jung, "Principles of Practical Psychotherapy," *The Practice of Psychotherapy,* CW 16, pars. 8ff.

30. Winnicott, pp. 185f.

31. Otto Kernberg, *Borderline Conditions,* pp. 227f.

32. Ibid., pp. 228f.

33. Ibid., p. 233.

34. Ibid., p. 237.

35. Ibid., p. 229.

36. Ibid., pp. 310f.

37. Splitting in psychoanalytic literature refers to a defense that is more primitive than repression. It corresponds generally to what analytical psychologists call dissociation, but especially denotes a situation in which contrary emotional states exist side by side without affecting one another. A patient may speak in a hateful and then loving manner, in quick succession, and see no contradiction. Equally, inferiority feelings and grandiose expressions coexist. On an archetypal level this corresponds to a situation in which the opposites, symbolized by the "world parents," have split apart and the principle of compensation is suspended (see Erich Neumann, *The Origins and History of Consciousness,* pp. 102ff).

38. Kohut, *The Analysis of the Self,* pp. 16f.

39. Paul Ornstein, "The Psychology of the Self," pp. 18f.

40. Searles, "The Self in the Countertransference," pp. 49f.

41. See, for example, E.S. Wolf's discussion of Searles' paper (note 40): "When I begin to recognize [my countertransference reactions] and begin to see them within the framework of the Psychology of the Self, [they] become lucid to me, and seem to fade away" (p. 57).

42. Kernberg, pp. 264f.

43. Béla Grunberger, *Narcissism,* pp. 13f.

44. Ibid., pp. 105f.

45. Ibid., p. 108.

46. Ibid., p. xviii.

47. Ernest Jones, *Papers on Psychoanalysis,* pp. 194f.

48. Grunberger, pp. 227f.

49. Ibid., pp. 102f.

50. Jung, "On Psychic Energy," CW 8.

51. Grunberger, p. 280.

52. Jung, "On Psychic Energy, " CW 8, par. 10.

53. Jung, "The Spirit Mercurius," *Alchemical Studies,* CW 13, par, 284.

54. Jung, CW 7, par. 122.

55. See, for example, the discussion by R.C. Zaehner in *Mysticism, Sacred and Profane,* pp. 21f.

56. An exception, where the symbolic approach can be invaluable, is in dealing with a mixed transference in which idealization is enforced. (See chapter 1, section 6.)

57. For example: An elderly man, suffering his entire life from a narcissistic character disorder, dreamed that he had to take a test—he had to weigh

the "jug of history." He did so and estimated its weight as much more than it actually was, and consequently failed the test. As with all narcissistic characters, his actual accomplishments were overshadowed by anxiety that he could not meet the next challenge. And like most, he was left with having actualized very little of his potential.

58. For Jung's descriptions of anima and animus, see *Aion,* CW 9ii, pars. 20ff. Anima and animus are archetypes, and any psychology of identity that does not employ them will be bogged down in an overly personalistic approach.

59. Ibid., par. 94.

60. See Schoek, *Envy,* for an exceptional sociological study of this.

61. Some narcissistic characters do have a highly developed spiritual sense. This follows from a successful integration of an idealized projection, or from archetypal experiences. But while their anima or animus functioning can then have a spiritual character, it will be undeveloped and archaic in human relatedness and in dealing with negative emotions. It will especially be unstable under the impact of exhibitionistic energies, which are usually keenly warded off for fear of inflation.

62. See Jung, "The Phenomenology of the Spirit in Fairytales," *The Archetypes and the Collective Unconscious,* CW 9i, pars. 384ff.

63. See Kohut, *Analysis of the Self,* pp. 260ff, for a discussion of the analyst's reaction to the idealized transference.

64. In *Two Essays,* Jung recalls a case characterized by an idealized transference (though he doesn't use this term) and describes his increasing frustration. He came to recognize the existence of an archetypal projection, which eventually was integrated by the patient (CW 7, pars. 206ff).

65. If the analyst is fearful of his own exhibitionism, out of concern that he become inflated, or equally from fear of his own exhibitionistic needs, he may go to the opposite extreme of being impassive, untouched and at times irritated. The lack of response can be just as wounding as the analyst's excitement over "being seen."

66. Jung, *Nietzsche Seminars,* part 1, lecture 4.

67. Jung, "Answer to Job," CW 11, par. 685. See also von Franz, *C.G. Jung,* pp. 77ff.

68. See Nathan Schwartz and Sandra Ross Schwartz, "On the Coupling of Psychic Entropy and Negentropy."

69. See Kohut, *Analysis of the Self,* pp. 27ff.

70. See Erich Neumann, *The Origins and History of Consciousness,* "The Uroboros," pp. 5ff and passim.

71. Kohut, *Analysis of the Self,* pp. 270ff.

72. Enfeebled ego consciousness is a result of what Erich Neumann refers to as matriarchal castration (*Origins,* pp. 384f).

73. See Guntrip, pp. 245ff, for a discussion of Winnicott's unpublished paper, "The Split-off Male and Female Elements to be Found Clinically in Men and Women."

74. Kernberg, p. 279.

75. See Jung, CW 12, par. 403.

76. This is discussed below in chapter 2, section 3.

77. Jung, CW 12, par. 306.

78. Jung, ibid., par 96.

79. Here by animus is meant that structural element of a woman's psyche which yields, among other qualities, the capacity for objectivity (an "observing ego"), discrimination, spirit and separation. In this way the animus functions positively, as an internal mirror, helping a woman reflect upon her ideas and actions as parts of her own personality instead of as introjected opinions. (See also above, note 58.)

80. Cf. the "pissing manikin" in Jung, CW 12, fig. 121.

81. Jung, "Flying Saucers: A Modern Myth," *Civilization in Transition,* CW 10, pars. 589ff.

82. See M. Esther Harding, *The Way of All Women,* chapter 1, "All Things to All Men."

83. See, for instance, "The Sea-Hare," *Grimm's Fairy Tales,* pp. 769ff.

84. See Raphael Patai, *The Hebrew Goddess,* pp. 219f.

85. See von Franz, *C.G. Jung,* p. 229.

86. Neumann, *The Child,* pp. 137ff.

87. Cited in Edgar Wind, *Pagan Mysteries in the Renaissance,* p. 77n. Wind lists this reference as pertaining to the Fountain Room at the Chateau d'Anet, but my research indicates that the pairs of opposites are actually in the Mirror Room.

88. See Neumann, *Origins,* pp. 102ff.

89. See H. Segal, *Introduction to the Work of Melanie Klein,* pp. 27f.

90. Neumann, *The Child,* p. 98.

91. See Kohut, *Analysis of the Self,* p. 22.

92. Louise Vinge, *The Narcissus Theme in Western Literature up to the Early Nineteenth Century,* pp. 7-11.

93. Neumann, *The Child,* p. 98.

94. See Edith Hamilton, *Mythology,* p. 30.

95. My summary of the tale in John Bauer, *Great Swedish Fairy Tales,* pp. 123ff.

96. Kohut, *Analysis of the Self,* p. 33, and Neumann, *The Child,* p. 156.

97. Vinge, p. 88.

98. C. Kerényi, *The Heroes of the Greeks,* p. 100.

99. Vinge, p. 100.

100. Ibid. p. 75.

101. Ibid., p. 147.

102. Ibid.

103. Ibid., pp. 149f.

104. Gerado Reichel-Dolmatoff, *Amazonian Cosmos,* p. 93.

105. Vinge, p. 208.

106. Ibid., p. 168.

107. Ibid., p. 20: "In Thespia, in Boeotia [the town is situated not far from Helicon] lived the boy Narcissus, very beautiful but proud towards Eros and those who loved him. His other lovers gave up but Ameinias alone begged persistently. But when Narcissus did not receive him, and even sent him a sword, he killed himself at Narcissus' door after begging the gods to become his avenger. When Narcissus saw his own face and figure in a spring he became in a strange way his own lover as the first and only one. Confused, and convinced that he suffered justly because he had despised Ameinias' love, he finally killed himself. After this the Thespians decided both to fear and honour Eros more at the public services, and also to sacrifice to him in private. The inhabitants of the area believe that the narcissus flower grew and spread from the soil on which Narcissus' blood was shed."

Canon's version of the myth has been analyzed by Spotnitz and Resnikoff in support of their central idea that aggression, self-hate and sadism underlie the character defenses in narcissistic disorders (*Psychotherapy of Preoedipal Conditions,* pp. 94-100).

108. Schoeck, pp. 122f.

109. Vinge, p. 166.

110. Ibid., pp. 12f.

111. J.G. Frazer, *The Golden Bough,* Part 2, pp. 77ff.

112. Kerényi, *Dionysos,* p. 265.

113. Ibid., pp. 358f (my italics).

114. Ibid., p. 270.

115. Vinge, p. 25.

116. Ibid., p. 37.

117. Ibid., pp. 38f.

118. Ibid., p. 57.

119. Ibid., p. 61.

120. Ibid., pp. 62f.

121. Ibid., pp. 66f.

122. Ibid., pp. 67f.

123. Ibid., p. 68.

124. Ibid., p. 80.

125. Ibid., pp. 125f.

126. Ibid., p. 127.

127. Ibid., p. 170.

128. Ibid., p. 186.

129. Lancelot Law Whyte, *The Unconscious Before Freud,* p. 43.

130. Vinge, p. 187.

131. Ibid., p. 189.

132. See Benjamin Farrington, *The Philosophy of Francis Bacon,* pp. 53f.

133. Vinge, pp. 183, 182.

134. Ibid., pp. 183f.
135. Ibid., p. 225.
136. Kerényi, in Jung and Kerényi, *Essays on a Science of Mythology,* p. 125.
137. Vinge, p. 288.
138. Ibid., pp. 281f.
139. Ibid., p. 283.
140. Ibid., p. 286.
141. Ibid., p. 287.
142. Ibid.
143. Ibid., p. 288.
144. Ibid., pp. 289f.
145. Ibid., p. 290.
146. Murray Stein, "Narcissus," pp. 48ff.
147. It is important to note, as Judith Hubback does in her review of Kohut's *Analysis of the Self,* that the narcissistic transferences are not archetypal transferences. They are a hybrid product of personal and archetypal factors (see below, chapter 3, section 3).
148. See Michael Fordham, *The Self and Autism,* pp. 90f.
149. See James Hillman, *The Myth of Analysis,* pp. 63f.
150. In A.'s case, discussed in chapter 1, section 7, I was able to have this kind of penetration during the initial phases when the "eagle" was attacking her. But as soon as this happened, she recoiled, saying, "I hate it when anyone gets that close!"
151. The term Goddess is used here to respect and specify the feminine dominant that ruled archaic cultures until it was suppressed by patriarchal developments. It is at times preferable to the designation "archetypal feminine" because it sets the imagery and affect referred to back into a time period unfettered by conceptual thinking. It also avoids the trap of envisioning this dominant of human experience as being "in the psyche," a problem I mentioned in the introduction. The energy of the Goddess is never "integrated into the psyche" and least of all into the ego. At best, the images and affect associated with her incarnate, leading to her symbolic appreciation within the ego, including an awareness of the vastness of her dimension. The Goddess herself is essentially unknowable. This is, of course, only a restatement of Jung's caution that we can never know the archetype per se, but only its images.
152. Sylvia Brinton Perera, in *Descent to the Goddess,* a study oriented toward the rediscovery of feminine instinct and image patterns, calls this power "feminine yang" (pp. 39ff).
153. See, for example, Michael Fordham et al., *Technique in Jungian Analysis.*
154. Rosemary Gordon, "Narcissism and the self," p. 251.
155. Jung, CW 7, pars. 8f.
156. G.R.S. Mead, *Thrice Greatest Hermes,* vol. 1, pp. 178ff.
157. Hillman, *Myth of Analysis,* pp. 258ff.
158. Claude Lévi-Strauss, *The Savage Mind,* pp. 17ff.

159. See Schwartz and Ross Schwartz, pp. 74ff.

160. Lévi-Strauss, pp. 20, 22.

161. Ibid., p. 17.

162. Ibid., p. 36.

163. Mead, pp. 197f.

164. Ibid.

165. See above, note 28.

166. That is the common trend, although it is true that Jung does at times refer to the body as body, rather than as a symbol for something else. For instance, in CW 13, par. 242, he writes that the Self and the unconscious are in the body, the same view that runs throughout the *Nietzsche Seminars*. For examples of the symbolic interpretation of the body, see: CW 14, pars. 295ff, where the motif of descent into the body is taken to mean a return to "hard reality"; CW 16, par. 478, where a corpse is interpreted as a "residue of the past"; CW 7, par. 35, for the body as symbol of the shadow; CW 16, par. 501, for the body as symbol of the ego. This way of interpretation is of course often valid in context, but it favors seeing images relative to the psychic rather than the somatic unconscious.

167. Jung, CW 16, par. 486.

168. Jung, CW 8, par. 10.

169. Norman O. Brown, *Life Against Death,* p. 313.

170. *Nietzsche Seminars,* part 3, lecture 5.

171. Jung, "Synchronicity: An Acausal Connecting Principle," CW 8, pars. 818ff.

172. *Nietzsche Seminars,* part 3, lecture 8.

173. Jung, CW 8, pars. 408ff.

174. Marie-Louise von Franz, *Number and Time,* part 4.

175. For example, *Nietzsche Seminars,* part 1, lecture 4.

176. For example, CW 16, par. 486.

177. *Nietzsche Seminars,* part 1, lecture 4, and passim.

178. Ibid., part 5, lecture 9.

179. Ibid., part 3, lecture 2.

180. Ibid., lecture 5.

181. Jung, *Mysterium Coniunctionis,* CW 14, pars. 654ff.

182. The phrase often occurs in Paracelsus, and carries the same sense as the motif of the "torture of the bodies" discussed by Jung in CW 13, pars. 439ff.

183. See Donald Lee Williams, *Border Crossings: A Psychological Perspective on Carlos Castaneda's Path of Knowledge,* chapter 4, "The Way of the Seer."

184. See Jung, CW 12, par. 360.

185. Ibid., par. 394.

186. Lévi-Strauss, p. 15.

187. Kohut, *Restoration of the Self,* p. 306.

188. Jung, *Psychological Types,* CW 6, par. 784.

189. Mead, p. 210.

190. W.F. Otto, *Dionysus,* p. 195.

191. See Rundle Clark, *Myth and Symbol in Ancient Egypt,* chapter 3.

192. Ibid. p. 158.

193. See Otto, *The Homeric Gods,* p. 78.

194. See Kerényi, *Eleusis,* p. 40, and James Hillman, *The Dream and the Underworld,* p. 45.

195. Clark, p. 121.

196. See Kernberg, pp. 248ff.

197. The notion of an induced reaction is commonplace in psychoanalytic thought, referred to as a "toxoid response" (Spotnitz, pp. 47ff) or as "projective identification" (Segal, p. 27; Rosemary Gordon, "The Concept of Projective Identification"). It is the same process Jung describes as *participation mystique* or archaic identity (CW 6, par. 781). By any name it is a form of psychic infection.

198. Clark, p. 111.

199. Ibid., p. 167.

200. Hillman, *Myth of Analysis,* p. 280.

201. Clark, p. 157.

202. D.P. Walker, *Spiritual and Demonic Magic,* pp. 159f.

203. See Jung, "A Psychological View of Conscience," *Civilization in Transition,* CW 10, pars. 850-851: "When one is talking with somebody whose unconscious contents are 'constellated,' a parallel constellation arises in one's own unconscious. The same or a similar archetype is activated, and since one is less unconscious than the other person and has no reason for repression, one becomes increasingly aware of its feeling-tone ... The psychoid archetype has a tendency to behave as though it were not localized in one person but were active in the whole environment."

204. See Hillman, *Myth of Analysis,* p. 275, and Brown, p. 308.

205. Mead, vol. 1, p. 196, n. 1.

206. See H. Elkin, "On Selfhood and the Development of Ego Structures in Infancy," p. 399, and M. Eigen, "Instinctual Fantasy and Ideal Images," pp. 131f.

207. C.A.P. Ruck et al., *The Road to Eleusis,* pp. 35ff and 75ff. See also Kerényi, *Eleusis,* pp. 177ff.

208. Winnicott, p. 176.

209. Segal, pp. 67ff.

210. Winnicott, p. 45n.

211. Kerényi, in Jung and Kerényi, pp. 123f.

212. Kerényi, *Eleusis,* p. 38.

213. Personal communication.

214. Otto, "The Meaning of the Eleusinian Mysteries," pp. 15ff.

215. A.'s case in chapter 1, section 7, is an example.

216. Vinge, p. 72.

217. Ibid., p. 74.

218. Ibid., p. 75.

219. Ibid., p. 96.

220. Ibid., p. 99.

221. Ibid.

222. Ibid., p. 18.

223. See above, note 107.

224. Vinge, p. 20.

225. Ibid., p. 34.

226. Danny Staples translation in Ruck et al., p. 59 (my italics).

227. Hillman, *Myth of Analysis,* pp. 258f.

228. Kerényi, *Dionysos,* pp. 110ff.

229. Ibid., and Otto, *Dionysus,* p. 202.

230. Phyllis E. Slater, *The Glory of Hera.* In spite of Slater's totally reductionist viewpoint—he sees Greek culture identified with its narcissistic shadow, rather than this quality being a dark side that accompanies any extreme, creative achievement—his study is a major contribution to our understanding of narcissistic structures in ancient Greece.

231. Unless this has occurred, the effect of emotional flooding is too severe, and often leads to a nonfruitful regression and/or hardening of defenses.

232. Eigen, "Instinctual Fantasy," pp. 131f.

233. See, for example, Otto, *Dionysus,* p. 56, where he is described as "the joyful one."

234. Kerényi, *Eleusis,* p. 29.

235. Jung, *Nietzsche Seminars,* part 3, lecture 2.

236. Kerényi, *Eleusis,* pp. 35ff.

237. Segal, chapter 6, and Elkin, pp. 403f.

238. See, for instance, von Franz, *Number and Time,* pp. 144f.

239. Kerényi, in Jung and Kerényi, pp. 123f.

240. Kerényi, *Eleusis,* pp. 98f.

241. Ibid., p. 45.

242. Ruck et al., p. 104.

243. Ibid., p. 106.

244. Kerényi, *Eleusis,* p. 114.

245. Ibid.

246. Kerényi, in Jung and Kerényi, p. 143.

247. Ibid., p. 142.

248. Ibid., p. 122.

249. Otto, *Homeric Gods,* pp. 105, 107.

250. Ibid., pp. 107f.

251. Ibid., p. 110.

252. Ibid., p. 111.
253. Ibid., p. 112.
254. Ibid.
255. Ibid., p. 118.
256. Kerényi, in Jung and Kerényi, p. 123.
257. Guntrip, pp. 163f.
258. Ibid., pp. 36f.
259. Eigen, "Abstinence and the Schizoid Ego," p. 497.
260. This is often due to experiences of parental envy (see chapter 1, section 5).
261. Jung, CW 12, par. 187.
262. Kerényi, *Eleusis*, p. 148.
263. Jung, CW 16, par. 8f.
264. Kernberg, pp. 264f.
265. Ibid., pp. 157f.
266. Guntrip, pp. 202f.
267. I F Masterson, *The Borderline Adult*, pp. 57f.
268. This was precluded in accordance with the psyche-soma complementarity described in chapter 3.
269. Elkin, p. 405.
270. Klein, p. 75.
271. Kohut, *Analysis of the Self*, p. 234
272. Kerényi, *Dionysos*, pp. 5ff.
273. Otto, *Dionysus*, pp. 133ff.
274. See Hillman, *Myth of Analysis*, pp. 283ff, for a discussion of Dionysian consciousness, of which narcissistic enfeeblement is a good caricature.
275. Jung, CW 14, par. 778.
276. Cf. Jung, "Psychology of the Transference," CW 16, par. 445.
277. Jung, "Individuation," CW 7, pars. 266ff. It should be noted, however, that in Stage Two an emerging Self and identity do not fit well into that aspect of Jung's view which envisions individuation as an unfolding of a preexistent wholeness, waiting to be discovered. The experience is rather of a numinous reality, always "outside" the ego and psyche as well as "inside," as a symbolic reality.
278. Jung, CW 6, pars. 812ff.
279. At times the divine aspect of the child will first appear, and then show shadow characteristics, like those of the masochistic child. Clearly we are dealing with two aspects of a single reality; the archetypal child is inevitably intertwined with actual experiences of infancy and early childhood.
280. Jung, CW 6, pars. 800f.
281. See Robert Stein, *Incest and Human Love,* p. 30.
282. Searles, *Countertransference*, pp. 56f.

Glossary of Jungian Terms

Anima (Latin, "soul"). The unconscious, feminine side of a man's personality. She is personified in dreams by images of women ranging from prostitute and seductress to spiritual guide (Wisdom). She is the eros principle, hence a man's anima development is reflected in how he relates to women. Identification with the anima can appear as moodiness, effeminacy, and oversensitivity. Jung calls the anima *the archetype of life itself.*

Animus (Latin, "spirit"). The unconscious, masculine side of a woman's personality. He personifies the logos principle. Identification with the animus can cause a woman to become rigid, opinionated, and argumentative. More positively, he is the inner man who acts as a bridge between the woman's ego and her own creative resources in the unconscious.

Archetypes. Irrepresentable in themselves, but their effects appear in consciousness as the archetypal images and ideas. These are universal patterns or motifs which come from the collective unconscious and are the basic content of religions, mythologies, legends, and fairytales. They emerge in individuals through dreams and visions.

Association. A spontaneous flow of interconnected thoughts and images around a specific idea, determined by unconscious connections.

Complex. An emotionally charged group of ideas or images. At the "center" of a complex is an archetype or archetypal image.

Constellate. Whenever there is a strong emotional reaction to a person or a situation, a complex has been constellated (activated).

Ego. The central complex in the field of consciousness. A strong ego can relate objectively to activated contents of the unconscious (i.e., other complexes), rather than identifying with them, which appears as a state of possession.

Feeling. One of the four psychic functions. It is a rational function which evaluates the worth of relationships and situations. Feeling must be distinguished from emotion, which is due to an activated complex.

Individuation. The conscious realization of one's unique psychological reality, including both strengths and limitations. It leads to the experience of the Self as the regulating center of the psyche.

Inflation. A state in which one has an unrealistically high or low (negative inflation) sense of identity. It indicates a regression of consciousness into unconsciousness, which typically happens when the ego takes too many unconscious contents upon itself and loses the faculty of discrimination.

Intuition. One of the four psychic functions. It is the irrational function which tells us the possibilities inherent in the present. In contrast to sensation (the function which perceives immediate reality through the physical senses) intuition perceives via the unconscious, e.g., flashes of insight of unknown origin.

Participation mystique. A term derived from the anthropologist Lévy-Bruhl, denoting a primitive, psychological connection with objects, or between persons, resulting in a strong unconscious bond.

Persona (Latin, "actor's mask"). One's social role, derived from the expectations of society and early training. A strong ego relates to the outside world through a flexible persona; identification with a specific persona (doctor, scholar, artist, etc.) inhibits psychological development.

Projection. The process whereby an unconscious quality or characteristic of one's own is perceived and reacted to in an outer object or person. Projection of the anima or animus onto a real women or man is experienced as falling in love. Frustrated expectations indicate the need to withdraw projections, in order to relate to the reality of other people.

Puer aeternus (Latin, "eternal youth"). Indicates a certain type of man who remains too long in adolescent psychology, generally associated with a strong unconscious attachment to the mother (actual or symbolic). Positive traits are spontaneity and openness to change. His female counterpart is the **puella,** an "eternal girl" with a corresponding attachment to the father-world.

Self. The archetype of wholeness and the regulating center of the personality. It is experienced as a transpersonal power which transcends the ego, e.g., God.

Senex (Latin, "old man"). Associated with attitudes that come with advancing age. Negatively, this can mean cynicism, rigidity and extreme conservatism; positive traits are responsibility, orderliness and self-discipline. A well-balanced personality functions appropriately within the puer-senex polarity.

Shadow. An unconscious part of the personality characterized by traits and attitudes, whether negative or positive, which the conscious ego tends to reject or ignore. It is personified in dreams by persons of the same sex as the dreamer. Consciously assimilating one's shadow usually results in an increase of energy.

Symbol. The best possible expression for something essentially unknown. Symbolic thinking is non-linear, right-brain oriented; it is complementary to logical, linear, left-brain thinking.

Transcendent function. The reconciling "third" which emerges from the unconscious (in the form of a symbol or a new attitude) after the conflicting opposites have been consciously differentiated, and the tension between them held.

Transference and countertransference. Particular cases of projection, commonly used to describe the unconscious, emotional bonds that arise between two persons in an analytic or therapeutic relationship.

Uroboros. The mythical snake or dragon that eats its own tail. It is a symbol both for individuation as a self-contained, circular process, and for narcissistic self-absorption.

Bibliography

Bauer, John, illus. *Great Swedish Fairy Tales.* Trans. H. Lundbergh. Delacorte, New York, 1973.

Brown, Norman O. *Life Against Death.* Wesleyan, New York, 1959.

Clark, Rundle, *Myth and Symbol in Ancient Egypt.* Thames and Hudson, London, 1959.

Cox, Harvey. *Turning East.* Simon & Schuster, New York, 1977.

Edinger, Edward F. *Ego and Archetype.* Putnam, New York, 1972.

Eigen, M. "Abstinence and the Schizoid Ego." *International Journal of Psychoanalysis,* vol. 54 (1973), no. 4.

———. "Instinctual Fantasy and Ideal Images." *Contemporary Psychoanalysis,* vol. 16 (1980), no. 1.

Elkin, H. "On Selfhood and the Development of Ego Structures in Infancy." *The Psychoanalytic Review,* vol. 59 (1972), no. 3.

Farrington, Benjamin. *The Philosophy of Francis Bacon.* U. of Chicago Press, Chicago, 1966.

Fordham, Michael. *The Self and Autism* (Library of Analytical Psychology, vol. 3). Heinemann, London, 1976.

———. "Defences of the Self." *Journal of Analytical Psychology,* vol. 19 (1974), no. 2.

———. In *New Developments in Analytical Psychology.* Routledge & Kegan Paul, London, 1957.

———. et al. *Technique in Jungian Analysis* (Library of Analytical Psychology, vol. 2). Heinemann, London, 1973.

Frazer, James George. *The Golden Bough* (Part 2: *Taboo and the Perils of the Soul*). St. Martin's, New York, 1963.

Gordon, Rosemary. "The Concept of Projective Identification." *Journal of Analytical Psychology,* vol. 10 (1965), no. 2.

———. "Narcissism and the self: Who am I that I love?" *Journal of Analytical Psychology,* vol. 25 (1980), no. 3.

Grimm's Fairty Tales. Routledge & Kegan Paul, London, 1975.

Grunberger, Béla. *Narcissism.* Trans. J. Diamanti. International Universities Press, New York, 1979.

Guntrip, Harry. *Schizoid Phenomena, Object Relations, and the Self.* International Universities Press, New York, 1969.

Hamilton, Edith. *Mythology.* New American Library, New York, 1969.

Harding, M. Esther. *The Way of All Women.* Putnam, New York, 1970.

———. *Woman's Mysteries, Ancient and Modern.* Harper & Row, New York, 1976.

Hillman, James. *The Myth of Analysis.* Northwestern U.P., Evanston, 1972.

———. *Puer Papers.* Spring Publications, Dallas, 1979.

———. *The Dream and the Underworld.* Harper and Row, New York, 1979.

Hubback, Judith. Review of *The Analysis of the Self* (Kohut). *Journal of Analytical Psychology,* vol. 18, (1973), no. 1.

Humbert, E. "The Self and Narcissism." *Journal of Analytical Psychology,* vol. 25, (1980), no. 3.

Jacobi, Jolande. *The Way of Individuation.* Trans. R.F.C. Hull. Putnam, New York, 1973.

Jacobson, Edith. *The Self and the Object World.* International Universities Press, New York, 1964.

Jacoby, Mario. "Reflections on Kohut's Concept of Narcissism." *Journal of Analytical Psychology,* vol. 26 (1981), no. 1.

Jones, Ernest. *Papers on Psychoanalysis* (4th ed.). William Wood, Baltimore, 1938.

Jung, C.G. *The Collected Works* (Bollingen Series XX). 20 vols. Trans. R.F.C. Hull. Ed. H. Read, M. Fordham, G. Adler, Wm. McGuire. Princeton U.P., Princeton, 1953-1979.

———. *Nietzsche Seminars,* 1934-1939 ("A Psychological Analysis of Nietzsche's Zarathustra"). 10 parts. Mimeographed seminar notes. Unpublished.

———. *Psychology of the Unconscious.* Trans. Beatrice M. Hinkle from 1911 German edition. Moffatt Yard, New York, 1916.

———, and C. Kerényi. *Essays on a Science of Mythology: The Myth of the Divine Child and the Mysteries of Eleusis.* Harper and Row, New York, 1949.

Kalsched, Donald. "Narcissism and the Search for Interiority." *Quadrant,* vol. 13 (1980), no. 2.

Kerényi, C. *The Heroes of the Greeks.* Thames and Hudson, New York, 1962.

———. *Eleusis* (Bollingen Series LXV-4). Trans. R. Manheim. Princeton U.P., New York, 1967.

———. *Dionysos* (Bollingen Series LXV-2). Trans. R. Manheim. Princeton U.P., New York, 1976.

Kernberg, Otto. *Borderline Conditions and Pathological Narcissism.* Jason Aronson, New York, 1975.

Keynes, Geoffrey, ed. *The Writings of William Blake.* 3 vols. London, 1925.

Kohut, Heinz. *The Analysis of the Self.* International Universities Press, New York, 1971.

———. *The Restoration of the Self.* International Universities Press, New York, 1977.

———. "Forms and Transformations of Narcissism." *Journal of the American Psychoanalytic Association,* vol. 14 (1966).

Lévi-Strauss, Claude. *The Savage Mind.* Weidenfeld and Nicolson, London, 1962.

Masterson, J.F. *Psychotherapy of the Borderline Adult.* Brunner-Mazel, New York, 1976.

Mead, G.R.S. *Thrice Greatest Hermes.* Watkins, London, 1964.

Neumann, Erich. *The Origins and History of Consciousness* (Bollingen Series XLII). Trans. R.F.C. Hull. Pantheon Books, New York, 1954.

———. *The Child.* Trans. R. Manheim. Harper, New York, 1976.

Ornstein, Paul. "The Psychology of the Self." *Issues in Ego Psychology*, vol. 2 (1979), no. 2.

Otto, W.F. *Dionysus*. Indiana U.P., Bloomington, 1965.

——— . "The Meaning of the Eleusinian Mysteries." In *The Mysteries: Papers from the Eranos Yearbooks* (Bollingen Series XXX-2). Ed. Joseph Campbell. Princeton U.P., Princeton, 1955.

——— . *The Homeric Gods*. Thames and Hudson, New York, 1979.

Patai, Raphael. *The Hebrew Goddess*. Avon, New York, 1978.

Perera, Sylvia Brinton. *Descent to the Goddess: A Way of Initiation for Women*. Inner City Books, Toronto, 1981.

Reichel-Dolmatoff, Gerado. *Amazonian Cosmos: The Religious and Sexual Symbolism of the Tukano Indians*. U. of Chicago Press, Chicago, 1971.

Ruck, C.A.P., R.G. Wasson and A. Hoffmann. *The Road to Eleusis*. Harvest, New York, 1978.

Satinover, Jeffrey. "Puer Aeternus: The Narcissistic Relation to the Self." *Quadrant*, vol. 13 (1980), no. 2.

Schoek, H. *Envy*. Trans. Secker & Warburg Ltd. Harcourt Brace, New York, 1969.

Schwartz, Nathan. "Narcissism and Narcissistic Character Disorders: A Jungian View." *Quadrant*, vol. 12 (1979), no. 2; and vol. 13 (1980), no. 2.

——— . "Personal and Archetypal Factors in the Transformation of the Narcissistic Character." *Journal of Modern Psychoanalysis*, vol. 5 (1980), no. 2.

——— . "Entropy, Negentropy and the Psyche." Unpublished Diploma Thesis, C.G. Jung Institute, Zurich, 1969.

——— , and Sandra Ross Schwartz. "On the Coupling of Psychic Entropy and Negentropy." *Spring 1970*.

Searles, Harold F. "The Self in the Countertransference." *Issues in Ego Psychology*, vol. 2 (1979), no. 2.

——— . *Countertransference*. International Universities Press, New York, 1979.

Segal, H. *Introduction to the Work of Melanie Klein*. Hogarth, London, 1964.

Slater, Phyllis E. *The Glory of Hera*. Beacon Press, Boston, 1968.

Spotnitz, Hyman, and Philip Resnikoff. *Psychotherapy of Preoedipal Conditions*. Jason Aronson, New York, 1976.

——— , and Phyllis Meadow. *Narcissistic Neuroses*. Modern Psychoanalytic Publications, New York, 1976.

Stein, Murray. "Narcissus." *Spring 1976*.

Stein, Robert. *Incest and Human Love*. Penguin, Baltimore, 1974.

Vinge, Louise. *The Narcissus Theme in Western Literature up to the Early Nineteenth Century*. Trans. R. Dewsnap. Lund, Gleerups, 1967.

Von Franz, Marie-Louise. *C.G. Jung: His Myth in Our Time*. Trans. Wm. H. Kennedy. Putnam, New York, 1975.

——— . *On Divination and Synchronicity: The Psychology of Meaningful Chance*. Inner City Books, Toronto, 1980.

——— . *Alchemy: An Introduction to the Psychology and the Symbolism*. Inner City Books, Toronto, 1980.

——— . *Puer Aeternus* (2nd ed.). Sigo Press, Santa Monica, 1981.

——— . *Number and Time.* Northwestern U.P., Evanston, 1974.

Walker, D.P. *Spiritual and Demonic Magic.* U. of Notre Dame Press, Notre Dame, 1975.

Whyte, Lancelot Law. *The Unconscious Before Freud.* Basic Books, New York, 1960.

Williams, Donald Lee. *Border Crossings: A Psychological Perspective on Carlos Castaneda's Path of Knowledge.* Inner City Books, Toronto, 1981.

Wind, E. *Pagan Mysteries in the Renaissance.* Norton, New York, 1968.

Winnicott, Donald W. *The Maturational Process and the Facilitating Environment.* International Universities Press, New York, 1965.

Wolf, E.S. Discussion of "The Self in the Countertransference" (Searles). *Issues in Ego Psychology,* vol. 2 (1979), no. 2.

Woodman, Marion. *The Owl Was a Baker's Daughter: Obesity, Anorexia Nervosa, and the Repressed Feminine.* Inner City Books, Toronto, 1980.

Zaehner, R.C. *Mysticism, Sacred and Profane.* Oxford U.P., New York, 1957.

Zimmer, Heinrich. *The King and the Corpse* (Bollingen Series XI). Ed. Joseph Campbell. Princeton U.P., Princeton, 1956.

Index

abandonment, fear of, 13, 53, 56, 63, 66, 156, 167
Abbadie, Jacques, 102
acausal processes, *see* synchronicity
active imagination, 64-65, 81, 109, 162, 167
Adler, Alfred, 10
Adone, L', 86
Adonis, 136
affects, 21-22, 38, 40-43, 53, 60, 64-65, 78-79, 93, 118, 134, 147-148, 150, 171-172; repressed, 64, 66
aggression, 37, 47, 52, 68, 108, 134-135, 174
alchemy, 19, 27, 35-37, 54-55, 58, 68, 79-80, 93, 114, 121-123, 129, 156
amplification, technique, 50-51, 56, 123
analysis, reductive, 15, 21, 37, 53, 56, 60, 123, 164, 178
analytical relationship, 25-28, 30-33, 37-38, 41-52, 56-65, 76, 113-132, 151-169; as container, 54-55, 60, 62-64, 68-69, 156, 165
anima, 25, 40, 42, 68, 85-86, 115, 172; -woman, 62, 111-112
animus, 25, 40, 42, 54-56, 58, 60-62, 65, 68, 79, 85-86, 111, 168, 172-173
Anubis, 118, 132
anxiety, 9, 46-47, 130, 167, 172
Apollo/Apollonian, 77, 124, 128, 134, 143-145, 151, 153
archetype(s)/archetypal patterns, 10-11, 13-18, 20-22, 25-28, 35-37, 40-48, 53-73, 78-79, 83-93, 95, 101-102, 105-106, 110-112, 119-121, 133-135, 141-145, 148, 155-168, 172, 175, 177
ascent, of spirit, 68-69, 92-94, 97-98, 121, 149-150

Bacon, Francis, 100
being, as feminine quality, 23, 40, 50, 60, 63, 67, 69, 71-72, 78-79, 105
Berchorius, 83
bird, in dream, 61, 64-65
black magician, 40, 65, 67-69, 71-72, 107, 131-132
Blois, Robert de, 81
Boccaccio, 140
body: 16-17, 24, 35-37, 40, 98, 110, 114, 118-122, 144, 176; awareness, 45, 47, 52, 69, 86, 92-93, 98, 108, 110, 114-132, 144, 148, 151-154, 158
bonding, infant-parent, 44, 46-48
borderline states, 15, 25, 31, 33-34, 114, 133, 144, 155-156, 161, 164

boredom, in analysis, 44, 50, 83, 125, 161
bride, false/true, 40, 67-69, 71, 82, 107
Brimo, 150
Brown, Norman, 119
butterfly, in dream, 58-59

Canon, 87, 140-141, 174
Castaneda, Carlos, 122
caterpillar, in dream, 58
Cerberus, 149-150
Cephisus, 76-83, 90, 92, 110, 145
chaos, 54, 56-57, 134, 145, 150
character disorders, 9, 53
child(ren): depressive position, 134-135, 144, 147-150, 162-163; Dionysian roots, 143-144; in dreams, 54-55, 63-64, 163, 166-168; as "fourth," 130; of God, 133, 159; importance of mirroring, 46-49, 72; inner, 157, 159-169, 179; of joy, 135, 153, 157, 159-164, 166-169; masochistic, 157, 159-169, 179; and mother, 43-48, 68, 71-72, 79, 82, 87, 93, 144, 147, 149-150, 161, 164, 168
Christ, 16-17
Claudanius, 141-142
complementarity, psyche-soma, 122-123
complexes, 12, 14, 25-26, 32, 64, 101, 106, 118, 125, 162-165
coniunctio, 19, 40, 71-72, 76, 82, 93, 144, 165
control, in transference, 48-53, 57, 78, 83-88, 150, 155, 158, 165
countertransference, 9-10, 20-23, 25-28, 30-33, 41, 43-44, 49-53, 63, 68-69, 80-81, 83-86, 113, 125-126, 131, 151-159
Cox, Harvey, 11-12, 16-18
creativity, 26-28, 40-41, 43-48, 51, 53-54, 63, 65, 69, 108-109, 111, 130, 166
criticism, sensitivity to, 38, 138

defense, narcissistic, 9-10, 13, 15-16, 19, 26, 28, 30, 33, 42-44, 48-49, 52, 67, 72, 76, 80, 83, 87, 95, 130, 134-135, 138, 155, 158, 163-164, 174
deintegration, 101
Demeter, 23, 120, 122-124, 133-138, 141-151, 155-157
Demophoon, 147
depression, 9, 21, 29-31, 39, 49, 52-53, 68, 134, 138, 142, 144, 148-150, 157, 159-164
depressive position, 134-135, 144, 147-150, 162-163
descent, into matter, 68-69, 86, 92-94, 98, 106, 114, 120-121, 144, 176

186

6. Descent to the Goddess: A Way of Initiation for Women.
Sylvia Brinton Perera (New York). ISBN 0-919123-05-8. 112 pp.

A highly original and provocative book about women's freedom and the need for an inner, female authority in a masculine-oriented society.

Combining ancient texts and modern dreams, the author, a practising Jungian analyst, presents a way of feminine initiation. Inanna-Ishtar, Sumerian Goddess of Heaven and Earth, journeys into the underworld to Ereshkigal, her dark "sister," and returns. So modern women must descend from their old role-determined behavior into the depths of their instinct and image patterns, to find anew the Great Goddess and restore her values to modern culture.

Men too will be interested in this book, both for its revelations of women's essential nature and for its implications in terms of their own inner journey.

"The most significant contribution to an understanding of feminine psychology since Esther Harding's *The Way of All Women.*"—**Marion Woodman,** Jungian analyst and author of *Addiction to Perfection, The Pregnant Virgin* and *The Owl Was a Baker's Daughter.*

Studies in Jungian Psychology
by Jungian Analysts

Quality Paperbacks

Conscious Femininity: Interviews with Marion Woodman
Introduction by Marion Woodman ISBN 0-919123-59-7. 160 pp. $16

Chicken Little: The Inside Story *(A Jungian Romance)*
Daryl Sharp ISBN 0-919123-62-7. 128 pp. $15

The Middle Passage: From Misery to Meaning in Midlife
James Hollis ISBN 0-919123-60-0 128 pp. $15

Getting To Know You: The Inside Out of Relationship
Daryl Sharp ISBN 0-919123-56-2. 128 pp. $15

Eros and Pathos: Shades of Love and Suffering
Aldo Carotenuto ISBN 0-919123-39-2. 144 pp. $16

Descent to the Goddess: A Way of Initiation for Women
Sylvia Brinton Perera ISBN 0-919123-05-8. 112 pp. $15

Addiction to Perfection: The Still Unravished Bride
Marion Woodman ISBN 0-919123-11-2. Illustrated. 208 pp. $18pb/$20hc

The Creation of Consciousness: Jung's Myth for Modern Man
Edward F. Edinger ISBN 0-919123-13-9. Illustrated. 128 pp. $15

The Illness That We Are: A Jungian Critique of Christianity
John P. Dourley ISBN 0-919123-16-3. 128 pp. $15

The Pregnant Virgin: A Process of Psychological Transformation
Marion Woodman ISBN 0-919123-20-1. Illustrated. 208 pp. $18pb/$20hc

The Jungian Experience: Analysis and Individuation
James A. Hall, M.D. ISBN 0-919123-25-2. 176 pp. $18

Phallos: Sacred Image of the Masculine
Eugene Monick ISBN 0-919123-26-0. 30 illustrations. 144 pp. $16

**The Christian Archetype: A Jungian Commentary on the Life
of Christ** *Edward F. Edinger* ISBN 0-919123-27-9. Illustrated. 144 pp. $16

Personality Types: Jung's Model of Typology
Daryl Sharp ISBN 0-919123-30-9. Diagrams. 128 pp. $15

The Sacred Prostitute: Eternal Aspect of the Feminine
Nancy Qualls-Corbett ISBN 0-919123-31-7. Illustrated. 176 pp. $18

The Cassandra Complex: Living with Disbelief
Laurie Layton Schapira ISBN 0-919123-35-X. Illustrated. 160 pp. $16

Close Relationships: Family, Friendship, Marriage
Eleanor Bertine ISBN 0-919123-46-5. 160 pp. $16

Jung Lexicon: A Primer of Terms & Concepts
Daryl Sharp ISBN 0-919123-48-1. Diagrams. 160 pp. $16

Add Postage/Handling: 1-2 books, $2; 3-4 books, $4; 5-8 books, $7

Write or phone for complete Catalogue of over 60 titles

**INNER CITY BOOKS, Box 1271, Station Q
Toronto, ON, Canada M4T 2P4** (416) 927-0355